Rowland E. P. Ernle

The pioneers and progress of English farming

Rowland E. P. Ernle

The pioneers and progress of English farming

ISBN/EAN: 9783337727765

Printed in Europe, USA, Canada, Australia, Japan

Cover: Foto ©ninafisch / pixelio.de

More available books at **www.hansebooks.com**

THE
PIONEERS AND PROGRESS
OF
ENGLISH FARMING

BY

ROWLAND E. PROTHERO

BARRISTER-AT-LAW, AND FELLOW OF ALL SOULS COLLEGE, OXFORD

LONDON

LONGMANS, GREEN, AND CO.

AND NEW YORK: 15 EAST 16th STREET

1888

All rights reserved

PREFACE

PORTIONS of the following pages have already appeared within the last three years, in the *Edinburgh* and *Quarterly Reviews*, and my thanks are due to the Publishers for their permission to utilise the material which has been previously published in these periodicals. The recent appearance of two of the Articles on which I have relied will, I hope, excuse the seeming conceit of my references to 'Rural France' (*Edinburgh Review*, October 1887) and 'The Tithe Question' (*Edinburgh Review*, January 1888).

The first part of the volume contains a brief sketch of Agricultural Progress, derived from sources so scattered or so obscure that its presentation in a connected form may prove of interest. In the second part, I have endeavoured to apply the results of history to the present conditions of English farming. I am fully conscious that the task is difficult, and that it is inadequately performed; but the fact that in any Session of Parliament, which is mainly devoted to British interests, Agriculture necessarily holds a prominent place, explains, though it may not justify, the attempt.

R. E. PROTHERO.

CONTENTS

CHAPTER I.

'SELF-SUFFICING FARMING.'

Light Soils the Sites of earliest Settlements—Nomadic Stage represented in 'Wild-field-grass Husbandry' of S.W.—Farming of Village Communities: 'Garstons,' Arable Fields, Meadows, Hams, Pastures—Traces of System at Present Day—Manors imposed on Village Communities at Norman Conquest—Divisions of Land and Classes on Mediæval Manors: Tillage, Crops, Harvest, Implements, etc.—Progress of Agricultural Classes illustrated from Castle Combe 1

CHAPTER II.

FARMING FOR PROFIT.

Social and Agricultural Crisis at Close of Tudor Period—Self-sufficing Farming supplanted by Farming for Profit, Common by Individual Ownership, Feudal Retainers by Rent-paying Tenants; Pasture displaces Tillage, Sheep the Plough; Commons and Open Fields enclosed—Ruin of Small Commoners and Labourers for Hire—Their Misery under the Tudors—Illustrations of Methods by which Commons were enclosed . 17

CHAPTER III.

THE SEVENTEENTH CENTURY.

Progress in Farming—Commencement of Agricultural Literature: Fitzherbert and Tusser—Arrest of Progress during the Civil War—Accumulation of New Sources of Agricultural Wealth: Turnips, Artificial Grasses, Drainage, Emancipation of Land from Feudal Tenures 29

CHAPTER IV.

TURNIP TOWNSHEND AND THE NORFOLK SYSTEM.

1700–60 the Golden Age of Agricultural Classes, followed by Period of Corresponding Adversity—Reaction during First Half of the Century from Pasture to Tillage, from Sheep to Arable Farming, from Encouragement of Wool to Bounties on Corn—Suffolk and Essex the Best Types of 17th Century Farming—Townshend's System revolutionises the Agriculture of Norfolk, and, through Norfolk, of England—Cultivation of Turnips and Clover 38

CHAPTER V.

BAKEWELL AND THE GRAZIER'S ART.

Improvements effected in Breed of Sheep and Cattle by Bakewell—His extraordinary Success with Sheep, and comparative Failure with Cattle—His Imitators: Ellman and Jonas Webb, Collings, Tomkins, and Quartley 48

CHAPTER VI.

ARTHUR YOUNG AND THE DIFFUSION OF KNOWLEDGE.

Vast Tracts of Waste and Unenclosed Land; Leases practically unknown; Ignorance and Prejudices of Farmers; Difficulties of Communication rendered almost insuperable by Condition of Roads; Traditional Practices regarded as Agricultural Heirlooms—Early Life of Arthur Young; his Exertions to remove Obstacles to Progress of Agriculture 55

CHAPTER VII.

ENCLOSURES OF OPEN FIELDS AND COMMONS FROM 1770 TO 1820.

Second Agricultural Crisis—Enclosure of Wastes or Open Fields, and Consolidation of Holdings an Economic Necessity owing to Growth of Manufacturing Population—Impossibility of introducing new Agricultural Methods among Open-field Farmers—Reports of Board of Agriculture, 1793—Enclosure of Commons indispensable for increased Supply of Food, but often injurious to Interests of Poor 64

CHAPTER VIII.

LARGE FARMS AND LARGE CAPITALISTS—MR. COKE, OF HOLKHAM.

PAGE

Manufactures create New Markets for Food, and encourage Investments of Capital in Land—Landlords take the Lead in Agricultural Improvements—Wheat Growing and Stock Feeding in Norfolk—Mr. Coke, of Holkham, as the Model Landlord—Holkham Sheepshearings—Effect of War Prices on Ownership of Land; Disappearance of Small Freeholders and Consolidation of Large Estates 77

CHAPTER IX.

SCIENCE WITH PRACTICE, 1812-45.

Agricultural Progress during present Century—1812-42, a Period of wide-spread Ruin and Protection—Unprecedented Dearness of Corn maintained by heavy Import Duties—Distress of Wage-earning Population, Ruin of Landlords, Bankruptcy of Farmers at the Close of War—Paper-money and Resumption of Cash Payments aggravate Distress—Machine-breaking, Incendiarism, and Agrarian Outrage—Clay Farms suffer most heavily—Necessity of Drainage; Science provides necessary Means: Blith, Young, Elkington, Smith of Deanston, Josiah Parkes, Land Improvement Loans—Stimulus given to Drainage by Artificial Manures—Manures ignored by Early Agricultural Writers; 'Nothing like Muck' means 'Nothing but Muck;' Discoveries of Sprengel, Liebig, Lawes, Henslow, Odams—Agriculture revived by general Industrial Progress, Legislative Aid, and improved Practices and Implements of Farming—Good Effect upon Farming of inflated War Prices, illustrated from Northumberland and the Life of John Grey of Dilston 86

CHAPTER X.

SCIENCE WITH PRACTICE, 1845-73.

Enclosure Act of 1845 and Free Trade inaugurate New Era of Intensive and High Farming—Caird's Pamphlet on High Farming—Period of Great Agricultural Prosperity—Its Causes—Characteristic of Time rather Diffusion than Invention of Improved Farming Practices—Services of Chemistry, Geology, Mechanics, and Steam—Effect of Union of 'Science with Practice' upon Farmers, and other Classes connected with Agriculture—Another Result of Union seen in Demand for Compensation for Unexhausted Improvements—Statistical Records of Agriculture; Sir James Caird and Sir John Lawes   104

CHAPTER XI.

AGRICULTURAL DEPRESSION, 1873–87.

New Element of Foreign Competition—Revival of old Complaints—Gold a Factor in previous Eras of Adversity or Prosperity, and a concurrent Cause in present Crisis with Foreign Competition, Reckless Trading and Over-production—Exceptional Demand for, and Decreasing Supply of Gold—Depreciation of Silver—Full Pressure of Foreign Competition only felt after 1873—Low Prices the Problem of Modern Farming—Effect of Crisis on Landlords, Farmers, and Labourers—No True Distinction on score of Property possible between Money invested in Land and Money invested in Funds—Danger of wild Theories of Land Nationalisation   .   115

CHAPTER XII.

PEASANT PROPRIETORS.

Peasant Proprietors the chief theoretical Remedy—Prevalence of Distress among the Class in France and Germany—Impossibility that Remedy can apply universally in England—Proof of this from Example of France; special Conditions for Success of Peasant Proprietary in Soil, Climate, or Domestic Industries—Objections against French System: excessive Subdivision, Mortgage Debts, and scattered Parcels of Land—Hardships of the Life of French Peasantry—Social and political Advantages of System—Peasant Proprietary in France not the Growth of Legislation—Futility of Attempts to create the Class in England   128

CHAPTER XIII.

LANDLORDS AND NATURAL GROWTH.

PAGE

Explanation of different Lines of Agricultural Development in France, Belgium, the German Empire, Austria, Russia, Denmark—Paucity of Number of Landowners in England—Agricultural Progress due in England to Private Capital and Enterprise—In France Government supplies Place of Landlords—State-directed Agriculture in France: Education, Horse-races, Shows, Veterinary Assistance, Drainage, Roads, Public Works . 141

CHAPTER XIV.

DISTRIBUTION OF LAND.

Number of Landlords; of Farmers and Size of their Holdings; of Agricultural Labourers—Distress not due to System of Land Tenure or Cultivation—Losses of Agriculturists counterbalanced by Gain of Middle and Wage-earning Classes—Measures of Agricultural Relief limited by small Numbers of Persons directly interested in Agriculture 155

CHAPTER XV.

PROTECTION AND TITHE RENT-CHARGE.

Protection in England at Commencement of Century, and in France and Germany at present Time—Improbability of Landlords and Farmers obtaining Protection—Unlikely that Tithe Rent-charge will be reduced — Object and Effect of Tithe Commutation Act of 1836—Proportion borne by Tithe to Rent less in 1888 than in 1836—Consequently no Ground for Demand for Reduction of Charge—Change in Incidence of Charge necessary—No final Solution of Difficulty except Redemption—Interests of Church and State best consulted by State Collection of the Charge, and gradual voluntary Redemption in better Times and at higher Prices 163

CHAPTER XVI.

LEGISLATIVE AID; LAND LAWS, LAND TRANSFER, EDUCATION, RAILWAY RATES.

PAGE

Former Feeling of Insecurity among Landlords fostered by doubtful Attitude of Legislature — Revived Confidence not impaired by Removal of Artificial Hindrances to Natural Growth of Small Owners—Reform of Land Laws and Establishment of Land Registration—Difficulties of cheap and easy System of Land Transfer—Lord Halsbury's Bill, 1887—Australian and Prussian Registries—Advantages of Land Registries—Agricultural Education in Great Britain and Ireland compared with that of France, and the Austrian and German Empires—Technical Teaching in Agricultural Matters especially needed in Rural Schools—Use of Ministry of Agriculture—Commencement of State Aid in England—Illustration of Working of System in France—Unfairness of present System of Differential Railway Rates, especially in case of Perishable Produce—Need for a Board of Control 177

CHAPTER XVII.

FISCAL RELIEF—LOCAL TAXATION.

During Protection Period Agricultural Land was heavily taxed because Consumers were heavily taxed for its Support— *Cessante ratione cessat et ipsa lex* — The Land Tax — The four old Rates before and after the Repeal of the Corn Laws—Increased Burden of Local Taxation in spite of Free Trade Prices—Comparison of Rates in 1841 and 1885—Enormous Growth of Local Debt—Need of Reform of Local Government—Suggestions for Relief of Agricultural Land from Local Taxation 201

CHAPTER XVIII.

SELF-HELP NOT PROTECTION.

Self-Help the true Remedy—Perishable Produce the main Source of Farming Profits—Signs of New Departure in these Directions—Co-operation necessary between Landlords and Tenants —Farmers not Free Agents in Contracts for letting and hiring

CONTENTS xiii

Land—Necessity of securing them against Rise of Rent based upon their own Outlay of Capital—Defects of Agricultural Holdings Acts of 1875 and 1883—Proposed Scheme to secure them Compensation—Freedom in Contract from Antiquated Restrictions—Sliding Scale in Rents—Reaction apparently imminent from Corn-growing to Meat and Dairy Farming—Advantages of diversified Husbandry 211

CHAPTER XIX.

AGRICULTURAL LABOURERS.

Agricultural Labourers as yet the smallest sufferers from Agricultural Depression—Improvements in their Moral and Material Circumstances—Three Wants of their present Condition—Peasant Tenancies; Means of providing necessary Capital—Good Prospects for Agricultural Labourers who become Small Farmers or secure regular Employment—Allotments—Probable Dismissal of large Numbers of Labourers—No possible Restoration of Balance between Demand and Supply of Labour except Emigration 224

CHAPTER XX.

CONCLUSION 236

APPENDICES

I. Prices of Wheat 243
II. Social Corn Laws 246
III. Agricultural Writers of the 16th, 17th, and first half of 18th Centuries 248
IV. The Corn Laws 252
V. Enclosures 257
VI. Questions of the Board of Agriculture, 1816 258
VII. Estimate of the Agricultural Population in 1688, and Census Returns of 1851, 1861, 1871, 1881 . . . 259

	PAGE
VIII. Production of Gold and Silver, 1851-86, &c.	261
IX. Value of Imports of Food	263
X. Statistics of Agriculture	264-5
XI. The Land of England and its Products, 1688, 1771, 1808, 1827, 1867, 1877, 1887	268
XII. Prices of Wheat and Import Duties, if any, in France, Belgium, Prussia, and England	274
XIII. Local Taxation	275
XIV. Allotments	277
XV. Wages of Agricultural Labourers	279
XVI. Prices of Provisions	281
INDEX	283

PIONEERS AND PROGRESS

OF

ENGLISH FARMING.

CHAPTER I.

SELF-SUFFICING FARMING.

The practice of English Agriculture was in its infancy solely determined by the growth of population. No rotation of crops was necessary till advancing numbers limited the extent of the unoccupied land. While people were few and land was abundant, grain crops were only raised on light soils. Dry uplands, where the least labour told the most, were first cultivated; rich valleys, damp and filled with forest growth, remained uninhabited. Sandy soils or chalky highlands are the sites of the oldest villages. Patches of the slopes of downs were cleared of self-sown beech, and sheltered dips tilled for corn; the high ground behind was grazed by the flocks and herds; the beech woods supplied mast for the swine. On Salisbury Plain, a century ago, there was no sign of human life except the proverbial 'thief or twain;' no contemporary mark of the hand of man but the gallows and their appendages. Yet here are to be found traces of numerous villages. The

B

sides of the Wiltshire and Sussex downs are scored with 'lynches,' terraces running horizontally, one above the other, along the slopes. Local tradition attributes their formation to spade husbandry. Marshall, in 1797, suggested, but only to reject, the operation of the plough; recently Mr. Seebohm has revived the same theory. Whichever view of their origin is correct, they indelibly indicate the sites of the earliest settlements, and the nature of the soil first selected for tillage.

'Wild field-grass' husbandry is a more primitive form of agriculture than that practised by village communities. Of both systems co-ownership and co-tillage are characteristic. The essential difference lay in this. In the common fields of the village, pasturage and tillage are permanently separated; grass-land always remains meadow or pasture; it is never broken up for tillage. Under the more primitive form fresh tracts of grass were successively taken in, ploughed, and tilled for corn. As the soil became exhausted they reverted to pasture. Such a practice may belong to some portions of the Celtic race, or to the nomadic stage of civilisation, the period when 'arva per annos mutant et superest ager.' In 1804 Marshall traced the 'wild field-grass' system in the south-western counties. In some districts, lords of the manor enjoyed rights of letting portions of the grass commons to be ploughed up, cultivated for corn, and after two years thrown back into pasture. And over the whole country from the Tamar to the eastern border of Dorsetshire he found open commons, such as the wide expanse of Yarcombe and the hills above Bridport, which from time immemorial had never known the plough, distinctly marked with the ridge and furrow. Other usages of the rural population, which a century ago were more peculiar to the south-west of England, suggest that in this district village communities never prevailed. The cultivated land is divided into little patches by the high Devonshire hedge; common parish fields can hardly be traced; fewer of the inhabitants are collected into villages, more are scattered in single houses. The small enclosures suggest that Devonshire was never peopled by Teutonic invaders; like Brittany, it is a country of hedges.

On this system the permanent separation of arable land from pasture hardly constitutes an advance in agricultural practice. It was probably introduced into this country by a people accustomed, like the Anglo-Saxons, to a drier and less variable climate. Yet this alien system for centuries governed the cultivation of two-thirds of England. Tufts of trees, conspicuous in the hedgeless expanse of land by which they were surrounded, marked the sites of villages, as they still do in the high table-land of the Pays de Caux. Within the 'tûn,' or enclosure, were the tofts and crofts of substantial peasants and the cottages and curtilages of the cottagers, 'fencèd al aboute with stikkes.' These were the only property held by the members of the township in several ownership. They were also originally the only permanent enclosures. But as agriculture advanced, yards ('gerstuns,' or garstons) for rearing stock, or for the oxen which could not 'endure his warke to labour all daye, and then to be put to the commons or before the herdsman,' were enclosed in the immediate proximity of the village. In these enclosures, or 'happy garstons,' as they were called at Aston Boges, were held the village merry-makings, the rush-bearings, the May-games, the summerings at St. John Baptist's Eve, the public breakfasts, and the distribution of bread and ale in Rogation week.

Beyond the village lay the common arable fields, including the driest and soundest land. These fields were two and three, or rarely four in number. If the former, one field lay fallow, the other under tillage for corn, or beans, or peas. The dual system was, when Fleta wrote, generally superseded by the three-field or trinity arrangement; yet it prevailed near Gloucester in the present century, and existed at Stogoursey in Somersetshire in 1879. From the reign of Henry III. to that of George III. the trinity fields received the unvarying triennial succession of wheat or rye, spring crops such as barley, oats, beans, or peas, and fallow. During this period a more scientific rotation was in some districts adopted. Thus at Aston Boges, in Oxfordshire, a fourth course was interposed. But, speaking generally, common field husbandry rather retrograded than advanced. For the strict supervision of the bailiff and the reeve, or the minute observance of common rules, was exchanged an anarchy which made the land, like that of Tully Veolan, resemble in the 'unprofitable variety of its surface a tailor's book of patterns.'

Each of the three arable fields was subdivided into shots, furlongs, or flats, separated from one another by unploughed, bush-grown turf balks. These flats were in turn cut up into parallel strips of about an acre apiece, coinciding with the arrangement of a ploughed field in ridges and furrows. Theoretically each flat was a square of forty poles, containing ten acres; in practice every variety of shape and admeasurement was found. But, though the pole from which the acre was raised varied from the thirteen and a half feet of Hampshire to the twenty-four feet of Cheshire, two sides of the flats always ran parallel. Thus each of the three arable fields resembled several sheets of paper, ruled with margins and lines. The separate sheets are the flats; the margins are the headlands running down the flats at right angles to, and across the ends of, the parallel acre strips which are represented by the lines. The strips appear under different names. In Scotland they were called 'rigs,' in the north of England generally 'oxgangs,' in Westmoreland 'dales,' and their possessors 'dalesmen,' in Cambridgeshire 'balks,' in Somersetshire 'landshires' or 'raps.' They generally contained an acre, but half-acres and even single poles or rods, called 'butts,' are found. Stray odd corners which did not fit in with the parallel arrangement of the shots were called 'crustæ,'[1] that is, pieces broken off, pightels,[2] 'gores,[3] fothers,[4] and pykes, because, as Fitzherbert explains, they were 'often brode in the one ende and a sharpe pyke in the other ende.' These strips, thus scattered over the arable fields, were fenced off for the separate use of individuals from seedtime to harvest. On Lammas Day separate use terminated and common rights recommenced; hence the strips were often called Lammas lands. After harvest the hayward removed the fences, and the cattle of the community wandered over the fields before the common herdsman. Sometimes each commoner herded his own flock. Richard Hooker, while he held the country living of Drayton Beauchamp in Buckinghamshire, was found by two of his former pupils, 'like humble and innocent Abel, tending his small allotment of sheep in a common field.' That no occupier might find all his land fallow in the same year, every one had strips in each of the three arable fields. If

[1] Registry of Worcester Priory (Camden Society), p. 18A.
[2] A pightel of land. Cf. Cullum, *History of Hawsted*, p. 77.
[3] As in Kensington Gore.
[4] Cf. Chaucer (Prologue, 530),—

'A ploughman, his brothur,
That hadde i-lad of dong ful many a fothur,'

where the word is generally taken to mean a load.

the holding was a virgate of thirty acres, there would be ten acres in each field. To divide equally the good and bad, well and ill situated soil, the bundle of strips allotted in each field did not lie together, but was scattered.

In the lowest part of the land—if possible along a stream—lay the 'ings,' or meadows, annually cut up into lots or doles, and put up for hay. These doles were fenced off for the separate use of individuals from Candlemas to Midsummer Day: from July to February they were open, common pasturage. Each lot was distinguished by a mark, such as the cross, crane's foot, or peel. Corresponding marks were thrown into a hat or bag and drawn by a boy. This balloting continued up to the present century in Oxfordshire and Somersetshire. No winter keep for stock was provided; the common field farmer could only fatten cattle at the wane of the summer. Then they had the aftermath of the meadows, the stubble or haulm of the arable fields. After Michaelmas they steadily declined, and only survived the winter in a state of semi-starvation. Hence worn-out oxen or aged cows were slaughtered in the autumn and salted for winter consumption. 'For Easter at Martylmas hang up a beef,' is the advice of Tusser.

On the outskirts of the arable fields lay one or more 'hams' or stinted pastures, supplying superior feed. Brandersham, Smithsham, and Wontnersham suggest that special allotments were made to those who practised crafts of general utility.

The poorest and most distant land of the township was left in its native wildness. It afforded timber for fuel or fencing, mast and acorns for swine, rough pasture for the ordinary live stock.

The common field system, thus briefly sketched, with

its arable, meadow, and pasture land, prevailed at some time or other throughout England except in the west, and underlies the disturbances in Skye. The following description of the crofters' holdings in 1750 might have been written, with but few alterations, of half the villagers in England in the eighteenth century:[1]—' A certain number of tacksmen formed a copartnery and held a tract of land, or township, for which they paid tribute to the chief, and each member was jointly and severally responsible. The grazing was in common. All the arable land was divided into ridges, assigned annually by lot among the partners. Each might have a dozen or more of these small ridges, and no two contiguous except by accident; the object being to give each partner a portion of the better and inferior land. The copartner appears to have had cotters under him, for whose work he paid.' In 1879, at Stogoursey, near Bridgwater, a village community were still cultivating 600 acres of land on similar principles. The prevalence of the system may still be faintly traced in England. Turf balks and lynches record the time when ' every rood of ground maintained its man.' Irregular and regular fences, straight and crooked roads, respectively suggest the wholesale or piecemeal enclosure of common fields. The age of the hedgerow timber sometimes tells the date of the change. The space devoted to hedges by agricultural writers of the eighteenth century denotes the abolition of open fields, and the minuteness of their instructions proves that the art of making hedges was still in its infancy. The scattered lands of ordinary farms, compared with the compact ' court,' ' hall,' or ' manor' farm, recalls the fact that the lord's demesne was once the only permanent enclosure. The crowding

[1] Letter to the *Times*, April 3, 1883.

together of the rural population in villages betrays the agrarian partnership, as detached farmsteads and isolated labourers' dwellings indicate the system by which it has been supplanted.

The relation of manors to village communities lies beyond the present inquiry. Two theories explain the origin of manorial rights and rights of common. The legal theory, in its crudest form, is that the lord of the manor is absolute owner of the soil of his manor, and that all rights acquired over it by freeholders and copyholders are acquired against him, and originate in his grant or sufferance. The historical theory is that self-governing, independent communities of freemen originally owned the land in common, and were gradually reduced to dependence by one of their members, who became the lord of the soil. If the second theory is correct, the legal position of the lord of the manor represents a series of encroachments which transformed the Mark of freemen into the Manor of villeins, and transmuted the customary rights of the villagers over the wastes into rights of user over the lord's soil. Questions like the origin and antiquity of manors, and the extent to which they prevailed before the Norman Conquest, have been to a great degree reopened by Mr. Seebohm's remarkable work,[1] in which the legal theory is practically supported by an historical argument. But whether the relation of manors to village communities represented encroachments by the lord or advances by the serf, whether the rights of agrarian associations underlay or were acquired against the manorial rights of the feudal baron—whether, in other words, the land-law of the noble was becoming the land-law of

---

[1] *The English Village Community*, London, 1883.

the people or the reverse, is here immaterial. Roughly
and generally speaking, the immediate lordship of the
land farmed by a village community, including the wastes
and commons, was, after the Norman Conquest, vested in
the lord of the manor, subject to regulated rights enjoyed
by its members.

During the three centuries after the Conquest the
manorial estate consisted of three portions—the demesne
land, the villein's land, and the commons. The demesne
land was originally intended for the lord's personal use;
it was his 'board land.' It therefore constituted the smaller
portion of the total acreage. Thus in 1222 the manors of
St. Paul's contained 24,000 acres, of which three-eighths
were in demesne. The demesne might be kept in hand
and cultivated by the agricultural services of the peasantry;
or let off in solid blocks to tenants, who also held land in
the common fields; or cut up into strips and intermixed
with other holdings of the villenage. The distinction between the 'terra dominica' and the 'terra villanorum' was
that the first, if let out, might be resumed each season at
will, but villein land was land of inheritance alienated in
perpetuity on payment of certain prædial services. Thus
the lord of the manor might keep his demesne in his own
hands, cultivating it as a home farm by the agricultural
services of the peasantry; or he might be a modern landlord, letting it out to tenants in separate farms at an annual
rent; or he might throw it into the farm of the township,
and become a shareholder with his tenants in the common
venture of the Agrarian Association.

The mass of the rural population lived in hereditary
subjection, holding land by labour-rent. Of this semi-
servile class, the villeins formed the aristocracy. The villein proper was no ordinary servant in husbandry, but,

like Chaucer's ploughman, had 'catel' of his own. He was obliged to contribute, at the rate of an ox for each half-virgate, to the manorial plough-team, which almost universally consisted of eight oxen. So tenacious was agricultural custom, that in the eighteenth century, whatever the soil or the weight of the plough, few farmers ploughed with less than this number. Villeins were distinguished from the inferior orders of their class by this obligation, and their uncertain services were gradually limited to boon-days or precations, and finally commuted for money. The continuous work of the farm fell to the inferior peasants, such as bordars and cottars, or actual serfs. The bordars were holders of a homestead, possibly a small croft of land near the village, and sometimes small pieces of the common arable fields. They aided the villein in cultivating the demesne, but were not owners of oxen. Their obligatory services were more continuous, more trivial, and more servile than those of villeins. Probably in actual labour the serf was not worse off than the bordar, and, like him, he might hold land; but his tenure was bondage, not prædial service. Out of these three orders sprang the small freeholder, the copyholder, and the wage-earning labourer.

The obligations of the peasantry varied not only with customs, but with seasons. Their most important services were the autumnal and Lenten seed-ploughings. Fallows were broken up about Hoketide, and ploughed and dunged for sowing wheat and rye about Michaelmas. Land was ploughed for oats, barley, and peas, after Epiphany; the crops sown and harrowed in March or April. The ploughman held the principal hale of the plough in his left hand, in his right a beetle to break the clods. A 'Dover-court' beetle was a necessary implement upon a farm in the time of Tusser; and Plot, whose 'Natural History of Oxfordshire' appeared in the seventeenth century, recommends its use after the land was harrowed. On some manors harrowing was one of the services which the villeins associated to render. But the implement was of the lightest and rudest description. Fleta gives the amount of wheat sown to the acre as two bushels, and the average yield at ten to twelve bushels. But, except on the best land, so small a seeding was rare. The quantity of seed for barley, oats, or rye was far greater. Probably the labour of sowing was performed by the bailiff himself, as, at the beginning of this century, it was performed by the farmer with his own hand.[1] All seed was sown broadcast, and the land, which was generally wet and foul, was more thickly seeded then than now. After the plots were sown and fenced, the hayward exacted a penalty from all trespassers, except messengers riding in haste. Corn was weeded in June, for the maxim was ancient,—

>Who weeds in May
>Throws all away.

In the fourteenth century, on the 220 acres of Hawsted Manor Farm, in Suffolk, sixty sarclers or weeders were employed on one day at 2*d.* apiece. In dry weather they were armed with a hook and a forked stick, in wet with tongs.

Nothing is more characteristic of the infancy of farming than the violence of its alternations. When roots and grasses were unknown, there was no middle course between incessant cropping and barrenness. The fallow was 'un véritable Dimanche accordé à la terre.' As with the land, so with its products. Feasting trode on the heels of famine. In the graphic language of ancient chroniclers, parents in

---

[1] Professor Rogers, *History of Agriculture and Prices*, i. 16.

1270 ate their own children when wheat rose to 336s. a quarter at the present value of money. Except in monastic granges, no quantity of grain was stored: a corn dealer was the 'caput lupinum' of the Legislature. Few remembered to eat within their tether, or to spare at the brink and not at the bottom. In August 1317 wheat was 80s. a quarter; in September following it fell to 6s. 8d. In 1557 the price of wheat was 53s. 4d.; after harvest it fell to 5s. Equally variable were the employments of agriculture. Months of indolence passed suddenly into intense labour. Harvestings in the Middle Ages were picturesque scenes of bustle and of merriment among the thousands to whom they meant the return of plenty. On 250 acres in Suffolk, towards the close of the fourteenth century, were grown wheat, oats, peas, barley, and bolymong, a mixture of peas or tares, and oats. The crops were cut and housed in two days. On the first day appeared thirty tenants to perform their 'bederepes,' and 244 reapers. On the second, the thirty tenants, and 239 reapers, pitchers, and stackers. Many of this assembly were the smaller peasantry on the manor; the rest were wandering bands of 'cockers' or harvesters, who had already begun to parade the country. A cook, brewer, and baker were hired to supply dinner at nine, and supper at five. Barley and oats, as well as peas and beans, were generally mown; rye and wheat were reaped. But the harvest, as in Roman times, consisted of two operations: the first was to cut the ears, the second to remove part of the straw for thatching. But the value of the straw of thin short corn hardly paid for the expense of removal, and the rest of the stubble was either grazed, or burned, or ploughed in.

The proportion of arable land was greatly in excess of grass land. The crops of the former were wheat, rye, oats, barley, beans, peas, and, in smaller quantities, flax and hemp. Roots or artificial grasses were entirely unknown. Of grain crops rye was the chief; it is the hardiest, grows on the poorest soils, makes the toughest straw. Rye was then the bread-stuff of the peasantry, as it still is in Northern Europe. It was generally mixed with wheat-flour. Bread so made was called maslin.[1] It retained its moisture longer, and, as Moryson ('Itinerary,' *temp.* James I.) says, was used by labourers because 'it abode longer in the stomach and was not so soon digested with their labour.' Wheat and rye were often sown together. Tusser condemns the practice, 'lest rye tarry wheat till it shed as it stand;' but it prevailed in Yorkshire in 1797 as a cure for mildew. By itself wheat was seldom sown. Barley was the drink-corn, as rye the bread-corn, of the Middle Ages; drage [2] was the commonest and best sort for malting. Oats were extensively cultivated in the north; but they were grey-awned, thin, and poor. The culture of vines is often quoted to prove a change of climate in the England of 1888. But it must be remembered that wine was then sweetened and flavoured with honey and spices; it was never drunk in its pure state; and therefore no theory can be founded upon the production of a liquid which may have resembled vinegar in its natural state. Little manure was used. In arable farms all the dung produced was thrown on the 'infield;' the 'outfield' was neglected. The right of folding was valuable to lords of the manor because their own land was thus enriched by the tenant's flock. Horses were scarcely used in agriculture. Oxen

---

[1] Lat. 'mixtilio.' Harrison, 'miscellin.' Yorkshire, 1797, 'mashel-son.' In the 'Compleat Farmer' (1760) it is called 'maislen;' but it is said to be 'ill-husbandry' to grow wheat and rye together.

[2] Lat. *drageum*, dredge: bigge; bere barley.

cost less, are shod only on the forefeet, do more on hilly ground; their gear and winter keep is less expensive: they are 'mannes meat when dead, while the horse is carrion.'

In the Middle Ages the monks both of England and of France were the pioneers of agriculture, and it was through their influence that marshes were drained, forests cleared, wastes reclaimed, and barren land reduced to cultivation. The 'strenuous idleness' of a baronial aristocracy revolted from farming. This contempt for bucolic life is illustrated by heraldry. Sport, war, religion, supply its emblems: agricultural implements and products are disdained till, like the garb of the Washbournes, the haywains of the Hays, the scythe of the Sneyds, they have been ennobled by martial use. The monks studied agriculture by the light of Varro and Columella. But their influence was sometimes opposed to progress. Corn was indispensable to monasteries, and its growth was often compulsory on monastic tenants. As the natural pastures of La Brenne in Berri were sacrificed to the desire of grain, so the ' fat vale' of Evesham was cut up into arable parcels, so small and scattered that no tenant could lay his holding down to grass. That their love of ale induced monks to compel the cultivation of barley where oats were more profitable is probably a slander. From 1350 onwards the relations of owner and occupier assume a modern aspect; leases become common; villenage and serfdom disappear: out of the Black Death and the French wars arise tenant farmers, copyholders, free wage-earning labourers. The first half of the fifteenth century most nearly realised the peasant's dream of Arcadia. Rural life in the preceding period must be studied, not in the holiday scenes of Chaucer, but in the realistic pictures of Langland. Between 1389 and

1444 the wages of agricultural labourers doubled: harvests were plentiful; beef, mutton, pork, became their food: sumptuary laws against extravagance of dress and diet attest their prosperity: the standard purity of the coinage was steadily maintained, and the number of shillings into which the pound was coined varied only between thirty and thirty-five. Fortescue attributes the success of the English against the French to the superiority of their diet. 'The people,' he says, ' be wealthye, and have al thynges necessary to the sustenaunce of nature, wherfor thay be mighty, able to resyste the adversaries of the realme, and to bett other realmes that do or will do them wrong.'

A concrete instance illustrates mediæval practices and the progress of the labouring classes. The Domesday Survey of the manor of Castle Combe in Wiltshire shows that the manor consisted of meadow, pasture, and arable land. The meadow was divided into strips held by the peasantry. The pasture, which was rough and wooded, was held in common. One thousand acres were under the plough, of which 400 acres were the lord's demesne, cultivated by thirteen serfs and labour-rents; the remainder was held by villeins, boors, and cottagers. The arable land was divided into two fields, North field and South field, among which were scattered twenty-five parcels of demesne land called 'dooles,' each comprising about four acres. There were no free tenants. In 1340 there were ten free tenants whose services were commuted for money payments, and who held between them 233 acres of arable land. The remaining tenants were still in bondage. Fifteen were customary tenants, holding 625 acres, partly by money rent and partly by labour services. Eleven other tenants held fifteen acres each by agricultural services; but in addition they held crofts, for which they paid rent in money. Eight 'Monday-men' held cottages and curtilages by labour-rent. These thirty-four tenants were all bondagers, but they could always commute their labour services at a money value, and provide substitutes. These they found in one another, or in twelve tenants of cottages who paid fixed rents. In 1352 all the labour-rents were commuted for money payments. In 1454 the 'dooles' of demesne land were let to five tenants who were responsible for the whole rent, though in practice they seem to have sublet. The customary tenants had increased to twenty; the Monday-men to fifteen. The manor was self-governing. The tenants elected the bailiff, the hayward, the sheep-teller, who counted the stock on the commons, the constables, ale-tasters, and other manorial officers. They also composed the 'leet-jury,' which disposed of small criminal offences, presented tavern-haunters or common idlers, made bye-laws regulating the maintenance of the merestones or butts, the repairs of the bridge or the sewers, the brewing and selling of ale and beer. And all this was done without the intervention of a lawyer or his fees.

CHAPTER II.

FARMING FOR PROFIT.

THE end of the wars of the Roses synchronised with social and commercial changes which produced the first great agricultural crisis. Up to the Tudor period the mass of English land was tilled upon the plan already described, which foreign legislators of the nineteenth century found to be still prevalent on the Continent. Without discussing further the origin of manorial rights, it may be repeated that at the Norman Conquest the feudal manors were superimposed upon agrarian communities. Henceforward the land was divided into the private demesne of the lord of the manor, the lord's wastes, and the tenemental land of the association. Rights of common were exercised not only over the commons, the soil of which was now vested in the feudal lord, but by each party respectively over the land of the other. If the lord of the manor farmed the demesne himself, his land was subject to the rights of common exercised over it by the manorial tenantry. If he farmed his demesne as a modern landlord, he multiplied retainers by letting it out in small portions to farmers who were often holders at the same time of tenemental land. If he threw the demesne into the common stock, he made himself a partner in the joint venture of the agrarian association. Demesne and commonable land was intermixed and cultivated in minute strips. So confused did the two portions become that on the estates of the Dean and Chapter of St. Paul's three acres could not be found by the land registrars. For this reason Fitzherbert, in his 'Book of Surveying,' impresses on the surveyor the need of accuracy, lest ' any parcell be loste, or imbeselde, or encroached by one from the other.' But between 1450 and 1560 an agricultural revolution was accomplished, which may be briefly described as a change from self-sufficing to profit-gaining agriculture, from common to individual ownership.

The first steps in this change were taken when lords of manors enclosed their wastes, or withdrew their demesne lands from the agrarian partnership, or when the partners of village communities agreed among themselves to extinguish their own common rights over the arable fields. On most manors three distinct rights of common pasture were enjoyed. 'There is commonly,' says Fitzherbert, 'a common close taken in out of the common fields by tenants of the same towne, in which close every man is stinted and set to a certaintie how many beasts he shall have in the same.' This enclosure of land that it might be common belongs to a later date, and is comparatively unimportant. Secondly, common rights were exercised over the lord's wastes, outwoods, moors, and heaths, 'which were never arable land,' and the soil of which was vested in the lord of the manor. Thirdly, rights of common were enjoyed over the land that lay fallow in rotation and over the common arable lands from harvest to seed-time, 'the plain champaign countrie,' to quote the words of Fitzherbert, 'where their cattle lie daily before the herdsmen.'

These are the rights of 'parcours' and 'vaine pâture,' which, in France, remained for centuries insuperable obstacles to agricultural progress. Upon the second and third class of rights depended the prosperity, if not the very existence, of agrarian associations; they afforded the only means of keeping live stock. It may be doubted whether, before 1236, lords of manors could by common law enclose wastes subject to rights of common; but, be this as it may, in that year the Statute of Merton sanctioned enclosures against all freeholders whose rights of common were derived from the owner of the soil. Fifty years later the right of enclosure was extended by the Statute of Westminster against commoners whose right was not derived from the lord of the manor. 'Many of the lordes,' says Fitzherbert at the beginning of the sixteenth century, 'have enclosed a great part of their waste grounds, and straightened their tenants of their common therein.'

The example of the landlord was often followed by the principal partners of the village farm. During the same period numerous agreements were entered into between the commoners to extinguish, temporarily or permanently, the right to graze the arable lands from harvest to seed-time. 'Licenses' were given to the tenantry 'to enclose part of their arable lands, and to take in new intakes or closes out of the commons.' Finally, lords of manors withdrew and enclosed their demesne lands which lay in the common fields, thus still further curtailing the right of common pasture. Fitzherbert says that, before 1530, 'the mooste part of the lordes have enclosed their demeyn landes and meadows, and kept them in severalties, so that their tenauntes have no common with them therein.'

This agricultural change was accelerated by a social and commercial revolution. The Hundred Years' war maintained the external features of a system which was completely undermined. It is this fact which gives the air of hollowness and artificiality to the reign of

Edward III. The feudal organisation of society was breaking up; land was regarded as a source not of power, but of wealth. The tendency set in strongly towards small convertible arable farms; tenants withdrew from the common farm of the township, and exchanged their scattered strips for solid tenements of from 10 to 120 acres; landlords found self-farming unprofitable, and divided their demesnes into small holdings let on lease, when agricultural services were commuted for money, and the Black Death had raised the rate of wages.

The withdrawal of the English landlord from the agrarian partnership exactly corresponds to the process which took place in the present century on the Continent. It was a change from common to individual ownership; land was divided between the lord of the manor and the association; rights of common, mutually enjoyed, were extinguished. In its results, manorial estates were consolidated, partly by withdrawal from the village farm, partly by the enclosure of wastes, and many of the agrarian associations were broken up. When these partnerships were dissolved, common-field farmers enclosed their strips and became peasant proprietors. Where the association lingered on, its farming steadily deteriorated, as well from the contraction of the area of the common farm as from the neglect of the 'field constraint' which had been mainly enforced by the landlord's officers. Yeomen were little affected by a change which slightly increased their numbers. The two classes that eventually suffered were the 'common-field farmers,' to use the eighteenth century description, and the cottagers or emancipated serfs, who had no share in the lands of the agrarian community, but lived as hired labourers, supplementing their wages by keeping cattle on the rough pasture. The change was at first advantageous to all the classes concerned. Wage-earning labourers obtained more constant employment, while more substantial farmers reaped advantages from the consolidation of their holdings. Such enclosures were warmly recommended by practical agriculturists like Fitzherbert, who advises every man to 'change fields with his neighbour, so that he may lay his lands together,' keep more cattle, improve the soil by their 'compostynge,' and rest his corn land when it becomes impoverished. A new conception of agriculture dawned on men's minds. Landlords recognised that the soil might produce rents now that they had ceased to need retainers; farmers were no longer content to produce enough for their own families, but desired to become growers as well as consumers. It is significant that the earliest corn laws were passed in the reign of Henry VI. Legislation to maintain the value of corn begins in 1436, and in 1463 foreign imports were forbidden[1] until prices reached the point at which export was prohibited.

But it was not long before commercial interests gave a new direction to agricultural tendencies, which proved fatal to the lower ranks of the labouring or land-holding population. The wars of the Roses were the suicide of feudalism, and in the reign of Edward IV. the spirit of trade breathed freely throughout England. If farmers were slow to recognise that 'the foot of the sheep turns sand into gold,' merchants were quick to see that money might be made by the growth of wool. But sheep could not be herded with success upon commons, and small holdings were incompatible with large flocks.

[1] No corn was to be imported until wheat was 6s. 8d., rye 4s., barley 3s. the quarter. These prices must have been high. (See table of prices of wheat, Appendix I.)

The growth of woollen manufactories raised the price of English wool, which commanded the market at home and abroad. Edward III. encouraged Flemish woolworkers to settle in England and improve domestic manufactures, which hitherto had aspired to nothing more than a coarse frieze. He settled his Flemings in every part of England, but especially in the eastern counties and the south-west. At the same time English wool was indispensable to the manufacturers of Flanders, who mixed it with the produce of Spain, so that Europe was clothed by English farmers. Wool was easy of transport, little liable to damage, subject to no duties. Baltic corn, on the other hand, competed successfully with English grain in foreign markets; as a merchandisable commodity corn was liable to every tax and damage. Arable farming was expensive and uncertain; sheep-feeding sure and cheap.

The high and certain profits of sheep-farming encouraged not only the consolidation of holdings, but a revolution in agricultural practice. Hitherto but little attention had been paid to grass farms. Now tillage gave way to pasturage. The new commercial aristocracy converted their land into parks or sheep-walks, where only a shepherd found employment. They encroached upon and enclosed the commons by force or connivance with the principal commoners. The purchase of common rights must have been rare, for in the reign of Edward VI. the Statute of Merton was re-enacted. Tenants were encouraged to consolidate their holdings, to exchange open fields for separate farms, to divide the common pasture with the landlord. Small tenants were evicted from their holdings on the demesne; farm servants who had boarded with them were dismissed; the cottages of the married labourers were pulled down. At the same time wastes and commons were enclosed and thrown into sheep farms. This contraction of the area of rough pasture inflicted a second and fatal blow on the interests of the small cottagers. The Statutes of Merton and Westminster only protected the interests of the freeholders, and so long as their consent was obtained no rights were recognised in other classes. The dissolution of the monasteries stimulated the process. The new landlords treated the royal grant as an excuse to override the customary and common rights of the existing tenants. The doggerel ballad ('Vox Populi Vox Dei,' 1549) laments the change:—

> We have shut away all cloisters,
> But still we keep extortioners;
> We have taken their lands for their abuse,
> But we have converted them to a worse use.

Legislation was powerless to check the reaction against tillage; it failed to compel landlords to limit their flocks and maintain their farm buildings. The main object of the Government was to prevent the depopulation of the country;[1] but exemptions were purchased from the restraining statutes, or their provisions were evaded. The destruction of farm buildings was forbidden, but it was easy to retain a single room for the shepherd; a solitary furrow driven across newly laid pasture satisfied the law that no fresh land should be converted from tillage; the number of sheep was limited by law, but flocks were held in the name of sons or servants. A petition in the reign of Henry VIII. states that 50,000 ploughs had been put down, each of which, on the average, maintained $13\frac{1}{2}$ persons. Thus, 675,000 persons were thrown out of work

[1] See Appendix II.

when the whole population of the country did not exceed five millions. Still more vain was the quaint pedantry of the law which gave arable land the precedence over all other lands, conferred privileges on beasts of the plough above other beasts, voided bonds to restrain tillage. 'Depopulatores agrorum' were denied the benefit of clergy, sanctuary, or Christian burial. In spite of every effort, England remained till the eighteenth century the sheep-feeding country she had become under the Tudors.

Advanced free traders might agree with Raleigh that England, like Holland, could be wholly supplied with grain from abroad without troubling the people with tillage. Many, however, looked no further than the immediate distress which these changes produced. Wage-earning labourers were thrown out of employment, tenant farmers were evicted from their holdings; crowds of small yeomen, copyholders, and cottars, who had eked out their livelihood by the produce of the stock which they maintained on the commons, were ruined. John Rous, the monk and antiquary of Warwick, was the first to protest against the conversion of the country into a wilderness, traversed only by shepherds and their dogs. Pole, Brinklow, More, Bacon, Strype, declaimed against a system which Latimer and Gilpin denounced from their pulpits. The cry of the people disturbed the learned quiet of Ascham, reached the ears even of Somerset and Edward VI. Their distresses broke to the surface in the numerous agrarian insurrections of the century. The sweating-sickness claimed its thousands; famine, rot, and murrain prevailed continuously. The high prices of necessaries, combined with the loss of commons and bad seasons, drove the small proprietors over the narrow border which separated them from starvation. Rents rose exorbitantly, till, for farmers at rack-rent, existence was a misery. There was an ominous growth of middlemen, 'leasemongers, who take groundes by lease to the entente to lette them againe for double and tripple the rente,' who battened on the earth-hunger of the people. In the reign of Henry VI. the average price of wheat was 6*s.* 8*d.* a quarter, of rye 4*s.*, of barley 3*s.* The daily wages of labourers without food from Easter to Michaelmas were 4*d.* Thus the labourer could then earn a quarter of wheat in 20 days, of rye in 12 days, of barley in 9 days. In 1595 the price of wheat was 20*s.* a quarter, of rye 13*s.* 4*d.*, of barley 12*s.* In the same year the wages of labourers were fixed by the Yorkshire justices at 5*d.* a day without food, from March 1 to November 1. Thus labourers could then earn a quarter of wheat in 48 days, of rye in 32 days, of barley in 28 days. Even those labourers who found employment worked for less wages than they received in the preceding century. They were compelled to accept the rate fixed by the employers; the arguments were whipping, branding, the galleys, or death. Thousands besides 'poor Tom' were whipped from 'tything to tything, and stock'd, punish'd, and imprisoned.' Legislators were bewildered by currency questions. Violent changes in the coinage aggravated distress. The nominal value of wages remained stationary while the purchasing power rapidly diminished. The standard purity of the pound of silver was, in the reign of Henry VIII., 18 dwts. of alloy to 11 oz. 2 dwts. of silver. The pound of silver was coined into 45 shillings. In the fifth year of Edward VI. there were 9 oz. of alloy to 3 oz. of silver. The pound of silver was coined into 72 shillings. In other words, the ounce of silver varied between 3*s.* 9*d.* in 1509 and 24*s.* in 1552. The standard of purity was restored in 1553, only to be again debased by Mary, and again restored by Elizabeth. As gold and silver poured into Europe from America prices rose throughout Europe. The rise was in England attributed to every cause but the true one, which was the lowering of the value of the precious metals. From 1459 to 1560 wheat averaged 9*s.* 2*d.* per quarter; from 1561 to 1601 it averaged 47*s.* 5*d.* But while the purchasing power of money was thus diminished, legislation prevented wages from following the rise in prices. Only human life was cheapened. The labour market was glutted; guild jealousies excluded peasants from trade. The poor-laws were passing from voluntary almsgiving to the compulsory support of the poor. There was no substitute for monastic bounty. Shakespeare drew no fancy picture, but one of which 'the country gave him proof and precedent,' of the 'bedlam beggars' who

>   from low farms,
> Poor pelting villages, sheepcotes, and mills,
> Sometime with lunatic bans, sometime with prayers,
> Enforce their charity.

Meanwhile large farmers profited by the low wages of agricultural labour and the high prices of agricultural produce. While Latimer laments the degradation of small yeomen, who, like his father, had farms of 'three to four pounds a year at the uttermost,' Harrison describes the rise of substantial farmers and the middle classes, and the chimneys, beds, sheets, pillows, pewter, tin, and silver, which for the first time appeared in their houses.

The process by which the commons were enclosed was often high-handed and oppressive. From the comparative silence of English records it cannot be concluded that a parliament of English landlords had no occasion to protect the interests of the cultivators of the soil. Sir Thomas

More speaks of 'husbandmen thrust out of their own, or else, by covin and fraud, or by violent oppression, put beside it, or by wrongs and injuries so wearied, that they be compelled to sell all.' The proceedings of Sir Giles Overreach in the 'New Way to pay Old Debts' did not entirely originate in the brain of the dramatist, and the peasant proprietor of a Naboth's vineyard would fall an easier victim than a lord of the manor.

> I'll buy some cottage near his manor,
> Which done, I'll make my men break ope his fences,
> Ride o'er his standing corn, or in the night
> Set fire to his barns, or break his cattle's legs.
> These trespasses will draw on suits, and suits expenses,
> Which I can spare, but will soon beggar him.
> When I have harried him thus two or three years,
> Though he sue *in formâ pauperis*, in spite
> Of all his thrift and care he'll grow behindhand.
> Then, with the favour of my man at law,
> I will pretend some title : want will force him
> To put it to arbitrament. Then if he sells
> For half the value he shall have ready money,
> And I possess the land.

But forcible enclosures of wastes or encroachments by squatters were not the only means by which common land passed into individual ownership. Voluntary agreements between commoners and proprietors of land were frequent, and bargains were often struck on equitable terms. Instances like the following extract from Kennet's 'Parochial Antiquities' (ii. 324) might be indefinitely multiplied :

'The said Edmund Rede, Esq., granted and confirmed to Thomas Billyngdon one close in Ardyngrave, in consideration whereof the said Thomas Billyngdon quitted and resigned his right to the free pasturage of four oxen to feed with the cattle of the said Edmund Rede and all right to any common in the said pasture or inlandys of the said Edmund.'

Here in the England of 1437 was the principle of commutation of rights of common applied by private contract. Sometimes these bargains were sanctioned by the Court of Chancery, or, where the Crown was interested, by royal license. No parliamentary confirmations are to be found before the reign of Charles II. Each party to the private contract possessed his block absolutely, instead of enjoying a perplexing variety of cross rights. Browbeating and bullying doubtless occurred, but attempted acts of oppression were frequently checked by the courts of law. Justice was not always perverted in the interests of landlords, nor were matters always 'ended as they were friended.' An interesting account of the attempted enclosure of the common fields at Welcombe, near Stratford-on-Avon, has been recently published by the late Dr. Ingleby, the well-known Shakespearian scholar. It is contained in a fragment of the private diary of Thomas Green, town clerk of Stratford in the first years of the seventeenth century. William Combe, lord of the manor of Welcombe, desired to enclose a portion of the hamlet which from time immemorial had been common fields. Lord Chancellor Ellesmere was an interested promoter of the scheme. Among the persons possessing rights over these common fields was William Shakespeare, who appears to have resisted their enclosure. Upon the petition of the commoners at Warwick Assizes, Chief Justice Coke made an order that 'noe inclosure shalbe made within the parish of Stratforde, for that yt is agaynst the Lawes of the Realme.'

CHAPTER III.

THE SEVENTEENTH CENTURY.

BUT though the change from common to individual ownership, from self-sufficing to profit-gaining agriculture, was accompanied with wide-spread distress, the sixteenth century, especially towards its close, witnessed a general impulse to the study and practice of farming. It was now that Herrera in Spain, Tarello in Italy, Heresbach in the Low Countries, Charles Estienne and Bernard Palissy in France, wrote upon agriculture. The gentry began to pay attention to farming. As Michel de l'Hôpital solaced his exile from court with his farm at Etampes, so Fitzherbert relieved his judicial labours with the cultivation of his land.

With the Tudor period begins the agricultural literature of England.[1] Besides Fitzherbert and Tusser, there were Turner, Googe, Sir Hugh Plat, Plattes, Markham, and others. 'Mayster Fitzherbert's Boke of Husbandry' was 'imprynted in 1523,' and in the same year appeared his 'Boke of Surveying.' The reputed author, a judge of the Common Pleas, treated his subjects in the most practical manner. His theory of the origin of the fluke in sheep survives in a more scientific form at the present day. The prevalence of the rot disquieted other agricultural writers. Harrison attributes it to 'gossamers, rowty fogs, mildews, and rank grass.' Leonard Mascall, who wrote on

[1] Appendix III., The early literature of agriculture.

the 'Government of Sheepe' in 1605, warns shepherds against plants grown 'on wet and marish grounds.' Tusser is the poet of agriculture. He embodies his experiences in doggerel verse, without any invocations of Pomona or Ceres. In his own life he illustrated the difficulty of combining the practical farmer with the contemplative poet. 'He spread his bread,' says Fuller, 'with all sorts of butter, yet none would stick thereon.' He was successively 'a musician, schoolmaster, serving-man, husbandman, grazier, poet—more skilful in all than thriving in his vocation.' His book was long recognised as a useful guide to farmers. In 1723, Lord Molesworth proposed that schools of agriculture should be established, in which 'Tusser's work should be taught to the boys to read, to copy, and get by heart.' Now it is only valuable as a storehouse of information respecting the domestic economy and rural life of our Elizabethan ancestors. Clover and artificial grasses were unknown to Tusser and Fitzherbert: the former mentions turnips as 'a kitchen-garden root to boil or butter.' Both advocate enclosures, and instance Essex and Suffolk to prove the superior cultivation under the newer system. Tusser's testimony that, in these two counties, beef and mutton were more plentiful, cheese and butter better, and all classes wealthier than elsewhere, is the more striking, as he was an Essex man and a Suffolk farmer. The proverbial 'Suffolk stiles' seem to point to the early extinction of parish fields; but both counties partly owed their pre-eminence to the possession of some of the highways between the Netherlands and London. Chaucer's merchant demands that the sea be kept clear between Orewell and Middleburgh. Yet it is significant that Fitzherbert and Tusser, representing the best theory and practice of agriculture of their day, ignore draining and dismiss manure or 'compass' with the briefest possible mention.

At the end of the seventeenth century the prospects of agriculture seemed brightening. As Hartlib, the friend of Milton and pensioner of Cromwell, puts it, 'ingenuities, curiosities, and good husbandry began to flourish.' 'The soil,' says Harrison, 'had growne to be more fruitful, and the countryman more painful, more careful, and more skilful for recompense of gain.' Wheat averaged 'on the welltilled and dressed acre' twenty bushels. Improved means of communication facilitated progress. Increased attention was paid to manuring. In Sussex, farmers purchased lime, fetched it from a distance, and burned it in kilns erected for the purpose. In Middlesex and Hertfordshire the sweepings of the London streets were bought up for the fields. In Cornwall, farmers rode many miles to get sand, and brought it home on horseback. In South Wales seaweed was extensively used. New materials for agricultural wealth accumulated, especially through the revival of gardening. Since the wars of the Roses this art had nearly expired. Herbs, fruits, and roots, which had been plentiful in the fifteenth century, had died out, or were thrown to the pigs. Even in 1650, Hartlib says that gardening was hardly known in the north and west of England. Hops were introduced into England in the reign of Henry VIII., though the old rhyme is hardly correct which says,—

> Hops, reformation, bays, and beer
> Came into England all in one year.

They were extensively cultivated in Suffolk in the time of Tusser. Onions, cabbages, carrots, parsnips, 'colleflowers,' were chiefly imported from Flanders; though Piers Plowman could command the two former vegetables, they were now rare except about Fulham and the Suffolk coast. Carrots were called Sandwich carrots, after the chief place of their cultivation. Turnips were scarcely grown except in gardens near London. Potatoes were still exotics, and luxuries of the rich. Both turnips and clover are urged on English farmers by Elizabethan writers. Googe, who knew the Low Countries, calls clover 'trèfle de Bourgogne,' and, after Heresbach, supposes it to be a Moorish grass, brought in by the Spaniards. In the same author's mention of a car armed with sharp sickles may be traced the first hint of the reaping machine.

The civil wars checked agricultural progress. Husbandry, if it did not actually decline, languished. It was a period of extreme distress. In 1651 Blith says that the poor farmers 'lived worse than in Bridewell;' Hartlib adds that but for foreign supplies the people must have starved. Wheat rose rapidly, till in 1648 it stood at 85s. the quarter. This rise was due to the deficiency not only of harvests, but of arable land. The average price from 1647 to 1651 was 77s. 7d.; the average taken from 1647 to 1700 was only 49s. 10d. Hartlib calculates that, in England and Wales, not more than four million acres were under tillage. While beef and mutton also rose to $3\frac{3}{4}d.$ per pound, daily wages without food advanced only 1d. upon the 3d. of 1444.

On the other hand, the materials of agricultural wealth rapidly accumulated, and the work of preparation continued almost uninterruptedly. To Sir Richard Weston, of Sutton in Surrey, formerly ambassador in the Palatinate, belongs the credit of the first successful cultivation of turnips and clover, the pivots of English agriculture. As Brillat-Savarin valued a new dish above a new star, so Young regards Weston as a 'greater benefactor than

Newton.' He did, in fact, give bread to millions. Blith and Hartlib followed him, but it was long, as the latter says, before clover emerged from 'the fields of gentlemen into common use.' Hartlib urges the adoption of roots and the folding of sheep, 'after the Flaunders manner,' as a means of improving sandy commons. He continually advocates the use of clover and ' Holy Hay or Saint foine,' and gives space to the following advertisement: 'Such as are desirous to buy any of the three-leaved grass, or lucern, spurry, clover-grass, and sinke-foile, what quantity they please, may have them at Thomas Brown's shop at the Red Lion in Soper Lane.' Twenty years later, Plot mentions clover and sainfoin among the unusual grasses cultivated in Oxfordshire. In 1669 Worlidge, after advocating enclosures and the cultivation of artificial grasses, urges turnips on farmers, 'although this be a plant usually nourisht in gardens and be properly a garden plant.' Still more explicit is Houghton (1682); he says that 'some in Essex have their fallows after turnips, which feed their sheep in winter, by which means their land is dung'd as if it had been folded; and these turnips, tho' few or none be carried off for humane use, are a very excellent improvement.' On the other hand, Blith derides turnips, which, he says, are only eaten by swine after they have been boiled.

Drainage was ably discussed by Blith. Writing as ' a lover of ingenuity,' he published his ' English Improver' in 1641. In 1652 a third edition of the work was published, under the title of 'The English Improver Improved.' In the interval Blith had become a captain and a courtier, and dedicated his book to the ' Right Honourable the Lord General Cromwell.' As remedies for the miseries of the agricultural population, he suggests the employment of more capital, the abolition of 'slavish customs,' the recognition of tenant right, the extinction of 'vermine.' Above all he insists on the necessity of drainage. It is characteristic of the age that he supports his argument from the Bible, and asks with Bildad, 'Can the rush grow without mire, or the flagg without water?' Blith deals not only with surface water, but the constant action of stagnant bottom water. No drain could, he said, touch the 'cold spewing moyst water that feeds the flagg and rush,' unless it was 'a yard or four feet deep,' provided with proper outfalls. His views are sound and advanced on a general scheme for drainage, in which landowners should be compelled to join for 'the commonwealth's advantage.'

When Blith wrote the drainage of the fens was a question of importance. The fen district was seventy miles long, in places thirty miles broad, and covered 680,000 acres. This was not land which had been under water since the Flood. Thorney was, in the time of William of Malmesbury, rich in vineyards and orchards, well wooded, productive, 'a very paradise of pleasure and delight.' The drainage works of the Romans had been carried on by the monks of Thorney, Crowland, Ramsey, Ely, Spinney. But latterly they had fallen out of repair. The district is naturally drained by the Cam, the Ouse, the Nene, the Welland, the Glen, and the Witham. But it was only in the maps that they ran into the sea. The river-beds were foul, the channels choked; the streams continually overflowed their banks. Twice a day tides drove back the fresh water, and prevented the discharge of the upland streams. The outfalls of the rivers silted up so rapidly, that in 1635, at Skirbeck Sluice, near Boston, a smith's forge and tools were found buried under sixteen feet of deposit. The country had thus become one vast deep fen, 'affording little benefit to the realm other than fish and fowl, and overmuch harbour to a rude and almost barbarous sort of lazy and beggarly people.'

The first drainage work of comparatively modern times was the cut from Peterborough to Denver, which, under the name of Moreton's leam, commemorates the famous Bishop of Peterborough. The whole district was surveyed at the close of the reign of Elizabeth, but it was not till 1606 that the first local Act was passed to reclaim the ring of Waldersea and Coldham. In 1630 the Earl of Bedford with thirteen gentlemen adventurers undertook to drain the southern fens. Though the Bedford level was the most completely executed work, the appliances could not cope with the rainfall of a wet season. Windmills were used to raise the waters of the interior districts to the level of the main river; Hartlib speaks of a 'Holland mill for dreyning set up at Ely, and kept by a certaine Frenchman.' But these clumsily constructed mills were inadequate. The work was partly done by Scotch prisoners taken at the battle of Dunbar, or by the Dutch prisoners of Admiral Blake. Other parts of the fens were in the same way partially reclaimed; others remained untouched till the present century. In some parts the works were never completed, or fell into decay, or were carried out by persons whom Blith characterises as 'mountebank engineers, idle practitioners, and slothful, impatient slubberers.' In many districts the mills and embankments were destroyed by the fenmen. The following stanzas are quoted from the doggerel poem of some fen Tyrtæus:—

Come, brethren of the water, and let us all assemble,
To treat upon this matter which makes us quake and tremble;

For we shall rue it, if 't be true, the Fens are undertaken,
And where we feed in fen and reed, they'll feed both beef and
    mutton.
The feathered fowls have wings to fly to other nations,
But we have no such things to help our transportations ;
We must give place (oh grievous case !) to hornéd beasts and
    cattle,
Except that we can all agree to drive them out by battle.
Wherefore let us entreat our ancient water nurses
To show their power so great as t' help us drain their purses,
And send us good old Captain Flood to lead us out to battle,
Then Twopenny Jack with scales on 's back will drive out all
    their cattle.

Owing to the inadequacy of the original works, and the 'riotous letts and disturbances of lewd people,' the east fen became once more a shaking bog or a chain of lakes fringed with reeds. The Wildmore and west fens were in 1793 so wet, that '40,000 sheep, or one per acre, rotted every year.' On Lindsey fen, in 1750, 'cows foraged midrib deep in water, swimming to their pasture from their hovels, and returning in the same way, and sheep were conveyed to pasture and clipped in flat-bottom boats.'

It is somewhat curious that foreigners should have taught the English the treatment of water. The Dutch drained our fens; paring and burning, irrigation, warping, canals, are all foreign importations. A colony of French emigrants, settled near Thorney, introduced paring and burning, and the paring plough was long known as the French plough. The irrigation of meadows is said to have been first practised in modern times by the notorious 'Horatio Pallavazene, . . . who robbed the Pope to pay the Queen.' Warping was brought from Italy to the island of Axholme in the eighteenth century, and by its means the peaty soils at the mouth of the Humber were converted into 'polders.' The great 'Canal du Midi' was completed in 1681, but for nearly a hundred years its example was lost on England.

Before the Revolution the country, as has been seen, possessed the means of recovering its strength and indefinitely increasing its productiveness. Enclosures facilitated the progress of improvements. New methods of cultivation were studied, new crops introduced from abroad. Turnips offered winter keep for cattle; with cultivated grasses, they supplied the means of enriching sands now profitable only as rabbit warrens: the same discoveries prevented the waste of land by exhaustive cropping and subsequent idleness under fallow. Drainage had been more practically discussed than it was destined to be again till the time of Smith of Deanston. The burdens of feudal tenures had been removed. Though the Crown had re-asserted its forest rights, the wild boar and the wolf disappeared in the reign of Charles II. But farmers were slow to profit by their improved position or to adopt new methods. No one, as Hartlib says, dared attempt innovations, lest he should be called 'a projector.' Little advantage was taken of the discoveries of experimental farmers; no general improvement was effected on the agriculture of the Georgics; no grazier formed a truer standard of the shape of cattle than Virgil or Columella.

CHAPTER IV.

AGRICULTURAL PROGRESS IN THE EIGHTEENTH CENTURY: TURNIP TOWNSHEND AND THE NORFOLK SYSTEM.

THE gigantic strides by which agriculture has advanced within the present century dwarf previous progress into insignificance; but the change between 1700 and 1800 was astonishing. While population doubled itself, the number of persons engaged in agriculture decreased not only relatively, but, up to 1770, actually. Before the end of the reign of George III. more than $6\frac{1}{2}$ million acres of land were enclosed. The area under cultivation had increased, but not in proportion to the growth of population; but the difference between the two does not alone measure the increased productiveness of the soil. England not only produced food for a population that had doubled itself, and grain for treble the number of horses, at a greatly reduced expenditure of labour, but during part of the period was, as M. de Lavergne says, the granary of Europe. From 1700 to 1764 the standard of living among all classes was considerably raised. The discovery of silver had spent its force, and the value of the precious metals hardened. But the coinage was greatly debased. Consequently there was a great inflation of nominal prices, which dissatisfied consumers without benefiting producers. But this difficulty had been successfully met by the statesmanlike action of the Government of William III. Population increased more slowly than the productiveness of the soil; poor rates fell below the figures of the preceding century; real wages were higher than they had been since the reign of Henry VI. Harvests were continuously prosperous; wheat, in spite of large exports, averaged, between 1713 and 1764, 34s. 11d. a quarter. There was little civil war or tumult, no rapidly increasing class of artisans, no glut of the labour market. Living improved among all classes. Instead of 'Martylmas beef,' the salted carcasses of half-starved oxen, 'euyll for the stone and euyll of digestyon, fitter to be used outside as a waterproofe than inside,' fresh meat was eaten by the peasantry. Wheaten bread ceased to be a luxury of the wealthy; rye was now chiefly grown as a forage crop. The oaten loaves of Lancashire only survived in the proverb 'That's noan jannock.' The barley meal of Cumberland gave place to wheaten flour. In 1760 wheat was the breadstuff of five-eighths of the population. The only drawbacks to agricultural prosperity were the 'most noted sheep rot' of 1735, and the cattle plague which broke out in Bohemia, devastated the north of France, and visited England three times during the period. Here the only remedy was to slaughter infected animals; the Government, paying one-third of the value, expended 135,000l. in a single year. The period was tasteless, coarse, and apathetic; but it was the golden age of the English peasant.

The next half-century witnessed a complete change. The Poor Law of 1733 had checked population. Cottages were razed to the ground, lest they should become 'nests for beggars' brats.' But no impediments could resist the effects of the prosperity of the previous period, or of the development of trade. Population sprang up with a bound; war raised necessaries to famine prices; bread, meat, cheese, beer, candles, were trebled; only clothing was cheapened.

The climate worsened after 1764; the mean average rainfall from 1741 to 1750 was 18½ inches; from 1771 to 1780 it averaged 26 inches. The harvests were as unprosperous as they had previously been favourable; the imports of grain exceeded the exports. In no part of the country did the purchasing power of wages rise with prices. The allowance system set a premium on large families, and so fostered the evil it was designed to alleviate. It was now that the South fell hopelessly behind the North. Before 1770 the rate of wages was lower in the North than in the South; now the position was reversed. Wages remained stationary in the South, eked out by mischievous allowances; while in the North they followed, though irregularly, the rise of prices. The introduction of machinery threw crowds of artisans out of work; the enclosure of commons again ruined thousands of small freeholders and copyholders. After 1814 the heavy fall of prices produced severe distress among landlords and tenants. Two years later the Board of Agriculture sent a circular letter throughout the counties to ascertain the state of the kingdom. The answers showed that landlords reduced their rents 25 per cent., struck off arrears, gave farms rent free for a year; that still great quantities of land were thrown up; that improvements were at a standstill, live stock decreased, and the country was filled with gangs of depredators; that everywhere 'bankruptcies, seizures, executions, imprisonments, and farmers become parish paupers,' were numerous. It is an extraordinary proof of the elasticity of the country that within ten years the social balance was restored.

The exertions of men like Townshend, Bakewell, Young, and Coke enabled farmers to meet the wants of a growing population. With their names is associated the agricultural progress of the century, which is comprised in improved methods of cultivation, the reduction of stock-breeding to a science, the enclosure of common field farms, the reclamation of commons and wastes, increased facilities of communication and transport, the invention of new implements, the application of new manures, the enterprise of capitalist landlords, the diffusion of intelligence among farmers. Within the period in question a class grew up which earned high wages and could afford to purchase farm produce. But for this wage-earning artisan class, agriculturists would have remained content to satisfy their own wants. The crisis at home and abroad gives peculiar interest to the advance of agriculture. England was sharing in that industrial movement which culminated politically in the rise of the new republic of America and the downfall of the ancient monarchy of France. It is more exciting to watch the political earthquake on the Continent; but it is more satisfactory to trace the peaceful operations of nature by which the face of society was changed in England. To measure the influence of agriculture upon the two movements is impossible; but here, at least till the close of the century, there was no gap between it and the general advance of industry.

After the English revolution a new stimulus had been given to arable farming. The exportation of British wool was forbidden, and home manufacturers could not take up the supply. At the same time duties were laid on foreign wheat, and bounties were offered for the export of corn.[1] Farmers

[1] Bounties on exports:—
1. From 1697 to 1706, 1,668,904 quarters of wheat, barley, oatmeal, malt, and rye were exported, which were valued at 1,874,994*l*. 10*s.* 6*d.*
2. From 1706 to 1726, 8,134,196 quarters were exported, valued at 8,429,704*l*. 14*s.*
3. From 1726 to 1746, 9,488,703 quarters were exported, valued at 10,080,224*l*. 7*s.* 3*d.* [In

were thus attracted back from pasture to tillage. The wars which ravaged the Continent and prevented foreign nations from sowing or harvesting their crops completed what domestic policy initiated. It was at this crisis that Lord Townshend began the Norfolk or four-course system of husbandry, long the model for all other counties. Townshend's political career had been useful, and from 1709 to 1730 he had held important offices of State. In his capacity of Secretary he had accompanied George I. to Hanover, where he had seen turnips grown as a field crop. In 1730 he abandoned to Walpole the exclusive enjoyment of power, devoted himself to farming, and, by causing 'two ears of corn to grow where but one grew before,' earned a better title to national gratitude than the whole generation of his political contemporaries put together.

Hitherto Suffolk and Essex had afforded the best examples of English farming. Suffolk was famous for its breed of Suffolk Punches, short compact horses, of about fifteen hands high, properly of a sorrel colour, unrivalled in their power of draught, though, as Cullum wrote in 1790, 'not fitted to indulge the rapid impatience of this

In the 1st period 552,867 quarters of wheat were exported.
,,   2nd period 2,518,213   ,,   ,,   ,,
,,   3rd period 4,461,337   ,,   ,,   ,,

4. Between the years 1746-65, 2,699,224*l.* 11*s.* 4¾*d.* were paid in bounties on the following exports:—(1) Wheat, 6,800,016 qrs.; (2) barley, 1,268,087 qrs.; (3) oatmeal, 67,186 qrs.; (4) malt, 4,977,303 qrs. (5) rye, 939,580 qrs.

In the whole period, 1697-1765, it is calculated that upwards of 33 million quarters were exported, the value of which exceeded 36,000,000*l.*

Burke's Act of 1773 reversed the old policy of bounties, and, before it was modified, England had become a consumer rather than a grower of corn. See Appendix IV. on the Corn Laws and the note there given on Bounties for Corn.

posting generation.' It was famous also for its dairy produce, especially its cheese, 'so hard that pigs grunt at it, dogs bark at it, but none dare bite it.' The mystery of its interior fired Bloomfield to sing of the Suffolk cheese which

> Mocks the weak effort of the bending blade,
> Or in the hog-trough rests in perfect spite,
> Too big to swallow and too hard to bite.

The southern part of the county was chiefly held in small farms, cultivated with the care and neatness of 'la petite culture.' Hollow drainage was practised earlier in Suffolk and Essex than elsewhere. The drains were wedge-shaped, filled with hazel boughs, bullocks' horns, ropes of twisted straw, stones, or peat. Bradley (1727) speaks of the Essex practice of making drains two feet deep at close and regular intervals throughout a whole field, filled with rubble or bushes, and covered over with earth; and he derives the term 'thorough-drainage' from an Essex word 'thorow,' meaning a trench to carry off the water. Crag, a calcareous shelly mixture of phosphates, was extensively used in the eastern part of Suffolk to fertilise the soil. The depth and size of the pits prove the antiquity of the practice. Ploughing was economically conducted: two horses only were used; oxen were unknown: 'no groaning ox is doomed to labour there' is the evidence of Bloomfield. The absence of oxen is an incidental proof of the early enclosure of the county, and of the prevalence of farmers rather than peasant proprietors. Yet, even in these favoured counties, successive corn crops were raised till the land ceased to bear, or weeds overpowered the cereals. Crabbe, himself a native of Suffolk, describes how

> Rank weeds, that every care and art defy,
> Reign o'er the land and rob the blighted rye.

Little effort was made to restore the fertility of the soil: roots were practically unknown; artificial grasses seldom, if ever, sown: scarcely any manure was used. Under a lease of 1753 a tenant on the manor of Hawsted was allowed two shillings for every load of manure which he brought from Bury and laid upon the land. But during a tenancy of twenty years only one load was charged to the landlord. The impoverished land was left to recover itself as best it could to grass. In the north-west corner of Suffolk tracts of moor and heath, alternating with blowing sands and rabbit-warrens, were interspersed with scanty patches of arable land, choked with weeds, in various stages of exhaustion.

Lord Townshend's estates were situated in Norfolk, then covered with rush-grown marshes, or sandy wastes where a few sheep starved, and 'two rabbits struggled for every blade of grass.' The brief but exhaustive list of its productions is 'nettles and warrens.' Six hundred thousand acres of Lincolnshire were either fen or wold. From Sleaford to Brigg, 'all that the devil o'erlooks from Lincoln town' was a desolate moor over which a land lighthouse, Dunstan pillar, guided travellers. There were no fences for miles, but the furze-capped sand-banks which enclosed the warrens. The high ground running from Spilsby to Caistor was similarly a bleak unproductive heath. From the edge of the wolds to the sea was a boggy wilderness. Both counties were as much additions to the profitable dominions of England as any warlike conquests. Young, in 1760, describes the effect of Townshend's Norfolk husbandry on a district near Norwich :—

'Thirty years ago it was an extensive heath without either tree or shrub, only a sheep-walk to another farm. Such a number of carriages crossed it, that they would sometimes be a mile abreast of each other in pursuit of the best track. Now there is an excellent turnpike road, enclosed on each side with a good quickset hedge, and the whole laid out in enclosures and cultivated in the Norfolk system in superior style. The whole is let at 15s. an acre, ten times the original value.'

It was not till the close of the century that this description of the improvements effected by the Norfolk system applied to the whole of the county. Still later was it before the methods which turned Lincoln heath from a rabbit-warren to a sheep market were generally adopted in Lincolnshire.

Among the improvements adopted by Townshend was the practice of marling. In ancient leases in Normandy tenants covenanted to marl. In England the practice had died out, owing, as Fitzherbert thought, partly to 'ydlenes,' partly to want of confidence between landlord and tenant. Markham says that marl was once largely used, since trees 200 or 300 years old grew in spent marl-pits, but that it had been discontinued after the wars of the Roses. Most of the agricultural writers of the seventeenth century, such as Hartlib, Houghton, Worlidge, Plot, agree with Markham in urging the revival of the practice. Farmers believed that marl was 'good for the father, bad for the son,' till Townshend proved its value on the light sands of Norfolk. The tide of fashion set once more in its favour, and farmers found another proverb for their purpose :—

> He who marls sand
> May buy the land ;
> He that marls moss
> Suffers no loss ;
> He that marls clay
> Throws all away.

By means of marl alone, Young calculated that 'three or

four hundred thousand acres of waste were turned into gardens.'

But Townshend's greatest achievement was the field cultivation of turnips and clover. A new vein of agricultural wealth was struck; turnips became the most active agents as well as the surest indicators of good farming. Clover and turnips had hitherto been grown as experiments. Tull brought the cultivation of roots to comparative perfection. 'I introduced turnips into the field,' he says, 'in King William's reign; but the practice did not travel beyond the hedges of my estate till after the peace of Utrecht.' A similar prejudice existed against clover. 'Farmers,' as Tull states, 'if advised to sow it, would certainly reply, Gentlemen might sow it if they pleased, but they [farmers] must take care to pay their rent.' Townshend was the first great landlord who proved the value of green crops as the pivots of agricultural improvement. He initiated the Norfolk system, the merit of which depends on the judicious alternation of roots and grasses with cereals. The introduction of green crops encouraged the farmer to observe what, in the absence of chemical manures, was the golden rule of never taking two corn crops in succession; saved him from leaving a portion of his land every year unproductive; enabled him to increase his live stock and maintain it without falling off during the winter. For the sands of Norfolk, turnips possessed peculiar value. Roots, fed off on the ground by sheep, fertilised and consolidated the poorest soil. Another portion of the crop, drawn off and stored for winter keep, enabled the farmer to carry more stock, supplied him with more manure, enriched the land, and trebled its yield. It thus became a proverb that 'a full bullock yard and a full fold yard makes a full granary.' Farming in a circle, unlike logic, proved a most productive process. Townshend adopted Tull's plan of drilling and horse-hoeing turnips instead of sowing them broadcast. He was an exponent of the maxim that 'the more the irons are among the turnips till the leaves spread across the rows, the better.' His advocacy of turnips earned him the nickname of Turnip Townshend, and supplied an example for Pope's Horatian illustrations—

> Why, of two brothers rich and restless, one
> Ploughs, burns, manures, and toils from sun to sun;
> The other slights, for women, sports, and wines,
> All Townshend's turnips and all Grosvenor's mines.

Those who followed Townshend's example realised fortunes. In thirty years one farm rose in value from 180*l.* a year to 800*l.*; another, rented by a warrener at 18*l.* a year, was let to a farmer at 240*l.*; a farmer named Mallet made enough off a holding of 1,500 acres to buy an estate of the annual value of 1,800*l.* a year. Some farmers were said to be worth ten thousand pounds. But the practice spread by very slow degrees. Many persons classed turnips with rats among Hanoverian novelties, and refused their assistance with Jacobite indignation. Nor was it possible to introduce roots or grasses among open field farmers on land which was common from August to Candlemas. But as the immense benefits of green crops became more evident the work of enclosure was accelerated. Besides the land enclosed by Acts of Parliament, thousands of acres were enclosed piecemeal by interchange among individual occupiers, or by agreement and redistribution in separate parcels among the whole body of commoners.

CHAPTER V.

AGRICULTURAL PROGRESS IN THE EIGHTEENTH CENTURY: BAKEWELL AND THE GRAZIER'S ART.

THE discoveries in the art of stock-breeding made by Bakewell, of Dishley, near Loughborough, in Leicestershire, produced even more startling results than Townshend's Norfolk system. Before his day the English farmer, like the Lord Chancellor, took his seat on the woolsack. British wool commanded the highest prices at home and in foreign markets; it had been the chief object of agriculturists for three centuries. The classification of sheep as long-woolled, short-woolled, and intermediate, shows that sheep as wool-producing animals had long been studied in England; the fleece, and not the carcass, was valued. Small animals, like the white-faced, hornless Ryeland sheep, were most profitable to farmers. In the reign of Henry VIII. 'Leemynster' wool fetched the highest, Cotswold the second price. Elynour Rummin, alewife of Leatherhead, received payment in kind for her customers, of whom

> Some fill their pot full
> Of good Lemster wool.

In 1783 Ryeland wool was sold at 2s. a pound, when ordinary wool fetched only 4d. Owing to the value of the fleece, Ryeland sheep were cotted in Herefordshire both summer and winter. Camden describes the cots in Gloucestershire as long, low-ceilinged buildings, three stories high, with slopes at the end of each floor, so that the sheep could mount to the topmost story. He characteristically derives the Cotswolds from this practice of cotting. But in the eighteenth century our farmers gained a start over other agriculturists by their readiness to detect and accept coming changes. When Louis XVI. was forming his flock of merinos at Rambouillet to improve French fleeces, English sheep-farming took a fresh departure, which had for its object, not wool, but butcher's meat.

Bakewell was an agricultural opportunist, 'un homme de génie qui a fait autant pour la richesse de son pays que ses contemporains Arkwright et Watt.' He was born in 1725, and died in 1794. He saw that the day was near when meat would be more valued in the ox than draught, or in the sheep than wool. He succeeded in producing beef and mutton for the million. Visitors gathered from every part of the world to learn from him what are now axioms of stock husbandry, and to see his famous black cart stallion, his bull 'Twopenny,' or his ram 'Two-pounder.' In appearance he resembled the typical yeoman who figures on Staffordshire pottery, 'a tall, broad-shouldered, stout man of brown-red complexion, clad in a loose brown coat and scarlet waistcoat, leather breeches, and top-boots.' In his kitchen he entertained 'Russian princes, French and German royal dukes, British peers, and sightseers of every degree.' He never altered the routine of his daily life. 'Breakfast at eight; dinner at one; supper at nine; bed at eleven o'clock: at half-past ten, let who would be there, he knocked out his last pipe.'

Before his day no true standard of shape was recognised. 'Cattle,' wrote Culley in 1809, 'were more like ill-made black horses than an ox or a cow; nothing would please but elephants and giants.' The favourite type were the gaunt Holderness breed, because they offered most space for the laying on of flesh. Oxen were prized for their power of draught; parish bulls were selected for those qualities which in Obadiah's pet were alleged to be wanting. No attention, except, as Hartlib allowed, in Lancashire and the northern counties, was paid to breed: it was a promiscuous union of nobody's son with everybody's daughter. Thus misshapen wall-sided beasts were scattered all over the country, and prizes were offered for the animal with the longest legs. Similarly sheep were tall, unthrifty beasts, valued for points which were absurd because they were useless. Wiltshire breeders demanded a horn which fell back so as to form a semicircle, in front of which the ear projected; Norfolk flockmasters valued the length and spiral form of the horn and the blackness of the face and legs; Dorsetshire breeders staked everything on the horn projecting forward, so that the ear was behind. Rams were, in fact, selected for horns, legs, and faces. Each county had its breed, unknown beyond its borders. Ryelands were limited to Herefordshire, old Norfolks to Norfolk, Southdowns to Sussex. The only exceptions were Welsh sheep, which were driven up to London for their mutton, and Hampshire downs, which seem to have been known in the seventeenth century as Hertfords. Bakewell's predecessor in sheep-farming was J. Allom, a breeder of local fame. His own experiments were made on the 'old Leicestershire' or Warwickshire sheep crossed with the Ryeland. Marshall thus describes the 'true old Warwickshire' ram:—'His frame large and loose; his bones heavy; his legs long and thick; his chine as well as his rump as sharp as a hatchet; his skin rattling on his ribs like a skeleton bound in parchment.'

With these unpromising materials Bakewell in 1750 began his uphill task. He discovered the principle of selection. He only used those rams and ewes that possessed the qualities which he wished to reproduce. As these qualities were perpetuated the breed was formed. His object was to breed animals which weighed most in the best joints, and quickest repaid the food they consumed. 'Small in size and great in value,' or the Holkham toast of 'symmetry well covered,' was his motto. He saw that the value of the sheep lay not in the length of the legs, but the size of the barrel; that the bones must be fine and the form compact, and that the true shape for profit was that of 'a firkin on as short legs as possible.' The great merits of his new Leicester sheep were their fattening propensities and early maturity. While other breeds required three or four years to fit them for market, the new Leicesters were prepared in two. Those who tried the Dishley sheep found that they throve where others starved, that while alive they were the hardiest, when dead the heaviest. Bakewell rapidly made a fortune. In 1755 he let his rams for the season at 16*s.* each; in 1789 a society was formed to extend his breed of sheep, which hired his rams at 6,000 guineas for the season.

Bakewell raised the new Leicesters to the highest pitch of perfection. But this was not all. His breed was best suited to the plains, but was ill adapted to hills or mountains. He had, however, shown the way in which breeds might be improved; imitation was easy. In a less immediate sense he was the creator, not only of the new

Leicesters, but of the Southdowns and the Cheviots. Following in his footsteps, Ellman of Glynde took up the Sussex sheep, and under his skilful care and that of Jonas Webb, of Babraham, the Southdowns competed for supremacy with the new Leicesters. Similarly the Cheviots were improved on Bakewell's principles. Before these breeds, fitted for the plain, the hill, and the mountain, native races, like the Northumberland 'mugs,' the foresters of Nottingham, the Morfe-common sheep, died away, like Red Indians before more civilised races. But gradually supporters rallied round other varieties. Bakewell's weapons were turned against himself: native sheep of other districts were improved by crossing with the Leicesters or the Southdowns; and though to these two breeds precedence will always be given on historical grounds, it may be questioned whether they have not been rivalled both in beauty and utility.

In cattle-breeding Bakewell was less successful. It was his material, not his system, which failed. He endeavoured to found his typical race on the Westmoreland cattle, the purest breed of the Craven Longhorns. He based his improvements upon the labours of two of his predecessors. Sir Thomas Gresley, of Drakelow House, near Burton, had in 1720 begun the formation of a herd of Longhorns. Webster, of Canley, commenced with some of the Drakelow blood; and Bakewell founded his experiments on two Canley heifers and a Westmoreland bull. But Bakewell could not produce the same results which he had developed in the new Leicester sheep. His cattle were good milkers, and little more. But it was by his example and practice that other breeds, with better natural qualities, were improved. Thus the Teeswater or Durham Shorthorns, both as dairy and meat-producing cattle, jumped into the foremost place. Charles Colling's Ketton herd was to cattle-breeders what Bakewell's new Leicesters were to sheep-farmers. In 1810 his stock was sold at an average price of 175 guineas. Similarly Tomkins, in 1769, took up and improved the Hereford cattle, from his two famous cows 'Pigeon' and 'Mottle.' By a pardonable anachronism Scott has assigned to the Laird of Killancureit 'a bull of matchless merit brought from the county of Devon (the Damnonia of the Romans, if we may trust Robert of Gloucester).' But the Devon cattle were only known as draught oxen for the plough in the days of Waverley. Mr. Coke of Holkham brought them into fashion early in this century, and their great breeder was Mr. Quartley.

Bakewell's success and the increasing demand for butchers' meat raised up a host of imitators. Breeders everywhere followed his example: his standard of excellence was gradually recognised. The foundation of the Smithfield Club in 1793 did much to promote the improvement of live stock. In 1710 the average size of the cattle and sheep sold in Smithfield Market was—beeves 370 lbs., calves 50 lbs., sheep 28 lbs., lambs 18 lbs.; in 1795 they weighed respectively 800 lbs., 148 lbs., 80 lbs., and 50 lbs. Part of this improvement must be attributed to Bakewell and his successors, part to the enclosure of the commons. So long as these existed the cattle were stunted, if not starved; and the stint, even if any limit was imposed, was disproportionately large. But local prejudices were hard to overcome; it was years before farmers ceased to value the shape and proportions which gratified the taste of their ancestors. It requires many blows to drive a nail through hearts of oak; or, as others might put it, the 'John Trot geniuses' of farming were hardly convinced even by interviews with the Shorthorns or new Leicesters which were paraded through the county. The formation of herds became a favourite pursuit of the wealthy. Flora MacIvor might herself have lived to see the day when country gentlemen were breeders of cattle without being 'boorish two-legged steers like Killancureit.'

Bakewell was a man whose energy and skill deserved success. He was unpopular in his day because of his secrecy; he had no confidant except an old shepherd. So lavish was his hospitality that before the end of his life he had to give up his farm, and died in comparative poverty. His irrigated water meadows, producing four crops a season, his miniature canal, by which the produce of the farm was conveyed to and fro, as well as his skill in stock-breeding, prove him to have been a man far in advance of his age as a scientific and practical farmer.

CHAPTER VI.

AGRICULTURAL PROGRESS IN THE EIGHTEENTH CENTURY: ARTHUR YOUNG AND THE DIFFUSION OF KNOWLEDGE.

BEFORE 1780 the Eastern counties and Leicestershire had alone profited to any substantial degree by improvements in agriculture or stock-breeding. The character of the farmers, the size of their holdings, the small number of open fields, the terms of land-letting, will explain the keenness of their spirit of progress. Young and Marshall agree that, in these counties, farms were large, and landlords and tenants enterprising. The farmers in Norfolk occupied 'the same position in society as the clergy and smaller squires;' in Lincolnshire 'many had mounted their nags and examined other parts of the country;' in Leicestershire they 'had travelled much and mixed constantly with one another.' Throughout these districts farmers were well educated, and possessed sufficient capital and confidence, though generally only holding at will or from year to year, to expend large sums of money on their land. In all the other counties agriculture languished, owing to the prevalence of wastes, the absence of leases, the ignorance of the people, the difficulties of communication, the obstinacy of traditionary practices.

The ancient forest of Sherwood, which recalled the days of Robin Hood and Little John, still occupied the greater part of Nottinghamshire; Rossendale, in Lancashire, was still a chace; nearly the whole of Derbyshire was a black region of ling; the land lighthouse of Dunstan pillar still guided the traveller from Sleaford to Brigg; Cambridgeshire and Huntingdonshire still defied the assaults of drainage; Northumberland was still overspread with forests of broom, in which a Scotch army might hide; from the northern point of Derbyshire to the extremity of Northumberland a line might be drawn for 150 miles as the crow flies, which passed across nothing but wastes. It was across this district that Jeanie Deans travelled in the reign of George II. Three quarters of Westmoreland, according to Bishop Watson, lay uncultivated. Hounslow Heath and Finchley Common were described in 1793 as wastes, fitted only for Cherokees and savages. That part of the East Riding called the Carrs, from Bridlington Quay to Spurn Point, and inland as far as Driffield, was an extensive swamp, which produced little but the ague; willow trees marked out the road from Hull to Beverley, and the bells rang at dusk from the tower of Barton-upon-Humber to guide the travellers. Though many farmers in the north were masters of from 5,000 to 40,000 sheep, and tenants of farms from 500*l.* to 2,000*l.* a year, they still milked their ewes, and were ignorant of the nature of a fold.

Half England was cultivated in very small farms, or by small peasant proprietors, or on the common field system. So late as 1794 it is calculated that, of 8,500 parishes, 4,500 were even then still farmed in common. Out of 84,000 acres of arable land in Bedfordshire, 24,000 acres were in open fields. In the 147,000 arable acres of Cambridgeshire, 132,000 were tilled in common; out of 438,000 acres in Berkshire, 220,000 were similarly cultivated. In Bucks 90,000, in Lincolnshire 268,000, in Huntingdon 130,000 acres were under this open field system. The Vale of Pickering, in Yorkshire, was farmed by the township, the common sheep-walks and pastures were overrun with bushes and weeds, the arable fields incessantly ploughed for an unvarying succession of crops, the meadows mown year after year without intermission or amelioration. At Naseby a few pasture enclosures surrounded the mud-built village; the open fields, tilled on the trinity system, were crossed and recrossed by paths to the different holdings, uneven, filled with cavernous depths of mire: the common pastures were in a state of nature, rough, full of furze, rushes, and fern. Bosworth Field, in 1785, was in wheat, as it had been three centuries before. In Oxfordshire and the neighbouring counties the common field system extensively prevailed. At Aston Boges, in Oxfordshire, the customs of the manor, 'used time out of mind,' were confirmed in 'ye 35th yeare of Queen Elizabeth, ano. dom. 1593.' The rules of cultivation which they laid down were carried out in the present century by the Sixteens, representatives chosen one from every four of the sixty-four yardlands [1] into which the manor was divided. In 1797 Rothwell, in Northamptonshire, contained 3,000 acres: 600 acres were small enclosures near the village; the remaining 2,400 acres were in three distinct fields of 800 acres each, partly arable, partly meadow, divided into eighty yardlands cut up into parcels, and scattered over the fields. Stewkley, in Buckinghamshire, was at the same time surrounded by three extended fields, one fallow, one wheat, one beans. There were 104 yardlands of thirty acres each. The main roads were rendered invisible by the driftways to the various properties. The Cotswolds,

---

[1] A yardland generally consisted of 30 acres.

from Broadway to Tetbury, and from Birdlip to Burford, lay unenclosed. Farmers were poor, ignorant, spiritless: holdings were small, wages low. On common fields it was impossible to introduce green crops, or to profit by the discoveries of Bakewell. Young had some reason for the conclusion that the 'Goths and Vandals of open field farmers must die out before any complete change takes place.'

In Essex and Suffolk leases for terms of years, with clauses as to management, were not unknown. But even landlords entertained prejudices against leases, because of the supposed want of reciprocity. In 1810 Young found many Oxfordshire landlords who never gave leases, because 'they told the farmer when he might begin systematically to exhaust the land.' Agreements, voidable on either side at six months' notice, were the rule in the country. Where a good understanding existed between landlord and tenant leases were not indispensable. But if tenants at will lost confidence, as in Yorkshire at the close of the century, 'good farming ceased, for fear the fields should look green, and the rent be raised.' Enterprise was impossible without certainty of return for outlay. Tenants at will adopted the routine of the district, and plodded along in the beaten track trodden by their ancestors. The Berkshire saying—

He that havocs may sit,
He that improves must flit,

expressed the popular belief that, if the tenant improved his land, he would be forced either to leave his holding or pay a higher rent. Leases for lives were the usual form, when the tenure was not at will or from year to year. But their utility was marred by the absence of any clauses of management or provision for the maintenance of buildings. In Devonshire leases were, as Fitzherbert advises, for three lives; but the landlord was often obliged, as the third life drew to its close, to put himself in as sub-tenant to save his farm buildings from irreparable ruin.

Still greater obstacles to agricultural progress were presented by an inert mass of local prejudice and an obstinate adherence to antiquated methods. The open field system provided sufficient for the occupiers who required nothing more. Where land was enclosed, the ignorance of the farmers made the dissemination of new ideas difficult. Not only could few read or write, but they entertained a not unjustifiable contempt for book-farmers. Few agricultural writers had had the practical experience of Fitzherbert; most wrote as if they had never travelled beyond the sound of Bow bells. Sometimes their books were too systematic or too general; sometimes their promises were so extravagant as to give literary agriculturists the reputation of quack medicine vendors. Ridiculous and valuable suggestions are intermixed. Here is the remedy, suggested by Hartlib or his editor Beati, for flukes in sheep: 'Take serpents or (which is best) vipers; cut their heads and tayles off and dry the rest to powder; mingle this powder with salt, and give a few grains of it so mingled to sheep.' Bewildered agriculturists fared ill between the bad scholarship, the inexperience, and the incorrect chemistry which was offered them in the name of science. In practice experimental farmers had often failed. Like ancient alchemists, they starved in the midst of their golden dreams. Tusser, teaching thrift, never throve. Gabriel Plattes, the cornseller who boasted that he could raise thirty bushels of wheat to the acre, died in the streets for want of bread. Jethro Tull, instead of gaining an estate, lost two by his horse-hoeing husbandry. Arthur Young failed twice in farm management before he began his invaluable tours.

Difficulties of communication impeded agricultural progress. Under the open field system the neighbourhood had no interest for the village; drift lanes to closes were alone important. Like ancient geographers, they knew their own district, while to all beyond they applied the description of impassable wastes or horrid sands. Some of the great highways were in good repair. Turnpike roads had been established in 1663; and in the reign of George II.

No cit nor clown
Can gratis see the country or the town.

Yet, in the eighteen miles of turnpike road between Preston and Wigan, Young 'measured ruts four feet in depth and floating in mud only from a wet summer,' and passed three broken-down carts. Essex in the time of Fitzherbert was famous for its bad roads. In the eighteenth century it worthily maintained its reputation. 'A mouse could barely pass a carriage in its narrow lanes,' which were filled with bottomless ruts, and often choked by a string of chalk wagons buried so deep in the mire that they could only be extricated by thirty or forty horses. 'Of all the cursed roads that ever disgraced this kingdom in the very age of barbarism none ever equalled that from Billericay to the "King's Head" at Tilbury,' was the suffering cry of Young in 1769. The roads of Herefordshire, says Marshall a quarter of a century later, were such as you might expect to find in the marshes of Holland or the mountains of Switzerland. Norfolk possessed such natural capacity for good roads, that Charles II. suggested it should be cut up to provide highways for the rest of the kingdom. Yet even in this county Young found 'not a yard of good road.' In remoter or more backward parts of England roads were impassable except for well-mounted horsemen, or wagons drawn by twelve horses. In narrow country lanes bells on the team were not an ornament, but a necessary warning. Roads were engineered on the principle that 'one good turn deserves another.' Farmers of one district knew the practices of the next as little as those of Kamtschatka. Outside their limited range were only

> Anthropophagi, and men whose heads
> Do grow beneath their shoulders.

This extreme isolation was a formidable obstacle. Yet the days when Gloucester seemed in 'the Orcades,' and York was a Pindaric flight from London, had advantages. In 1800 it took fifty-four hours for 'a philosopher, six shirts, his genius, and his hat upon it,' to reach London from Dublin.

Traditional practices were agricultural heirlooms, which farmers guarded with jealous care: ocular proof of the superiority of new systems failed to wean them from the routine of their ancestors. Hartlib complained that in Kent he had seen 'four, six, yea, twelve horses and oxen to one plough;' nor were the teams diminished a century later. By immemorial custom in Gloucestershire, two men and a boy, with a team of six horses, were employed for ploughing. Mr. Coke sent a Norfolk ploughman into the county, who, with a pair of horses and a Norfolk plough, did the same amount of work in the same time. But though the annual expenses were thus diminished by 120*l*. it was twenty years before neighbours profited by the lesson. In 1780 a Norfolk farmer settled in Devonshire, where he cultivated turnips on the newest methods. His crops were larger and finer than those of other farmers;

yet at the close of the century none had followed his example. Young, in 1768, says that clover and turnips were unknown in many parts of the country. Clover was not sown in Northumberland before 1752, turnips did not appear till eight years later. The first root crop in Cumberland was grown in 1755 by Mr. Howard of Corby. Even where turnips were cultivated, drill husbandry was unheard of; broadcast sowing still prevailed; hoeing was hardly practised out of the eastern counties. As to Jethro Tull, Young adds, 'farmers knew not that such a man existed.' In Devonshire, till nearly the end of the century, the spade was of the shape known to card-players, and crops were carried, or 'led,' from the fields, packed in crooks arranged on the backs of horses. When Davies wrote his report on Wiltshire in 1811, turnips were almost unknown, though sheep were the sheet-anchor of the agriculture of the county. In 1812 Strickland surveyed the East Riding of Yorkshire. In that year wheat had reached 122s. the quarter; but much of the land was still in open fields. Irish farmers at the end of the eighteenth century still used sledges, still sowed their potatoes broadcast, still 'walked backwards before their teams, striking them in the face when they wished them to advance,' still 'drew their ploughs and harrows by their horses' tails.' 'Indignant reader,' exclaimed Young, 'this is no jest of mine, but cruel, stubborn, barbarous truth.' Yet in 1634 an Act was necessary in England 'agaynst plowynge by the taile.'

The useful work of studying the agricultural practices of England and disseminating the results of scientific experiments was undertaken by Arthur Young. His name is ignored in many works on agriculture, notably in the article in the new edition of the 'Encyclopædia Britannica.' France has better appreciated his merits. In the phrase of

M. Lesage, his latest translator and editor, she has made an adopted child of his work. Young was born in September 1741, at Bradfield Hall, near Bury St. Edmunds. His father was a Prebendary of Canterbury. From Lavenham School he passed, at the age of seventeen, into a wine merchant's office at Lynn. On the death of his father, in 1763, he returned home as his mother's bailiff; but his experiments proved so unsuccessful that he was removed from the management of the estate. From various causes he failed twice in farming on his own account before he devoted himself to those tours, in the course of which he has drawn his spirited sketches of England, Ireland, and France. He first visited France in 1787, on the invitation of the Duc de la Rochefoucauld-Liancourt, whose two sons had been partly educated in his neighbourhood at Bury St. Edmunds. Young was a man of keen observation and considerable culture, familiar not only with the writings of English agricultural writers, but with those of De Seres, De Châteauvieux, and Du Hamel. He possessed great talents for description, but little power of generalisation. His arguments in favour of corn bounties, and his depreciation of science, prove him to have shared the prejudices of the day. Yet he was one of the most enlightened and useful pioneers of agricultural improvement that the century produced. His enthusiasm is always genuine if it is sometimes extravagant, as when he praises the plumpness of Rubens's female portraits with the eye of a grazier, or remarks of a fine Correggio, 'A fine picture is a good thing, but I had rather it had been a fine tup.' In 1793 he was appointed secretary to the new Board of Agriculture. He died in London in February 1820, having been for ten years totally blind.

CHAPTER VII.

AGRICULTURAL PROGRESS IN THE EIGHTEENTH CENTURY—
THE SECOND AGRICULTURAL CRISIS—ENCLOSURES OF
OPEN FIELDS AND COMMONS FROM 1770 TO 1820.

THE second agricultural crisis was due to the reaction from pasture to tillage in the latter half of the eighteenth and the beginning of the nineteenth centuries. England returned from sheep to arable farming under new conditions and changed circumstances, which rendered it a matter of national necessity to break up open fields, consolidate small holdings, and enclose wastes and commons. Without large farms, capital, and increased production, it would have been impossible for England to feed her growing population, or to attain her commercial prosperity.

The blow fell in the first instance on the agrarian associations which still farmed the common fields. When Young commenced his tours few counties had changed their external features or agricultural practices for centuries. Hitherto the slow increase of a rural population had been the sole incentive to improvement. Watt, Arkwright, and others changed the condition of society with the suddenness of a revolution. Population was advancing by leaps and bounds; a market was opened for agricultural produce. The farmer lay down at night confident that he could supply his family with food; he woke in the morning to hear the clamour of crowded manufacturing cities for bread and meat. Self-sufficing agriculture was an anachronism. How was the new condition to be met? Arthur Young was ready with his answer. 'Large farms and large capital' was his interpretation of the problem set by the manufacturer to the agriculturist. He proclaimed a crusade against open fields. As a practical farmer, the sight of good land yielding poor crops gave him pain; but he had better grounds for his hostility. Here and there the villagers had appointed field-reeves to direct agricultural operations; but, speaking generally, the farming of the old agrarian communities had deteriorated since the sixteenth century. They could make no use of improved methods of cultivation, rotations of crops, or machinery. Enterprising men were hampered by the apathy of less active partners. If one farmer drained his land, the others stopped up the main drain so that his land was swamped. The strips were too narrow to admit of cross-harrowing or cross-ploughing. No winter crops could be grown because common rights of pasture were enjoyed over the arable fields. Half the day was wasted in going to and fro between the different parcels; the expense of reaping or carting was enormously increased when crops lay in little, remote, and distant strips. Innumerable footpaths to the various closes cut up and contracted the available land. Litigation was perpetual, since self-interested farmers ploughed up the common balks or headlands, moved their neighbours' landmarks, and filched their land or crops. As Tusser said two centuries before of common field farmers,—

> Some champions agree
> As wasp doth with bee.

The manure of the live stock was wasted on the commons

instead of enriching the land of individual owners. Without a general agreement among a large body of small, suspicious, and ignorant independent proprietors, alternate husbandry could not be adopted by the open-field farmer; turnips and clover, the philosopher's stones which turned sand into gold, were beyond his reach. Where no interest was individual, no private person would improve, drain, or reclaim wastes; no would-be follower of Bakewell could pursue the science of stock-breeding. The pastures on which the live stock of the township fed generated the rot; promiscuous herding propagated infectious disorders. On every common were crowded together half-starved horses, cattle, and sheep, a disgrace to their respective breeds, a fruitful cause of disease, because no individual farmer could improve his breed of live stock. Not only was the arable land badly tilled, but the wastes and commons were a standing reproach, from a productive point of view, to the rural economy of the country. It is not surprising that Young should have demanded a general system of enclosure.

His crusade against the old common-field system was assisted by other causes. It required little to turn a peasant proprietor into a wage-earning labourer. Every step in the industrial development of the nation tended to the consolidation of farms, the extinction of the common-field system, and the disappearance of small owners. Commerce drew the peasantry to centres of trade. Even in the reign of Charles II. petitions were presented against the denudation of country districts and the consequent scarcity of agricultural labour. Thousands of the rural population were attracted from agriculture to manufacture; the small farmer no longer had the aid of his family in the cultivation of the soil, and he could not afford to pay wages.

Formerly he had no need for money; home production satisfied his domestic wants: exchange or mutual accommodation supplied whatever he could not fashion for himself. Wealth only existed in its simplest forms; natural divisions of employment were not made, because only the rudest implements of production were used. The rapid development of manufacture caused its complete separation from agriculture; the application of machinery to manual industries completed the revolution in social arrangements; a division of labour became an economic necessity. The farmer and the artisan became mutually dependent; barter no longer sufficed, but money was absolutely necessary. Hitherto the rude implements required for the cultivation of the soil, or the household utensils needed for the comfort of daily life, had been made at home. The farmer, his sons, and his servants, in the long winter evenings carved the wooden spoons, the platters, and the beechen bowls; plaited wicker baskets; fitted handles to the tools; cut willow teeth for rakes and harrows, and hardened them in the fire; fashioned ox-yokes and forks; twisted willows into the traces and other harness gear. Travelling carpenters visited farmhouses at rare intervals to perform those parts of work which needed their professional skill. The women plaited the straw for the neck-collars, stitched and stuffed sheepskin bags for the cart saddle, wove the straw or hempen stirrups and halters, peeled the rushes for and made the candles. The spinning-wheel, the distaff, and the needle were never idle; coarse home-made cloth and linen supplied all wants; every farmhouse had its brass brewing kettle. The very names of spinster, brewster, baxter, webster, showed that the women spun, brewed, baked, and wove for the household. All the domestic industries by which cultivators of the soil increased their incomes, or escaped the necessity of selling their produce, were now supplanted by manufactures. Basket or brush making, pillow lace, straw plait for hats, hand-loom weaving, spinning silk, hemp, or wool, stitching gloves for the trade of Hereford or Leominster, the woollen or worsted manufacturers of Norfolk and Suffolk, the broadcloth trade of Gloucestershire and Wiltshire, the iron manufacturers of Kent and Sussex, the baizes of Colchester and Sturminster, were gradually centred in the cities of the north, instead of being disseminated through the villages of the south. A change of fashion, like the decay of the taste for Derbyshire 'ribs,' brought Brandreth to the gallows. The cheapness of manufactured goods encouraged the dependence of the farmer on the manufacturer; the separation of the two industries was essential for the perfection of both. The gigantic increase of the population, together with the withdrawal of a large part of the labouring classes from agriculture, demanded the utmost development of the resources of the soil. Small farmers and peasant occupiers were picturesque obstacles to improvement, whose removal was necessary and inevitable.

On agricultural grounds the open-field system was indefensible; enclosures indisputably increased both rent and produce. The arguments used in its support are based on the damage done to the poor, and the depopulation of enclosed parishes. 'A Country Gentleman,' who, in 1772, wrote a pamphlet upon 'The Advantages and Disadvantages of Inclosing Waste Land,' did not exaggerate the profits of enclosure. He says that rich open-field land was often let in its open state at 6s. to 7s. per acre. Open farms were divided into two, three, or four fields: if three, one field lay fallow, depastured by sheep; the second was wheat or barley; the third, beans, peas, or oats. He drew up the following table of the probable results of enclosure :—

Description of Land	Present Rent	New Rent to Landlord	Net Profits to Farmer
		£	£
1. 1,000 acres of rich open fields	6s. per acre	300	360
Do. ten years after enclosure	15s. ,,	750	500
2. 1,000 acres of poorer land	4s. ,,	200	300
Do. ten years after enclosure	8s. ,,	400	370
3. 1,000 acres of rich common pasture	2s. ,,	100	240
Do. ten years after enclosure	15s. ,,	750	500
4. 1,000 acres of heaths and moors	1s. ,,	50	60
Do. ten years after enclosure	8s. ,,	400	370

Within the next half-century these predictions were abundantly confirmed by results; rents and production were more than quadrupled, and farmers grew rich upon war prices.

In 1793 the Board of Agriculture was constituted, with Sir John Sinclair as president, and Arthur Young as secretary. The first object of the Board was to collect information respecting the agriculture of the country. For this purpose a series of questions were circulated among farmers, many of which related to open common fields. At the same time Commissioners drew up reports of the agricultural conditions of each county. The facts collected in these reports are invaluable to students of agricultural history. They establish beyond all controversy the enormous advantages of enclosed over open-field farms. Tenants lived comfortably on enclosed land, rented at 10s. 6d. an acre, who had starved on open farms at 2s. 6d. an acre; enclosed land was cheaper at 20s. than open land at 8s. The effect upon a district near Norwich of enclosures and the Norfolk system has been already illustrated.[1]

[1] See p. 44.

'The vast benefit,' says Arthur Young,[1] 'of enclosing can, upon inferior soils, be rarely seen in a more advantageous light than upon Lincoln Heath. I found a large range which formerly was covered with heath, gorse, &c., and yielding, in fact, little or no produce, converted, by enclosure, to profitable arable farms; let, on an average, at 10s. an acre; and a very extensive country, all studded with new farmhouses, barns, offices, and every appearance of thriving industry; nor is the extent small, for these heaths extend near seventy miles.' Nor were these exceptional cases; they might be paralleled in every county in the United Kingdom.

But enclosures aimed at more than the extinction of open-field farms. Wastes and commons were also to be fenced and reclaimed. In 1773 Arthur Young drew attention to the extent of land lying waste in his 'Observations on the Present State of Waste Lands of Great Britain.' The Report of the Committee of the Board of Agriculture upon Enclosures states that twenty-two million acres of land lay waste, of which England had 6,259,470 acres, Wales 1,629,307 acres, Scotland 14,218,224 acres. To this report is annexed a valuable sketch of the old law of wastes and commons, presented by the Surveyor-General of Woods and Forests. The surveyor held that the common law annexed rights of common to all manors because of the inducement they afforded cultivators to till their land as arable farms, but that since the introduction of roots and artificial grasses no such need existed. If commons were unlimited, lords of manors might enclose; if stinted, commoners were often owners of the soil. The earliest method of enclosure was by writs of partition or admeasurement. But the proceedings were so costly that they were little

---

[1] *Agricultural Survey of Lincolnshire*, 1799, pp. 77-8.

used. In more modern times commons were divided by consent of the interested parties, or by private Acts of Parliament. Here, again, formidable obstacles impeded enclosures. It was difficult to obtain the consent of persons whose interests were opposed; but four-fifths of the commoners, the lord of the manor, and the tithe-owner must agree before a Parliamentary sanction could be obtained. Cottagers were attached to the idle system of keeping a few half-starved cows upon the commons; small freeholders feared the legal expense; small common-field farmers dreaded a rise of rent; landlords hesitated to invest capital for the benefit of tithe-owners; tithe-owners were unwilling to take land in exchange for their tenths of the produce. Finally, the expenses of private Acts were almost prohibitive. A General Enclosure Act was imperatively needed, but if such a measure was passed, ' what,' as a reporter asks, ' would become of the poor but honest attorney, officers of Parliament, and a long train of &c. &c., who obtain a decent livelihood from the trifling fees of every individual Enclosure Bill? The waste lands in the dribbling, difficult way in which they are at present enclosed will cost the country upwards of 20 millions to these gentry, which under a general Enclosure Bill would be done for less than one million.' Partly from social causes, partly in consequence of the recommendations of the Board of Agriculture, partly through the zeal of Arthur Young, but *mainly through the necessity which presses upon a protectionist country, engaged in a European war, to feed its growing population out of its home resources*, the first general Enclosure Act was passed in 1801. From 1777 to 1793, 599 Enclosure Acts were passed. Between 1793 and 1809 the number rose to 1,052. It has been calculated that $4\frac{1}{2}$ million acres of land were thus added to the cultivated area of the country in England and Wales alone.

The agricultural and economical aspects of the question favoured enclosure, but the social arguments were less conclusive. It was, indeed, urged that enclosure of commons would benefit the morality of the country. The commoners are described as a 'most wretched' class, relying on a precarious and vagabond subsistence, eked out by pilfering. Their 'miserable huts' are 'seldom or never abodes of honest industry,' but harbour 'poachers and thieves of every description.' Forests, like Epping or Hainault, were the resort of 'the most idle and profligate of men; here the undergraduates in iniquity commence their career with deer-stealing, and here the more finished and hardened robber retires from justice.' On the other hand, it was said that enclosures depopulated the country, were often needlessly created, and inflicted irreparable damage upon the poor.

The depopulation of the country by enclosures was not confirmed by experience, because the object of the change was rather the increase of tillage than, as in the sixteenth century, the extension of pasturage. Arthur Young, in 1801,[1] proves by statistics, that of thirty-seven enclosed parishes in Norfolk, population had risen in twenty-four, diminished in eight, and remained stationary in five. In some few instances, no doubt, land was enclosed and ploughed which would have been more profitable as open pasture, but these cases were rare and exceptional. The real strength of the argument against the enclosure of commons lay in the injury they often inflicted upon the poor. The 'Country Gentleman,' whose pamphlet has been

[1] *Inquiry into the Propriety of applying Wastes to the Better Support and Maintenance of the Poor.*

already quoted, recognises this as an inevitable result. The landlord, the farmer, and the nation must gain by enclosure, but 'the small common-field farmer' must become 'a hired labourer.' He recommends that the lot of these 'reduced farmers' be rendered as easy as possible 'by laying to their cottages a sufficient portion of land to enable them to keep a cow or two.' Had this advice been followed, England might have escaped the deplorable effects of the poor-law in the next fifty years.

The claims of commoners were frequently disregarded by Commissioners. Young strongly advocated enclosures, but he laments the disastrous effect of the change upon the general condition of the labouring population. He instances numerous enclosures which, without adequate compensation, deprived commoners of their live stock, made it difficult or impossible to procure milk for their children at any price, cut off their chief incentive to frugality, reduced them to hired labourers solely dependent upon their weekly wages. 'Many kept cows that have not since,' is his oft-recurring summary of results. Out of thirty-seven parishes he found only twelve in which the position of the poor was improved by the enclosure of commons.[1] Many commoners received no allotment because they failed to prove their legal right; others were assigned too little land to keep a cow, and both land and cow were sold to wealthy farmers; others were bought out for comparatively small sums before the award was made; others sold their allotments because they could not spend the sums necessary to enclose their portions; in some cases allotments were made to the owners and not to the occupiers of cottages. On the other hand, in some parishes the interests of the poor were carefully protected; they were not required to give strict proof of their legal

[1] Arthur Young, *On Wastes*, 1801.

rights, and were allotted sufficient land for the summer and winter keep of their cows. Wherever this plan was adopted the poor rate remained low, even during the troubled times of the French war. Men of that generation, who knew what it was to keep and to want a cow, preferred the cow to parochial relief of 5*s.* or 6*s.* a week.

Against these individual losses must be set the national gain. Without the enclosure of commons England could never have fed her growing population, or gained the first place in the race for industrial supremacy. 'Where,' asks Arthur Young, ' is the little farmer to be found who will cover his whole farm with marl at the rate of 100 or 150 tons per acre? who will drain all his land at the expense of 2*l.* or 3*l.* an acre? who will pay a heavy price for the manure of towns, and convey it thirty miles by land carriage? who will float his meadows at the expense of 5*l.* per acre? who, to improve the breed of his sheep, will give 1,000 guineas for the use of a single ram for a single season? who will send across the kingdom to distant provinces for new implements, and for men to use them? who will employ and pay men for residing in provinces where practices are found which they want to introduce into their farms?' Nor was the commoner without compensation in more certain employment and higher wages. If it is unpractical sentiment to regret the enclosure of commons, the rural poet of Dorsetshire may be invoked to tell the greatness of the loss to the labouring population.

 Thomas (*loq.*):   Why, 'tis a handy thing
   To have a bit o' common, I do know,
   To put a little cow upon in spring,
   The while woone's bit ov orchard grass do grow.
 John: Aye, that's the thing, you zee. Now I do mow
   My bit o' grass, an mëake a little rick;
   An' in the summer while do grow,

My cow do run in common vor to pick
A bläde or two o' grass, if she can vind 'em,
Vor tother cattle don't leave much behind 'em.
An' then, bezide the cow, why, we do let
Our geese run out among the emmet hills;
An' then, when we do pluck 'em, we do get
Vor seäle zome veäthers an' zome quills;
An' in the winter we do fat 'em well,
An' car them to the market vor to zell
To gentle-volks.   .   .   .
An' then when I ha' nothèn else to do,
Why, I can teäke my hook an' gloves, an' goo
To cut a lot o' vuzz and briars
Vor hetèn ovens or vor lightèn viers;
An' when the childern be too young to eärn
A penny, they can g' out in zunny weather,
An' run about, an' get together
A bag o' cow-dung vor to burn.

The change came at a difficult crisis. An artisan class was arising, and population shifting from the south to the north. Commoners and open-field farmers could not readily adapt themselves to altered conditions, or join in the keen struggle for existence which was commencing. At the same time the prices of necessaries were doubled during the war; yet wages remained the same. It was this combination of circumstances which rendered the poor-law system so fatal. And the law was most unwisely administered. The weekly earnings of labourers were supplemented from the poor rate with such a sum as in the opinion of the magistrates would support their family; a shilling or eighteen-pence was paid for each child. This bounty upon production threw single men upon the rates, because employers calculated that labourers with the largest families required least wages. While the war swelled farmers' profits, ratepayers paid their labour bill. Wages were regulated not by services, but by wants. Such a system promoted early marriages, encouraged a superabundant population, increased the number of illegitimate births, annihilated distinctions between good and bad workmen. It was now that the south fell hopelessly behind the north. As population centred round the coal-fields, the manufacturing industries of the south dwindled, and its cloth and iron workers swelled the number of the indigent poor. After the peace of 1815, disbanded soldiers, sailors, and militia-men added to the number of the discontented and unemployed. Thousands of artisans were discharged as machinery was introduced into manufactures. Thus the balance between the demand and supply of labour was completely overthrown, and the distress of the wage-earning populations from 1810 to 1820 was only paralleled by the miseries of the sixteenth century.

CHAPTER VIII.

LARGE FARMS AND LARGE CAPITALISTS—MR. COKE OF HOLKHAM.

A LARGE expenditure of capital was needed to bring into cultivation the newly reclaimed commons or the barbarously cropped and impoverished open fields. But in order to derive full profit from the outlay it was necessary to obtain access to the new markets. Agriculture and manufacture agreed in demanding increased facilities of transport and communication. The demand created the supply. Hitherto the charges for the conveyance of heavy goods had been practically prohibitive. Except in the summer, farmers were confined to the nearest markets and deprived of the stimulus of competition. The impassable condition of the roads led to the widest differences in the prices of neighbouring districts. Meat varied with the distance from London; within fifty miles of the capital it was 4d., beyond that limit 2d.; as the distance increased prices fell, and farmers at Horsham were glad to take five farthings a pound for mutton. Food rotted upon the ground in one parish, while in the next there was a scarcity. The corn-law legislation of the eighteenth century provided for variations of prices in twelve different districts of England and Wales. Between 1760 and 1780 all the main roads were repaired, while Brindley's construction of the Bridgewater Canal established a canal mania, only paralleled by the railway mania of this century. Within a few years

England was better provided with means of inland navigationt han any country except Holland. At first new means of communication depressed the wage-earning labourer. Wages were generally low where food was cheap; increased facilities of transport equalised the price of meat, bread, cheese, butter; but wages were slow to follow the rise of prices, and it was fifty years before the balance was restored.

Increased facilities of communication accelerated the rapid development of manufactures. When once the home markets were thrown open, agriculture received an extraordinary stimulus from the high prices of farm produce, and the increased demand consequent on a growing population and an improved standard of living. Napoleon became the Triptolemus of the farmer. The stoppage of foreign grain supplies, war prices, the corn laws, made land a profitable investment for capital. Even the fall of prices in 1814 only excited agriculturists to renewed efforts. New implements were tried; labour was economised by the inventions of Small and Meikle; cattle shows and ploughing matches were held throughout the country; prizes were offered to local breeders; farmers' clubs and provincial societies were established. Great landlords took the lead in improvements. It is said that Walpole always opened the letters of his farm steward before he broke the seals of letters on State affairs. Bolingbroke caused his house at Dawley to be painted with trophies of ricks, spades, and prongs, and read Swift's letters between two haycocks with his eyes to heaven, not in admiration of the dean, but in fear of rain. The later generation were more earnest or more practical. In 1723 a society of 'Improvers in the Knowledge of Agriculture' had been formed in Scotland; in 1777 the Bath and West of England Society was instituted, the Highland Society in 1784, the Smithfield Club in 1798. In the latter year Pitt, at the instigation of Sir John Sinclair, created the Board of Agriculture, with Young as secretary. 'Farmer George' contributed articles under the signature of Ralph Robinson to Young's 'Annals of Agriculture,' kept his model farm at Windsor, and experimented in stock-breeding. So far Byron's epigram may be accepted—'A better farmer ne'er brushed dew from lawn.' Lord Rockingham at Wentworth, the Duke of Bedford at Woburn, Lord Egremont at Petworth, and crowds of other landlords, followed the King's example. Fox in the Louvre was lost in consideration whether the weather was favourable to his turnips at St. Anne's Hill. Burke was seen by Young experimenting in carrots as a field crop on his farm at Beaconsfield, though he directed his sarcasm against the Duke of Bedford's devotion to agriculture. Lord Althorp, in the present century, worthily maintained the traditions of his official predecessors. During a serious crisis of affairs, when he was Chancellor of the Exchequer, John Grey of Dilston called upon him in Downing Street upon political business. Lord Althorp's first question, eagerly asked, was 'Have you been at Wiseton on your way up? Have you seen the cows?' No new book escaped the vigilance of agriculturists. Miss Edgeworth's 'Essay on Irish Bulls' had not been published three days when it was ordered by the secretary of the Bath and West of England Society of Agriculture. Nor were the clergy less enthusiastic. An archdeacon, finding the churchyard cultivated for turnips, rebuked the rector with the remark, 'This must not occur again.' The reply, 'Oh no, sir, it will be barley next year,' proves that the eighteenth-century clergy were at least zealous for the rotation of crops.

Large farms and large capital found in Mr. Coke of Holkham their most celebrated champion. In 1776 he came into his estate, with 'the King of Denmark' as 'his nearest neighbour.' The refusal of a tenant in 1778 to accept a lease at an increased rent threw a quantity of land on his hands. Excluded by his politics from court and Parliament, he thenceforward devoted himself to farming. His energy was richly rewarded. Dr. Rigby in 1816 ('Pamphleteer,' xiii. p. 45) stated that the rental of the Holkham estate rose from 2,200l. in 1776 to 20,000l. in 1816.

When Mr. Coke took his farm in hand, not an acre of wheat was to be seen from Holkham to Lynn. The sandy soil grew nothing but rye. No manure was purchased; the little muck that was produced was miserably poor: a few Norfolk sheep and half-starved milch cows were the only live stock. He determined to grow wheat. He marled the land, purchased large quantities of manure, trebled his live stock. At the end of nine years his object was attained. He saw that on land like that of Norfolk muck was everything. The Flemish saying applied equally to the eastern counties: 'Point de fourrage, point de bestiaux; sans bestiaux, aucun engrais; sans engrais, nulle récolte.' In 1772 the value of bones as manure had been accidentally discovered by a Yorkshire foxhunter, who was cleaning out his stable. Coke profited largely by the discovery. He also introduced into the country oil-cake and other artificial foods, which, with roots, enabled the Norfolk farms to carry increased stock. Under his advice and example stall-feeding was extensively practised. Cattle and sheep were sent up half fed to the Norfolk fairs, to be bought by graziers and fattened for the London market. On 'Bullocks' Hill, near Norwich, during the great fair of St. Faith's, were assembled drovers of every county, with Galloway Scots, Lowland Scots, Highlanders, and Skye cattle, besides beasts from less remote districts. The grass lands, on which the beef and mutton of our ancestors were raised, were deserted for the sands of the eastern counties; the metropolis drew its meat supplies from Norfolk. The cattle were sent up to Smithfield under the care of drovers, who took a week on the journey. The busiest time of the year was from April to June. The quantity of animals fattened on nutritious food gave the farmer the command of the richest manure, fertilised his land, and enabled him not only to grow wheat, but to verify the maxim, 'never to sow a crop unless there is condition to grow it luxuriantly.'

Coke also improved the live stock of the county. On his own estate, after patient trial of other breeds, he adopted Southdowns and North Devons. But his efforts were not confined to the home farm. Early and late he worked in his smock-frock, assisting his farmers to improve their flocks and herds. Grass lands were wholly neglected till he gave them his attention. If land wanted seeding, farmers threw indiscriminately on the ground a collection of seeds, drawn at haphazard from their own or their neighbours' ricks, containing as much rank weed or rough grass as nutritious herbage. It was a mere chance whether the farmer aided the sour or the sweet grasses in the struggle for existence. Stillingfleet, in 1760, distinguished the good and bad herbage by excellent illustrations of the kinds best calculated to produce the richest hay and sweetest pasture. Coke was the first farmer who appreciated the value of the distinctions. During May and June, when the grasses were in bloom, he gave his botanical lessons to the children of his tenantry, who scoured the country to procure his stock of seed.

Convinced of the community of interests among owner, occupier, and labourer, Coke stimulated the enterprise of his tenants, encouraged them to put more capital and more labour into the land, and assisted them to take advantage of every new invention or discovery. His farm buildings, dwelling-houses, and cottages were models to other landlords. By offering long leases of twenty-one years, he guaranteed his tenants a return for their outlay and energy. 'My best bank,' said one of his farmers, 'is my land.' At the same time he guarded against the mischief of a long unrestricted tenancy by regulating the course of cultivation. In all the leases of his estates he inserted covenants for the adoption of the Norfolk system of husbandry. Though clauses of management were then comparatively unknown, his farms commanded the competition of the pick of English farmers. Even Cobbett, in spite of his prejudices against landlords, was compelled to admit the benefits which Coke's tenants derived from his paternal rule. 'Every one,' he wrote in 1821, 'made use of the expressions towards him which affectionate children use towards their parents.'

One great obstacle to improvement remained. Farmers of the eighteenth century lived, thought, farmed, like the farmers of the sixteenth. The Holkham sheep-shearings did much to break down traditions and prejudices. These meetings began in 1778, in Mr. Coke's own ignorance of farming matters: he annually invited small parties of farmers to his house to discuss agricultural topics and aid him with their advice. In 1818 open house was kept at Holkham for a week; hundreds of persons assembled from all parts of Great Britain, the Continent, and America. The mornings were spent in inspecting the farms and the stock; at three o'clock six hundred persons sat down to dinner; the rest of the day was spent in toasts and speeches. Among the pupils was Erskine, who abandoned the study of Coke at Westminster

Hall to gather the wisdom of his namesake at Holkham. At the sheep-shearings were collected practical and theoretical agriculturists, farmers of different districts, breeders of every stock. The Duke of Bedford, Lord Egremont, and other landlords established similar meetings in different parts of the country.

National necessities demanded the extinction of the open-field farmer, and the enclosure and reclamation of wastes and commons. The same causes during this period brought the same fate upon the small freeholders or yeomen. More substantial than the open-field farmer or the cottager, they maintained their struggle for existence with more tenacity. The evidence of the Agricultural Commission of 1833 proves that they still existed in almost every county. But their numbers were already diminished. The social advantages of landownership combined with high profits to give land a fancy value. In Cheshire, during the French war, agricultural land fetched as much as forty years' purchase. Yeomen consulted their pecuniary advantage by selling their estates; capitalists gratified both their tastes and their speculative instincts by buying land. It was manifestly the interest of small freeholders to sell their properties, the size of which prevented their taking full advantage of the price of corn, and to employ their capital in farming hired land. Those who remained on their own estates were for the most part ruined. War prices and the corn laws made farming a gambling speculation; the wheat area alternately contracted and expanded; violent fluctuations in the value of farm produce upset all calculations. Many yeomen mortgaged their estates to make extravagant provision for their children, to buy more land, to enclose and improve their properties, or to erect better farm buildings.

Prices fell, but the debt remained. The struggle was brief; farming deteriorated, buildings fell into ruins, finally the estate was sold. The purchasers were not yeomen, for after 1820 small capitalists ceased to invest their savings in land, but neighbouring squires or successful manufacturers. In Shropshire their capital dwindled, and they were forced to sell. In Wiltshire their farming retrograded and their buildings fell into bad repair. In Yorkshire the number of small proprietors diminished: formerly, if one small freeholder went, another took his place; now this ceased to be the case. In Worcestershire the small owners were obliged to sell, and men of their own class ceased to buy land after 1812. In Kent and Somersetshire many freeholders retained their land by practising the most rigorous self-denial, and by entirely ceasing to employ labour; but all who had mortgages or annuities to pay were forced to sell their properties. Everywhere large landed properties were built up on the ruin of small landowners. It was only in counties like Lancashire, where the prices of dairy produce had not fluctuated during the war, and where huge markets sprang up at the doors of the farmer, that yeomen weathered the storm. The agricultural gain, derived from the extinction both of the common-field farmer and the small freeholder, was at the time great and undeniable. 'One-horse farmers' on heavy soils had to struggle with the inconvenience of borrowing and lending horses. Hours were wasted before the teams could be collected and baited; the process of ploughing was interrupted by frequent turns in small fields; the area of cultivation was unduly encroached upon by hedgerows; the methods of farming were antiquated, the implements old-fashioned; without stock, capital, or machinery, living from hand to mouth, unable to buy manure, or cake, or any but the poorest sheep and cattle, the small yeoman could not hope to compete with the large tenant farmer. On social grounds the removal of small proprietors was a deplorable necessity. But the alternative was the starvation of millions of artisans.

CHAPTER IX.

SCIENCE WITH PRACTICE, 1812 TO 1845.

If the present century has not proved uniformly prosperous to farmers, it has witnessed a miraculous advance in the scientific practice of agriculture. Farming has advanced with gigantic strides. Vast capital has been expended on farm buildings and drainage; new tracts of land have been brought into cultivation. Steam and machinery have lightened the toil, lessened the cost, and increased the amount of production. Systems of cultivation are better adapted to the requirements of soil and climate; more live stock is kept, and it is both better bred and better fed. The farmers' resources of crops, winter food, manures, appliances, are infinitely increased. New means of transport and communication bring markets to the remotest door. But the chief improvement has been the diffusion of intelligence and education; the work inaugurated at the Holkham sheep-shearings has gone on apace. The 'rough-shod race' no longer despise science. Bucolic life was the pastime of the town, the relaxation of statesmen, the inspiration of poets; but farmers neither asked nor allowed scientific aid. Now good farming combines scientific knowledge with practical experience. The dawn of the new era was marked in 1812 by Davy's lectures before the Royal Society, and the adoption by that body of the motto 'Science with Practice.' Progress does not depend on chance-directed discoveries by unlettered rustics, but on experiments conducted by the rich and learned. History shows that unaided agriculturists have by sheer doggedness conquered most formidable difficulties. Foreign competition is a more insidious foe than the open revolt of nature's 'wayward team;' but the forces arrayed on the side of English agriculture are now indefinitely multiplied. Within the last century capitalists, mechanics, architects, geologists, chemists, physiologists, botanists, have been enlisted on the side of the farmer. The agricultural progress of the present century is, in fact, summed up in the application of science and capital to the cultivation of the soil.

In the years 1812 to 1845 is included one of the most disastrous periods of English farming. It is also the period of Protection.[1] Inflated prices raised rentals and the standard of living, and vastly increased the area under corn cultivation. Prices fell when the war terminated. Contracts of all kinds had been made in the expectation that those prices would continue. Landlords declared that their ruin was inevitable if rents were reduced, and farmers, holding under leases, felt the full pressure of the crisis. These facts came out in the Reports of the Select Committee on the Corn Trade, which sat in 1814, and increased Protection was the result. Farmers had learned that fortunes were to be made by growing corn, and once more expectations and rents rose together. But wheat steadily declined. For a few years farmers paid their exorbitant rents out of capital; but the end could not be long deferred. Again Select Committees sat in 1821-2. It was shown that rents had increased not less than 70

[1] See Appendix IV., The Corn Laws.

per cent. on the rentals of 1790. Agriculturists demanded that foreign corn should be prohibited; but the Committee of 1822 hinted that Protection was undesirable, and proposed nothing. Violent fluctuations in prices continued to overthrow all calculations; the wheat area now swelled and now shrivelled, and the sliding scale of 1829 only increased the speculative character of the farmer's trade. Select Committees sat again in 1833 and 1836, and evidence was given that farmers had lost all they had, and were working on the road; in the weald of Kent and Sussex there was scarcely a solvent tenant. The last ten years proved more prosperous; but the improvement was mainly due to better farming, the growth of population, the alteration of the poor laws, and the Tithe Commutation Act of 1836. Such is a brief epitome of the agricultural history of a period which will be examined in more detail.

The advance made in farming between 1812 and 1845 was effected in the face of almost unexampled distress. During the years 1773 and 1793 English imports and exports of grain balanced each other, and these twenty years mark the turning-point when the nation passed from growers into consumers of corn. Within the next two decades of years the war and deficient harvests forced up the price of agricultural produce. While the East drained England of its bullion, Pitt's issue of paper money inflated prices. As bank notes circulated in greater quantities, prices rose higher and higher. Wheat in 1800 and 1801 was driven up to the unprecedented height of 110s. 5d. and 115s. 11d.; for the five years 1809–13 it averaged 103s. 10d. Buyers of land paid forty and forty-five years' purchase, raised heavy mortgages on their estates, charged them extravagantly with annuities, and loaded them with legacies and portions for younger children. Yet the land seemed to stand the strain. Rents were doubled and cheerfully paid by farmers who made fortunes out of the war prices. Throughout the war the efforts of legislators were directed to the maintenance of high prices of home-grown grain. Heavy duties were imposed on foreign corn in 1804; they were increased in 1813, again in 1814, and again in 1815. It is, however, noteworthy that the last increase was not passed without a protest from ten peers, entered upon the journals of the House. The same policy was continued from 1815 to 1845. One argument, strongly urged upon Parliament throughout the whole period of Protection, was that, if prices fell, the land newly brought under the plough must necessarily fall out of cultivation. An extraordinary stimulus was thus given to enclosures;[1] 601 Acts were passed between 1810 and 1814, and at the same time the wheat-growing area was enormously increased. During this war period money was drawn together in masses in the hands of saving farmers and traders. A significant proof of the growing wealth is afforded by the amount of capital paying legacy duty, which rose from 1,116,680l. in 1797 to 33,118,281l. in 1820.

But while all who sold produce profited by the artificial prices of commodities, the wage-earning population sank lower and lower. Agricultural labourers had lost their commons; their wages were supplemented not by their industry, but by their pauperism; and the poor rates exactly doubled between 1801 and 1813.

At the close of the war distress prevailed over the whole of Europe. Throughout the progress of the struggle England, owing to her insular position, had suffered less

[1] See Appendix V., Enclosures.

than other countries. Its termination found her with a national debt of over 900,000,000*l*., an excessive taxation levied to meet the war expenditure, falling prices and dwindling industries, a disordered currency, a fictitious credit, and a mass of unemployed labour. 'Peace and plenty' proved a ghastly mockery. Distress had always succeeded the close of war. In 1764 and again in 1784 farmers suffered severely from the sudden diminution of the demand for their produce. In 1815 the distress was proportionately increased by the length of the struggle and the exertions which the country had made. England lost the monopoly of trade which she had enjoyed during the war; her manufactures exceeded the demand; warehouses were overloaded, markets overstocked; produce was unsold or unpaid for; iron furnaces were blown out, cotton mills closed; the coal trade languished; the shuttles stood still in Lancashire and Yorkshire. Distrust and speculation replaced wholesome and natural commerce. Side by side with commercial depression went agricultural distress. The bitter cry of the landowners was heard in the House of Commons, and in 1815 the monopoly of the home market was secured to British growers unless wheat was above 80*s*. But the sudden fall of prices in 1814 and 1815, consequent on over-production and the diminished value of the currency, had already spread ruin and bankruptcy among the agricultural classes. In 1816 the Board of Agriculture issued a circular letter inquiring into the general conditions of agriculture.[1] The answers, to which reference has been already made, reveal the gravity of the crisis. Landlords lost, by reductions alone, 9,000,000*l*. on their rentals of the preceding years; many farms were thrown up; notices to quit poured in. Large tenants, farming on borrowed capi-

[1] See Appendix VI., Questions of the Board of Agriculture.

tal, had become parish paupers; bankruptcies, seizures, executions, imprisonments for debt, were universally prevalent. The evidence laid before the Select Committee of 1821 confirms the truth of these reports. In Dorsetshire, for instance, fifty-two farmers, cultivating between them 24,000 acres, failed between 1815 and 1820. Rents were lowered in Somersetshire by a third, and the small farmers were reduced in point of diet to the condition of labourers, and the latter were compelled to subsist on bread and potatoes. In Sussex, again, rents fell, upon an average, 53 per cent. Even on large farms in Norfolk tenants suffered severely, and put down their chaise and riding horse. The blow fell the more heavily on the southern counties, among other reasons because the old practice of lodging and feeding labourers in farmhouses had been discontinued during the war, and money wages could only be paid by unprofitable sales of produce. Rents fell into arrear; tithes and poor rates remained unpaid; improvements were discontinued; live stock dwindled, and gangs of poachers and depredators kept the country in continual alarm. Numerous tradesmen, innkeepers, and shopkeepers, who depended on farmers for their principal custom, were involved in the same ruin. War prices were gone, war taxes remained. Out of falling profits owners of land were unable to meet augmented taxation and heavy charges; occupiers could not pay rents which had been raised upon fallacious estimates of agricultural prosperity, and were slowly and reluctantly reduced. Meanwhile the credit of the paper currency was undermined; bank notes were discounted at a loss, and guineas sold at a premium. The failure of numerous county banks, which between 1797 and 1814 had increased in number from about 200 to 940, added to the ruin of country districts. As the year 1816 advanced, bad seasons created a scarcity; wheat rose suddenly from 52*s.* in January to 103*s.* in December; the potato crop, which had recently become important in England, failed ; and the perpetual floods of the spring and summer were succeeded by a winter of appalling severity. The army and navy had been reduced, the militia disbanded, the store, commissariat, and transport departments placed upon a peace footing. To this mass of unemployed labour were now added thousands of artisans and agriculturists. Starvation stared them in the face. Distress bred discontent, and discontent disturbances which were fostered by political agitators. While the Luddites broke up machinery, gangs of labourers avenged the fancied conspiracy of farmers by burning stacks, ricks, and farmhouses, or destroying the shops of butchers and bakers.

Peace seemed only to aggravate every form of distress. At such crises the currency is often made the sole scapegoat for conditions which result from many causes. But one great cause of the general depression was the paper money, upon which had been built up extravagant ideas of the national wealth. Till cash payments were resumed financial equilibrium could not be permanently restored. The process by which the paper money was withdrawn extended over the first twenty years after the conclusion of the peace; but its general course was directed by Lord Liverpool's adoption of the single gold standard, and Peel's Currency Bill of 1819, to which the House of Commons agreed without a dissentient voice. The withdrawal of the paper money produced the same result as a drain upon the precious metals. A variety of causes combined with the resumption of cash payments to send down prices with startling rapidity.[1] Landowners, who had raised money upon their land, found themselves confronted by ruin. Their reluctance to reduce rentals involved hundreds of tenants in their fall. The alternative was hard. Petitions show that where mortgagees foreclosed upon estates the land was sold for sums which barely, if at all, recouped the charges. In 1819 Cobbett's ominous prophecy respecting the Currency Bill seemed in danger of literal fulfilment: 'Before this Bill could be carried into complete execution a million of persons at least must die of hunger.'

The cheapness of food abated distress among the manufacturing population, but it aggravated the difficulties of farmers. For the next fifteen years the attention of Parliament was continually called to the landed interests. Resolutions were passed at county meetings demanding relief; innumerable pamphlets proved that three pounds did not now go as far as two had done during the war,[2] and asked for remunerating prices for agricultural produce; petitions covered the table of the House, and select committees sat in 1820, 1821, 1822, 1833, and 1836. But within twenty years after the peace had been readjusted to diminished prices, and agriculture slowly began to share in

[1] *Table showing the Fall of Prices*, 1819–22.

Dates	Wheat per quarter		Mutton per stone (8 lbs.)				Beef per stone (8 lbs.)			
	s.	*s.*	*s.*	*d.*	*s.*	*d.*	*s.*	*d.*	*s.*	*d.*
Jan. 1819 . .	64 to	84	5	0	to 6	4	4	0	to 5	0
July 1819 . .	58 ,,	80	4	6	,, 5	2	4	6	,, 5	4
Jan. 1820 . .	54 ,,	70	3	4	,, 4	4	3	4	,, 4	8
July 1820 . .	58 ,,	81	4	2	,, 5	2	3	6	,, 4	6
Jan. 1821 . .	40 ,,	62	3	0	,, 4	0	3	2	,, 4	2
July 1821 . .	36 ,,	63	2	2	,, 3	4	2	8	,, 3	8
Jan. 1822 . .	30 ,,	66	2	2	,, 3	2	2	0	,, 3	0
July 1822 . .	30 ,,	56	1	10	,, 2	6	2	0	,, 2	10

[2] The following illustration from 'A Letter to a Member of Parlia-

the general revival of trade, yet the period left its mark not only in the extinction of small landowners, but in the retrogression of farming. On heavy clays less capital and less labour were expended; wet seasons prevented farmers from getting upon their land, and led to the discontinuance of manure, excessive cropping, and the impoverishment, even the abandonment, of heavier soils. Wages had been lowered and labourers dismissed; Swing and his proselytes were at work, and in 1830-1 agrarian fires blazed from Dorsetshire to Lincolnshire. To add to the difficulties of the clay farmer, the rot of 1830-1, which is described as the most disastrous on record, 'swept away two million sheep.' Much of the land was in miserable condition. Ploughed up when corn was high, it was badly laid down again when prices fell. Some was cultivated as 'up and down land,' tilled for two or three years, and then abandoned, according to variations in the price of wheat. A general want of confidence prevailed between landlords and tenants, and recent experience created a profound distrust of leases. Rents had been reduced from 25 to 30 per cent., and large arrears had accumulated; poor rates

---

ment' is interesting as showing some of the ordinary expenses of living in 1822 :—

	£
A person has an estate of, per annum	500
(His family consists of himself, wife, four children, one man and two women servants.)	£
Education of his children with their clothing	160
Assessed and parochial taxes	30
Servants' wages	25
Own and wife's clothing	35
Deduct a third of his income	166
	416

Remain to bear the expenses of housekeeping, &c.	84

What is to become of this class and all under?

were enormously increased. Farmers on light lands suffered comparatively little. Prices were low; but the spread of drill husbandry, artificial manures, better rotations of cropping, and improvements in the breed both of cattle and sheep enabled them to farm with profit. A good machine was driving out a bad one. Fifty years before, clay lands were the corn and beef producing districts of the country, while the light soils of Norfolk lay uncultivated. Now the parts were reversed. This revolution in farming had been mainly effected by turnips, and only drainage could enable clay farmers to hold their own against their rivals. The Commission which was appointed in 1836 received evidence upon the condition of the landed interests. They made no report, but the majority of the witnesses confined the distress to clay farmers. Signs of returning prosperity became faintly visible. Manufacturing progress began to tell upon agriculture; the new system of poor laws had already reduced the rates; wool, mutton, and beef had risen in price; barley and oats were selling briskly and at higher rates: wheat was low, but the price resulted partly from defective harvests in 1838 and 1839, partly from improved and extended cultivation. The 'rebellion of the belly' at Birmingham and Newport (Mon.) in 1839 and at Sheffield in 1840 was the result of the rise in prices by which the farmers profited.

The drainage of clay farms was the crying need of the day, and the Tithe Commutation Act of 1836 encouraged landlords and tenants to expend capital without fear that tithe-owners would share the profits. At the nick of time science provided the necessary means.

Drainage had been ably discussed by Walter Blith in 1641, and it had been insisted upon by Young as a necessary preliminary to agricultural improvement. But hitherto farmers had been baffled by insuperable difficulties. Over-wetness, which arose from water issuing to the surface in consequence of subterranean interruptions to its course, had been admirably dealt with by a Warwickshire farmer named James Elkington at the close of the eighteenth century. His services in tapping springs were in great request in the midland counties, where his crowbar was compared to the rod of Moses. He received a Parliamentary grant of a thousand pounds; but his success so largely depended on experience, that his secret was but imperfectly reduced to rules by Johnstone.[1] Only springy or spouty land was drained, and only those spots which were considered dangerous to cattle. A trench was cut deep enough to reach the bed along which the water filtered before it encountered the obstacle that forced it to the surface, and was then filled with stones to within $2\frac{1}{2}$ feet of the surface. But in draining the soil of its surface water the ordinary method was to throw the land into ridges from two to four feet high. As the headlands were often similarly dammed up, the furrows became standing pools of water. The height of these ridges was sometimes extraordinary. In Gloucestershire, while Marshall stood in a furrow, a man of middle height, crossing the field towards him, was lost to sight in every furrow. But this practice served other purposes besides drainage. On grass lands it provided a variety of herbage. Many farmers believed that it increased the surface. It was also employed on light chalky loams where it was not required for warmth or dryness, because in common fields continually fallowed, if the lands had lain flat, the soil would have been run together like lime

---

[1] *An Account of the most improved Mode of Draining Land according to the System practised by Mr. James Elkington.* By John Johnstone, Land Surveyor, Edinburgh, 1797.

by a 'pash' of rain. The effect of this drainage was to wash the soil bare from the ridges into the furrows, and thence into the adjoining stream; thus the high parts were too poor, and the lower too wet, to yield crops. If the rain descended with any force, it ran along the surface, carrying with it the manure and the richness of the soil. Every river flowed turbid after a storm, laden with the wealth of the land.

The discoverer of the science of thorough drainage was Smith of Deanston. It had indeed been extensively practised in Essex, Suffolk, and Leicestershire, where land was drained by trenches filled up with haulm, ling, straw, or turf, and covered over. The practice of this system has been traced back in Essex to 1644; but in the nineteenth century it had hardly travelled out of the eastern counties. Smith of Deanston had watched the effect of turf furrow-drains in carrying off bottom water on the flat clay lands of Stirlingshire. In 1806 he went to reside in Perthshire. There it occurred to him that the same system might be employed to carry off the surface water which stagnates on clay soil, rendering the land cold and tenacious in wet seasons, hard and unworkable in dry weather. In 1823 he began to try the experiment on a small farm at Deanston, and from 1834 onwards made known his extraordinary success to agriculturists.

The advantages of his system were at once evident, and now scarcely need remark. The soil cannot retain by attraction more than a certain amount of water; it must get rid of the rest by evaporation or superficial discharge. If the water runs off the surface, the land is deprived of one of the richest of fertilising agencies. Not only is rain heavily charged with ammonia, carbonic acid, and other gases, but it is the only carrier of heat downwards. The land is also robbed of its own natural fertility as well as of artificial means for its enrichment. If the soil rids itself of the surface water by evaporation, its temperature is chilled. A wet cloth wrapped round a bottle in hot weather acts as a refrigerator; the same effect is produced upon the soil by evaporation. But Smith's system made rain a friend and not an enemy. In winter undrained land is saturated with water; in summer, baked so as to exclude all air; in frost, bound in a coat of iron. The object of Smith was to change the texture of the soil, to draw off the water and admit the air, and thus to communicate that divisibility and mellowness which farmers call friability. Drainage gave the farmer twice as many days on which he could work his land; it increased the efficacy of his farming operations and of his manures; it secured an earlier seed-time and an earlier harvest, raised the average produce, and lessened the expenses of working. On pasture land its benefits are not less obvious. Drainage destroys coarse aquatic plants, increases the sweetness and nourishment of the herbage, and affords a full bite to cattle weeks before undrained land.

Much remained to be effected in the details of drainage after Smith had demonstrated its principles. But within the next ten years Josiah Parkes (1843) had brought his practical and scientific knowledge to bear upon the subject, the necessary appliances had been simultaneously provided by Reed's cylindrical pipes (1843) and Scragg's machine (1845) for their manufacture, and the necessary capital was offered to landlords upon easy terms by loans provided under the Act of Parliament of 1846.

Drainage chiefly helped one class of farmers, new manures assisted all. In the infancy of agriculture little or no attention was paid to the use of manure. Fitzherbert and Tusser hardly mention the subject. Plat is the first writer who treats of it at any length. Salt sand, salt water, salt weeds, and everything of a saline quality had been strongly recommended by Gervase Markham in his 'Farewel to Husbandry,' written in the reign of James I.; Gabriel Plattes considered that 'sal-amoniake' formed a good mould in which to set corn; the use of salt had been urged upon farmers by Lord Bacon. But, as a rule, a little half-rotted straw was the only substance used. On the sea-coasts farmers might employ seaweed and sand, but the prohibitive prices of land carriage prevented their use in the interior. Lime, chalk, marl, crag, gypsum, rags, coal ashes, and the sweepings of London streets [1] were used by farmers who found their natural manures upon the spot; but their use was necessarily local. 'Nothing like muck' was the proverbial saying, because nothing but muck was obtainable. The one exception up to this time was bone, which had created a new industry. Now, however, as railways cheapened costs of conveyance, and drainage enabled the soil to benefit by fertilising substances, science provided portable means of enriching lands. Sprengel led the way by investigating the properties of soil, and Liebig brought chemistry to bear on the composition of new stimulants in the shape of manure. From 1835 onwards the use of nitrate of soda and guano gradually spread. The manufacture of British guano supplied a cheaper and hardly less valuable substance than its Peruvian rival. In

[1] The manures enumerated by Hartlib (*Legacy*, 1652) are—'(1) Chalke; (2) Lime; (3) Ordinary dung; (4) Marle; (5) Snaggrett [shelly earth from river beds]; (6) Ouse from marsh ditches; (7) Sea Weeds; (8) Sea Sand; (9) Folding of Sheepe; (10) Ashes; (11) Soote; (12) Pigeon's and hen's dung; (13) Malt dust; (14) Salt and lime; (15) Grassy turf and brakes; (16) Fish; (17) Urine; (18) Woollen rags; (19) Denshyving, or paring and burning; (20) Mixing of lands; (21) Lupines, and ploughing green plants into the ground.'

1840 Liebig recommended, and in 1843 Sir John Lawes obtained superphosphate of lime by dissolving bone-dust in sulphuric acid.[1] Geology contributed its quota In 1843 Professor Henslow proved that coprolites, similarly dissolved, would produce the required superphosphate. Eight years later Odams showed the value of the blood and refuse of London slaughterhouses. The use of guano, phosphatic, and ammoniacal manures completely revolutionised the old rules of cropping. It stimulated not only produce, but drainage. Manures and drainage acted and reacted upon one another; the first encouraged the second. Both together enabled farmers to carry more stock, and taught the lesson that he who puts most into the land gets the most out. Manure, like charity, proved a blessing alike to the giver and receiver.

Other changes helped to mitigate the force of the blow from which English farming tottered. Railroads, steam navigation, joint-stock banks, assisted agriculturists in their difficulties. Parliament passed Acts for the Amendment of the Poor Law, the Commutation of Tithes, the Repeal of the Beer Duty, the Enfranchisement of Copyholds, the Enclosure of Common Fields, and reduced forty millions of taxation.[2] Agricultural implements were improved or more widely diffused. Small's plough, the subsoil plough, Meikle's threshing machine, and the drill machine rendered labour more effective. The art of 'setting corn' is said by Sir Hugh Plat to have originated with a 'silly wench,' who accidentally dropped some wheat seeds

---

[1] The declared value of bones imported into the country in 1814 was under 550*l*. In 1837 it had risen to 255,000*l*. In 1815 the quantity of rape cake and linseed cake was only 16,000 cwt.; in 1837 it rose to 800,000 tons. In 1841 the guano imported was only 1,700 tons; in 1847 it amounted to 220,000 tons.

[2] The poor rates fell in England from 6,317,255*l*. (1834) to 4,044,741*l*. (1837).

in holes into which she ought to have dibbled carrots and radishes. Tull suggested a machine for the purpose; but even in 1788 drills were only 'getting into use' in the first agricultural counties, like Norfolk and Suffolk. 'Mine,' says Mr. Samuel Taylor in that year,[1] ' was one of the first invented.' The inventor was the Rev. Mr. Cooke, and it made its first appearance at Aspul, in Suffolk. But, adds Mr. Taylor, 'it was at this time rare to see a piece of drilled corn.' In 1839 the use of an improved implement was explained to the Royal Agricultural Society as 'a machine to lay the seeds in regular rows;' but it made its way slowly into general use. New attention was paid to plants and grasses. It was now[2] that swedes, cabbages, and Kohl rabi were cultivated, and that the mangel-wurzel was introduced. Dr. Chevallier cultivated selected and assorted qualities of barley seed; Colonel Le Couteur, in Jersey, did the same for wheat, and the Lawsons in Edinburgh for grasses. During the same period veterinary science made gigantic strides, and valuable stock was no longer sacrificed to ignorant quacks. County societies were formed for the extension of agricultural knowledge, and the encouragement of stock-breeders by cattle shows. In 1819 the Board of Agriculture had expired: the formation of the Royal Agricultural Society in 1838 marks the revival of better times. The first meeting of this society, which was designed to act as the heart of agriculture, was held at Oxford in 1839. Meanwhile the schoolmaster was abroad, and in 1842 the Royal Agricultural College at Cirencester and the Agricultural Chemistry Association were founded.

[1] Memoir of Samuel Taylor of New Buckenham, Norfolk, reprinted from the *Farmer's Magazine*, April 1841.
[2] Both swedes and Kohl rabi are mentioned by Young at the end of the previous century.

Nor were the inflated prices of the war without permanent advantage to the agriculture of the county. The history of farming in Northumberland strongly illustrates this brighter aspect of a gloomy period. John Grey of Dilston,[1] the Black Prince of the North, one of the most skilful and enterprising agriculturists of the day, played a conspicuous part in the change. Born in 1785, and early called, through the death of his father, to the management of property, he lived in the midst of the agricultural revolution. When his father first settled in Glendale the plain was a forest of wild broom. He took his axe, and, like a backwoodsman, cleared a space on which to commence his farming operations. The Cheviot herdsmen were then described as 'ferocious and sullen,' the people as uneducated, barbarous, and ill-clothed. The country was wholly unenclosed, without either roads or sign-posts. The cattle were lost for days in the forests of wild broom. But the character of the soil, on which landlords alternately plundered or starved, attracted skill, enterprise, and industry. Men of the same stamp as the Messrs. Culley settled in its fertile vales, and by their spirited farming revolutionised whole districts which, like the rich vale of the Till, were wildernesses of underwood. The value of land was doubled, if not quadrupled, by the use of turnips and artificial grasses upon tracts which had previously produced naked fallows, or crops of peas choked with weeds. Money made by farming was eagerly re-invested in the reclamation of wastes; commodious buildings were erected, new roads were laid out, threshing machines, worked by water or by horses, were introduced as flails proved too slow a process for the increased produce. During the wars of the French Revo-

[1] *Memoir of John Grey of Dilston*, by Josephine E. Butler. Edinburgh, 1869.

lution profits increased rapidly, and with them rose competition and rents for land. Long leases were given and large farms, and every rood of soil was put in requisition; large stones were dug up and removed in order to obtain an arable surface; bogs were drained, and open lands enclosed. The fall of prices brought reductions of rent, failure of tenants, changes of ownership and occupancy. But the high state of cultivation which was stimulated by unexampled prosperity was maintained. A substitute for high prices was provided by the increased produce which resulted from manure, drainage, subsoil ploughing, and other results of the union of science with practice.

Similar changes might be noted in almost every county. One other instance will suffice. Before Mr. Pusey's Committee on Tenant Right in 1848 a witness was asked what had been the increase of produce in Lincolnshire in consequence of improved farming. He replied: 'The increase has been from almost nothing to thirty-two and thirty-six bushels of wheat to an acre. It was formerly little more than a rabbit warren, only thirty-five years ago.'

CHAPTER X.

SCIENCE WITH PRACTICE, 1845-1873.

THE year 1845 divides the two periods of 'Science with Practice.' It inaugurated a new era. It marks the transition from farming by extension to farming by intension. Hitherto British farmers had mainly supplied the wants of a growing population by increasing the area of cultivation. After the General Enclosure Act of 1845 they were practically excluded from this resource. They could only meet new demands by developing to the utmost the productiveness of the soil. It is true that within the last forty years upwards of 800,000 acres have been taken into cultivation in England and Wales; but this increase is counterbalanced by the agricultural land which has been occupied by the growth of towns, roads, and railways. The farming area remains, roughly speaking, what it was in 1845. Between 1801 and 1851 the population of Great Britain and Ireland increased by ten million new claimants for food, and the old supply of land was supplemented by four million additional acres. After 1845 British farmers were driven to depend for profits upon high farming. For the next thirty years they held their own by superior science against the vast corn-fields of Russia, the virgin soils of America and Canada, the alluvial plains of Egypt, and the favourable conditions of labour which enable India to grow grain with unequalled cheapness. During that period home-grown wheat was not displaced, but only supplemented by imported corn; the production of wheat did not decline, nor was its place supplied by foreign produce; imports did not increase faster than consumption. The serious question to be considered is whether English farming in 1888 is still in this position.

So long as Protection lasted, landlords and farmers were unable to resist the gambling spirit which it fostered. An upward tendency in prices raised rents and encouraged reckless competition for farms. But latterly the rise of prices proved only the flicker which precedes extinction. Corn-law rents and free-trade prices ruined farmers; Peel's sliding scale of 1842 gave them no relief; the reduction of their labour bills revived incendiarism. Finally, in 1846, Protection was abolished, and England adopted the principle of Free Trade. A period of great distress followed, in which rents were completely revised. Adverse seasons and fear of the consequences of free trade intensified the crisis. Mr. (now Sir James) Caird's pamphlet on 'High Farming the Best Substitute for Protection,' which was published in 1848, suggested the true remedy. The cessation of the free-trade panic, the revival of confidence, the diffusion of agricultural improvements, the expansion of trade, the increase of the precious metals owing to the discovery of gold and silver mines in Australia and California, and the Crimean war, helped the landed interests out of their difficulties. The cost of living, as regards the working classes, lessened; the raw materials of manufacture were cheapened; the rate of discount was lowered; new markets opened in the East, and the increase of our merchant shipping diminished the cost of transport. For the next fifteen years England enjoyed peace while Europe and America were at war, and the full effect upon prices of a free-trade policy only began to be felt in 1873. From 1846 to 1877 no proposition to inquire into the state of agriculture was laid before Parliament, if we except the inquiry into tenant right of 1848, and into land improvements in 1873. After the Crimean war the rentals of land rapidly and steadily increased; between 1857 and 1878 they rose not less than 20 per cent.; and the capitalised value of the increase was calculated at upwards of 260 millions.

This prosperity was claimed by the Manchester school as their achievement. Apart from the impulse of despair which it gave to farmers, there can be no doubt that free trade encouraged the best form of high farming. Corn fetched so low a price that, regarded as a separate department, corn-growing ceased to pay. But the rise in the price of meat enabled farmers to grow corn at a profit in conjunction with stock-feeding. Free trade forced them to adopt a mixed husbandry of corn and cattle, and made corn pay through the intervention of green crops and live stock. Here, again, the question now to be considered is whether these favourable conditions still exist. There can, it is feared, be but one answer. 'Down corn, up horn,' was the principle on which farming profits depended. Now both are down together. After the adoption of free trade the farmer's chief resource was to sell corn in the shape of meat; but the recent fall in the prices of stock has checkmated his industry.

The period from 1812 to 1845 had witnessed the preparation for, rather than the adoption of, high farming. The reports made to the Royal Agricultural Society in the early years of its existence, the letters of Sir James Caird as 'Times' Commissioner in 1850, the letters of the Commissioner of the 'Morning Chronicle' in the same year, the evidence given before Mr. Pusey's Parliamentary Committee on Agricultural Customs, supply abundant materials for estimating the progress of English farming since the Commissioners of the Board of Agriculture published their Reports from 1800 to 1812. The general impression made by the comparison is that farmers, speaking generally, had made but little use of the new materials of agricultural wealth which science had placed at their command. In each county high farming was rather the exception than the rule; at least one-half of the occupiers of land had made little advance upon the open-field farms of the eighteenth century. The characteristic of the period 1845–73 is not the invention of novelties, but the wider diffusion of the best practices.

The repeal of the corn laws acted as a spur to the energies of farmers; and from 1853 to 1873 they were encouraged by a succession of prosperous seasons, to which the years 1866 and 1867 were the chief exceptions. If harvests were deficient, farmers were consoled by high prices. Wheat during the twenty years succeeding 1848 averaged little below the prices of the last twenty years of Protection, and the last six years of the period approached them even more closely.[1] The Crimean war and the civil war in America stopped supplies from the Baltic and the New World; the great demand for grain for France raised the markets in 1871; the heavy rainfall and deficient harvest of 1872 brought wheat to 57*s.* per quarter; and thus foreign imports, though relieved in 1869 of the shilling duty, failed to force down the prices of English grain. At the same time the ravages of the cattle plague raised the prices of meat in 1872–3 to a figure which

---

[1] For 20 years preceding 1848 the average price of wheat was 57*s.* 4*d.*
  For 20 years succeeding 1848 ,, ,, ,, 52*s.* 2*d.*
  For five years 1869-70-71-72-73 ,, ,, ,, 53*s.* 5*d.*

rendered stock-feeding and corn-growing highly remunerative.[1] Even when corn was low the high prices of meat maintained the balance.

It would be a tedious because monotonous task to enumerate in detail the improvements effected in agriculture during this period. Roots and artificial grasses remained the great pivots of high farming. They enabled the farmer to keep more stock, enrich his land with more manure, and thus trebled the growth of corn by bringing into use not only rich soils, but light lands which had been previously valueless; they drew his attention to comparative degrees of maturity in sheep and cattle, and led him to devote himself to breed, precocity, and fattening propensity; they compelled tenants of stiff wet lands to drain carefully and thoroughly; they revolutionised the old systems of cultivation by demonstrating the advantages of autumn tillage. Not last nor least of their merits is the continuous employment they provide for agricultural labourers, who are no longer dismissed at the approach of winter, but earn their wages all the year round. Fresh

[1] *Average Prices of Butchers' Meat (per stone of* 8 *lbs.) at the Metropolitan Cattle Market for* 1843–6 *and for* 1870–3.

Years	Beasts								Sheep							
	Inferior		2nd class		3rd class		4th clas		Inferior		2nd class		3rd class		4th class	
	s.	*d.*	*s.*	*d.*	*s.*	*d.*	*s.*	*d.*	*s.*	*d.*	*s.*	*d.*	*s.*	*d.*	*s.*	*d.*
1843	2	8¾	3	2½	3	7	3	10¼	3	0½	3	5	3	10	4	1
1844	2	7¼	3	1	3	5¾	3	10¾	2	11	3	5¾	3	8¼	4	0½
1845	2	9¾	3	5¼	3	9	4	1¼	3	4¼	3	10¼	4	3¾	4	9
1846	2	8	3	1¼	3	7¼	4	0	3	7¾	4	1	4	5½	4	10
1870	3	7	4	4½	4	11½	5	4	3	6	4	2¾	5	0¾	5	7¼
1871	3	11¼	4	10¼	5	4½	5	8½	4	1	4	10	5	10½	6	5
1872	3	7½	4	4½	5	3½	5	8	4	5½	5	4	6	2½	6	8
1873	4	9	5	3½	5	10¼	6	0	5	2¼	5	11	6	6¼	6	9½

discoveries increased their utility: swedes and mangel-wurzels on the one side, spring vetches from the other, fill the gap which intervened between moisture-loving, frost-dreading turnips and later green crops. Geology and chemistry gave their invaluable aid to tillers of the land. Geology taught the reasons which govern the superfluity or the absence of bottom water, furnished definite classifications of soils, ascertained the composition of their different strata, explained the principles that control their capabilities and degrees of fertility. Chemistry reveals by its analyses the elements on which agricultural values of land depend, suggests how to remove differences or supply deficiencies, equalises the characters of soils, restores the properties which different plants exhaust, and, in a word, assists every branch of husbandry, from the manuring of the land to the production of milk, from the growth of corn to the fattening of cattle. The triumph of chemistry is summed up in the system of successive cropping without impoverishment which has been established by the experiments of Sir John Lawes and Dr. Gilbert. Mechanical inventions completed what geology and chemistry had commenced. The soil is not only improved by drainage and artificial manures, but by subsoil and trench ploughs and deeper cultivation; it is more easily tilled by the lighter and better implements which replaced the cumbrous plough with its shoe-like share fitted on to the wooden chip, and which, working at the lightest possible draught, show clean-cut, level-edged, unbroken rectangular furrows. Instead of the hawthorn tree which Markham recommended for a harrow, new implements are adapted for light or heavy lands, as well as clod-crushers, and horsehoes and scarifiers to cleanse the foulness of the land. Thus the soil is better prepared for the reception of the seed, and the seed itself is not only better selected and assorted, but it is more effectively sown by drills, which have supplanted the elaborate directions for hand-sowing given by Fitzherbert, and realised the wildest dreams of Worlidge, Evelyn, or Tull. Nor is mechanical invention content to improve the preparation, the tillage, and the sowing of the crops. It also supplies means by which they can be secured. Harvesting by hand has given place to mowing, reaping, tedding, and binding machines; cumbrous wagons have yielded to lighter carts; elevators have diminished the labour of stacking; the flail is supplanted by threshing and corn-dressing machines, which not only thresh the grain quicker, but leave less in the straw. Lastly, the application of steam to agricultural implements has immeasurably increased their efficiency, and instead of horse or water power the plough can now be driven, or the corn threshed. by a strength that never tires or slackens. Nor has science confined its efforts to the treatment of arable land. It has done much to improve the management of grass; and in no department of agriculture has it achieved more marked results than in stock breeding and feeding. Stalls and yards which fifty years stood empty were filled with fat or store beasts. More stock was bred; and it is better bred, better fed, and more comfortably kept; while the use of oil-cake enabled the farmer to enrich his store of manure, increase his supply of winter keep, and carry more head upon his farm. And here, too, machinery economises his labour; it crushes his corn, breaks his cake, chaffs his fodder, pulps or slices his turnips, steams or boils his food. Stall-feeding avoids the waste that is inevitable in yards; each animal receives an equal portion of food instead of being starved by the strongest, eats at its leisure, ruminates unmolested, and rests undisturbed. Three beasts were fatted upon land which, as pasture, barely supported one. During this period, from 1845 to 1873, most of these practices and appliances became widely known if not generally adopted. At the same time commodious buildings were erected; holdings were enlarged; small fields were thrown together, admitting light and air to the land, economising the time of the labourer, and saving expenses of repairs and gates.

But the most conspicuous improvement was the change among farmers themselves. The class rapidly advanced as it was recruited from men of skill, enterprise, and capital, open to new ideas, quick to accept new discoveries, able and willing to try experiments. Good roads, good homesteads, good crops, good stock, and good farmers became the rule rather than the exception. The union of science and practice has, in other respects, borne abundant fruit. It has created a new industry, and a new class of persons connected with farming; it has not only increased the amount, but lessened the cost of production, and thus freed the rural population to supply the demand for artisan labour; it has attracted capital into the land, and made the recognition of tenant right an indispensable necessity. Between 1851 and 1881 agricultural students increased from 104 in 1851 to 728 in 1881, agricultural implement proprietors and workers from 55 to 4,260, the land drainage service from 11 to 1,695. On the other hand, though the produce as well as area under cultivation is greatly increased since 1801, the agricultural population has declined. In 1811 it was 34 per cent. of the whole; in 1821, 32; in 1831, 28; in 1841, 22; in 1851, 16; in 1861, 10; in 1871, and still more in 1881, not only relatively but actually the total number [1] of agricultural

[1] See Appendix VII., Census Returns of Agricultural Classes.

labourers has considerably decreased. Whether this result is satisfactory may be doubted; but it is indisputably a remarkable proof of the progress of scientific agriculture. Another sign of the change is tenant right. In the days of Protection English farming was conducted upon a system which required little or no capital. Farmers brought nothing upon their holdings in the shape of costly manure or expensive feeding stuffs; they laid down no pipes for drainage, and used no manure beyond that which was produced upon the farm; their premises were dilapidated and poverty-stricken. They themselves were men of little enterprise, capital, or intelligence, farming by rule of thumb and from hand to mouth, investing in no improvements, aiming at nothing more than to make both ends meet. The essence of ancient tillage was exhaustion followed by fallow. Nothing was spent in replacing the productive qualities which the crops had withdrawn. All this was now reversed. The essence of the modern system was restoration of fertility; and tenants had at their command a host of resources, the use of which entailed a large expenditure of capital without immediate profits. High farming extracts more from the land; but it also puts more into it and increases instead of diminishing its value. Common law gave no compensation to outgoing tenants except for their way-going crops, and everything affixed to the soil belonged to the landlord. Under such circumstances tenants had little encouragement to expend money in manures, drainage, or a course of skilful farming: without capital, improvements were impossible; but capital is proverbially too shy to be attracted where no security is forthcoming. The necessary outcome of the changed system of farming had been recognised by Mr. Pusey in 1848. Before that time the cry for tenant right was unheard, not because greater confidence existed between landlord and tenant, but because the protection of the right was not required. Three-quarters of a century ago tenants were not compensated for their outlay because outlay was never made, or because profits covered the risk. From 1800 to 1820 land was clayed, chalked, or manured without any security for the tenant's outlay. The 'custom of the country' intervened on his behalf, but partially and ineffectually. It was proved before the Parliamentary Committee of 1848 that in three counties only, Lincoln, Leicester, and Glamorgan, did the custom of the country afford the tenant any redress, if he received a notice to quit before he had repaid himself for his outlay, or found his rent raised upon improvements which he had himself effected. Even then it was doubtful whether the prevalent usage of the district could have been successfully pleaded in a law-court, though it was often accepted in arbitrations. The demand for tenant-right, which has resulted in the Agricultural Holdings Acts of 1875 and 1883, is rather a significant proof of improved farming than of distrust between landlords and tenants.

To this same period appropriately belong the first records of practical and experimental agriculture. In 1864, upon the motion of Sir James (then Mr.) Caird, it was determined to procure statistical information respecting agriculture, the acreage under cultivation, and its food supplies, whether bread or meat. At first considerable difficulty was experienced, especially in the Midland and Southern counties, in procuring complete returns, which were regarded as portents of increased taxation. But the returns are now approximately correct, and have repeatedly proved their value. We are no longer at the mercy of guesswork, which often travels wide of the mark. Arthur

Young calculated the acreage of England and Wales at forty-six million acres, and Pitt adopted his estimate as the basis of his Property tax. It is now accurately known [1] how many acres are arable or pasture, what are the crops cultivated, and what the livestock which they carry. And the same information, in less detail, is also supplied with reference to our foreign competitors. Of equal, if not higher, value are the reports of experimental agriculture which are from time to time issued from Rothamsted, the most important station connected with farming in Europe or America. No branch of experimental agriculture or agricultural chemistry can be discussed without reference to the investigations of Sir John Lawes and Dr. Gilbert. It is difficult to estimate the enormous influence which their experiments have already exercised upon farming, or to assign limits to the increased productiveness of the soil which England might have witnessed but for the disastrous period of 1873–87.

[1] From these statistics it appears that the total area of England and Wales is 37,319,221 acres, of which, in 1887, 27,823,207 acres are under crops, bare fallow, or grass.

CHAPTER XI.

AGRICULTURAL DEPRESSION, 1873 TO 1887.

THE causes of the present as contrasted with previous depression are partly new and partly old. The sketch which has been given of agricultural progress shows that a succession of bad seasons or a revolution in the science of farming have produced widespread distress and necessitated changes of front which can only be effected with heavy loss. But the new element now for the first time present is foreign competition.

Though the circumstances are partially new, most of the literature on the subject is old. A large class of persons have always doubted the reality of farmers' troubles. In 1651 Blith said that the chief cause of the depression was the 'high stomachs' of the farmer. In 1816 people argued that if farmers drank sound beer instead of sour claret, and their wives returned from the piano to the dairy, they would still be wealthy. It was reserved for an imaginative poet in 1801 to charge them with soaking five-pound notes instead of rusks in their port wine. Then, as now, the complaint was heard that fundholders escaped taxation. Why, asks a pamphleteer of 1822, should landowners, who only get $3\frac{1}{2}$ per cent. for their purchase, while 'moneyed men' obtain 5 per cent., be despoiled of a third of their income by a taxation which the moneyed interest escapes? Then, as now, the sufferers were not silent. The cry was heard that the taxes and the prices ruined farmers, and it was maintained in 1816 that wheat could not be grown at a profit under 54s., and that, if the tenantry had their lands rent free, they could not subsist under present conditions. Then, as now, political agitators were prepared to use depression to foment discontent. In 1766 a writer says that the ' sober industrious poor ' are the real sufferers from high prices; but ' who,' he asks, ' ever heard of any of this character mixing themselves with mobs,' made up of the ' drunken, lazy, and abandoned,' whose case was misrepresented, exaggerated, or rather ˙created by certain senseless and injudicious writers in the common newspapers?' In the last century, as well as this, every politician at a coffee-house had his infallible nostrum; theorists elaborated impracticable schemes, which were supported by the ignorant and used by the factious; oppositions, themselves sitting in the cold shade of poverty, bewailed the miseries of the poor; dowagers at quadrille tables inveighed against the cruelty of Parliament in disregarding the voice of the people; quiet old gentlemen from the depths of their armchairs recommended military executions of butchers, bakers, poulterers, and fishmongers as the most effective remedy. If we are to believe half what we see in print, times have been as bad before. Let the reflection encourage us in facing present difficulties.

For the last fourteen years the country has been passing through a crisis of prolonged, if not unexampled, severity. Three previous epochs stand out conspicuously as periods of agricultural depression. In the last half of the sixteenth century, at the close of the seventeenth century, and during the years 1813–36, the disordered state of the currency constituted an important factor in the distress. Similarly the distress in 1765–73 was partly due to the excessive value which was attached to gold. Similarly, too, the most prosperous era of the present century, 1854–73, synchronised with a large increase of the precious metals consequent upon the discovery of gold and silver mines. The presence of this factor alike in adversity and prosperity suggests that the crisis of 1873–87 is largely affected by questions of the currency. The influx of gold raises prices because the purchasing power of money is relatively diminished by its abundance, and sellers benefit by the enhanced value of their produce. But it also stimulates commercial activity, and thus its tendency to raise prices is balanced by increased production and consequent cheapness. So, on the other hand, the withdrawal of large quantities of precious metals necessarily lowers prices, because the dearness of money increases its purchasing power, and consequently buyers gain by the seller's loss. The passage from this broad and simple principle to its detailed application is bewildering in its intricacy. If, as appears certain, currency questions enter largely into the present depression, it is greatly to be regretted that those who speak with authority on this most recondite subject have not translated their technical language into a tongue which is more intelligible to ordinary understandings.

But it is not contended that the currency alone has produced the present crisis. A glance at the history of the past twenty years reveals, not only what has become of the gold, but numerous concurrent causes of financial depression.

The failure of Messrs. Overend & Gurney in 1866 was the first symptom of the rottenness of our commercial prosperity. Reckless trading had spread widely. Insolvent firms glutted the markets with goods in order to manufacture credit, and deprived legitimate traders of their reasonable profits. Banks engaged in business which lay outside their proper sphere, and linked their fortunes with unscrupulous adventurers. The crash came in 1878, but it had long been inevitable. Events of such magnitude as the Civil War in America, the Franco-Prussian War, and the French payment of the Prussian war indemnity necessarily exercised a prodigious influence on the commercial world. Prices rose inordinately in England during the excited period from 1871-3. To this rise two circumstances mainly contributed. The American War had cut off cotton supplies for four years, and during that period all the old produce was sold off, while an actual scarcity was created. Consequently in 1869 capital flowed into the new channel literally in torrents. So, again, an extraordinary demand was created for coal and iron to develop the railways of Germany and the United States, while the opening of the Suez Canal gave a stimulus to the shipbuilding trade.

In 1873 the reaction came, though it did not reach England till a year later. Quantities of capital were locked up in unremunerative railways; taxes had been largely increased to provide for war expenses or maintain huge armaments; reckless speculation had followed the triumph of Germany. A railway panic set in in America, and disastrous failures occurred at Vienna, as well as in Germany and the United States, and they were followed by a fall in wages and in the prices of coal, iron, and other articles. When the reaction reached England it was aggravated by a series of bad harvests, as well as by the political difficulties to which the revival of the Eastern Question gave rise. In 1875 great failures like those of Im Thurn & Co., or Alexander Collie, and the default on the Turkish debt aggravated the depression, which was intensified by strikes, labour disputes, reductions of wages, and the discharge of operatives. The following year brought no increase of trade, but rather diminished both wages and confidence. Throughout 1877 prices fell; trade shrank and financial disasters became general. But the full extent to which the commercial prosperity of the country was undermined was not suspected till the colossal failures of the Glasgow, South Wales, and West of England Banks in 1878. The country has not yet recovered the blow, although trade now stands on a sounder footing through the drastic purging it has undergone.

It is impossible to determine what proportion of the existing commercial depression is directly due to the diminished and diminishing supply of gold. But a diagnosis of the disease detects characteristic signs of a crisis arising out of the gradual decrease of monetary stock. A sudden exportation of cash may produce a short crisis as severe as it is transient. A slow reduction of the stock of money blights and paralyses trade, produces languor, and stifles energies. One puts a pistol to the head of commerce, the other drains its lifeblood. And these signs are accompanied by an exceptional demand for gold, and a palpable falling off in its supply. Within this period the paper currencies of the United States and European nations were replaced by specie payments. In 1871 the German Empire, which had hitherto adopted the single silver system, adopted the single gold standard with a subsidiary silver coinage; America hoarded stores of gold in order to resume metallic money; Sweden, Norway, and Denmark substituted gold for silver in their currency. This drain upon the gold of the world, in addition to the ordinary consumption through wear and tear or works of art, was not met by an increased supply. On the contrary, Sir

Hector Hay's evidence before the Silver Commission of 1876[1] shows that the production of gold was steadily decreasing, and the evidence laid before the Select Committee on Depression of Trade in 1885[2] establishes the same fact. To untrained eyes it also appears significant that in the years 1877-81 the exports of gold from England exceeded the imports by 11,160,000*l*.[3] As gold became dearer, prices fell; its purchasing power increased, and produce was cheapened by the scarcity of the precious metals. At the same time silver was depreciated in value. The resumption by America of a double standard temporarily raised its price, but it fell again, partly absolutely owing to the increased yield of silver mines, partly relatively to the enhanced value of gold. Under ordinary circumstances the silver of the world is absorbed in the East. But the process has been extraordinarily slow. Meanwhile, as it appears to unscientific observers, the English farmer suffers both from the glut of silver and the famine of gold.[4] The Indian rupee, once worth 2*s*., is now worth scarcely 1*s*. 5*d*. Corn producers benefit by the fall in paying wages; and merchants importing Indian produce can afford to speculate in the exchange, and undersell home markets. The use of a single gold standard possesses undoubted merits, but it is complicated by our possession of an Eastern empire which has adopted the single silver standard.[5]

[1] See Appendix VIII. Table 1.   [3] *Ibid.* Table 3.
[2] *Ibid.* Table 2.   [4] *Ibid.* Table 4.
[5] The disturbance in the wheat trade in fact results from the dislocation between the values of English gold and Indian silver, though England has the advantage in the exchange. The British currency gives a fixed value of $2\frac{4}{11}d.$ to the grain of fine gold. When the Indian rupee was 1*s*. $10\frac{1}{2}d.$, $10\frac{1}{2}$ grains of fine gold purchased 165 grains of fine silver; now 8 grains of fine gold purchase the same amount of silver.

The general depression was aggravated by the collapse of agriculture, consequent, in the early part of the period, upon a succession of bad harvests. An inclement autumn in 1872 and an unfavourable spring counterbalanced the fine harvest weather of 1873, and the crop fell below the average. The harvest of the next year was excellent and abundant, but it was the last of a cycle of prosperous seasons. Wheat began to fall in 1875, and a succession set in of unsettled seasons with bleak springs and rainy summers. Farmers found everything cheap to sell and dear to buy. The harvests of 1875-6-7 fell far below the average both in quantity and quality. The average price of these three years was 51s. as against 57s. 5d. in the preceding three years. The potatoes failed, the fruit crop ran short, and the cattle plague was rife. In 1877 land agents began to complain that eligible tenants for vacant farms were scarce. The heavy losses which farmers had suffered from three bad seasons in succession, cattle plague, and scanty hay and root crops, were not compensated by the fine season of 1878. The full force of American competition made itself felt when agriculture at home was already thus enfeebled. The Civil War had delayed the impending pressure; it was now accelerated and intensified by the commercial panic in America in 1873, which drove thousands of the working classes out of trade, and settled them down as farmers in the Western States. A general move was made from the Eastern States towards the West. Land was taken up with extraordinary rapidity; population sprang up with a bound in districts which were unclaimed and uninhabited except by the large stockowners, who pastured their herds on open prairies which now yield abundance of corn. The effect was at once felt in the price of grain. The series of bad seasons culminated when the sunless, ungenial 1879 produced the worst harvest within living memory. Meanwhile America enjoyed crops of most exceptional abundance, and, taking advantage of the agricultural collapse in England, flooded the country with her produce. Some conception of her profits may be formed from the ease with which she carried out her resumption of cash payments.

Foreign competition, coming on the back of unprosperous seasons, completed the ruin of English farmers. They were unable to recover themselves, and went from bad to worse. The modern problem is low prices. The margin of profit on the staple produce of agriculture sank to nothing. Wheat-growing ceased to pay; the keeping of more stock on arable land barely met the expense of artificial food; the reconversion of tillage to pasture glutted the milk market; meat farming suffered from the severe competition of America. Added to all these difficulties was the heavy burden of local taxation; labour was dearer and less effective; men were obliged to be employed where boys had sufficed; railway companies carried foreign goods at preferential rates, which compelled English farmers to pay part of the bill for carriage of their foreign competitors. Many remedies were proposed, some the results of wide, others of limited experience. Each suggestion, fortified by instances of its successful adoption, was recommended to the country at large. Investments in fish-farming or jam-making at the best could afford only local relief. As to this large class of remedies, the most that was to be said was that farmers must sit loosely to routine, and welcome assistance from whatever quarter it came. [No general cure for distress exists, except favourable seasons, increased supplies of money whether metallic or paper, revival of trade, curtailment of production by the shifting of capital, diminution of foreign competition, adjustment of standards of living to decreased incomes, restored courage, and the adaptation of farming practices to new requirements.

Recent seasons proved less inclement, and trade less languid; but two of the principal causes of the crisis operate with scarcely diminished force. Foreign supplies pour into the country in increasing volume.[1] Agriculture bears upon its face every sign of a depressed industry. The soil remains weakly farmed, undermanned and understocked, partly because capital has dwindled, partly because of the ravages of cattle disease, partly because farmers are compelled to realise something, even if sales are premature. Land is going back; it is falling out of condition, if not out of cultivation, and farmers are too poor, too weak, and dispirited to restore or maintain it. Its produce per acre is diminishing, and the number of sheep has decreased by more than two million since 1875.[2] High farming at present prices appears waste of money; agriculture cannot hold its own by intension against extension. The progress of centuries seems thrown away; the instrument becomes useless just when it is perfected and able to double the existing produce of the soil. From every point of view but the farmer's, the brightest spot in the general gloom is the cheapness of food. Free trade has at least secured the country from the horrors of famine.

In the face of past losses and present prices landlords have reduced their rentals to little more than the amount which they reached in 1836. And still 'Let the landlords come down with the rents,' in the apprehension of many, solves every difficulty and closes every argument. Not

[1] The growth of this prodigious trade from 1866 is shown in Appendix IX.
[2] See Appendix X., Statistics of Agriculture, 1867-87.

every landlord is a Dives; the majority sit at the rich man's gates. Many of them succeed to land encumbered by settlements and mortgages; they cannot dispose of their property, for land is a drug in the market; rates and taxes swallow up what is left from interest and rent charges, and the so-called landowner becomes an agent between his tenants and the mortgagees and taxgatherers. Anyone who has lived in the country can call up before his eyes numerous families who have curtailed their expenditure, diminished their establishments, let or closed their houses, or become absentees on the Continent. But among farmers arrears, bills of sale, liquidations, bankruptcies kept ever in advance of reductions and remissions of rent. It is, of course, impossible to determine the exact amount of their loss. In 1875 their capital might be placed at something between 230,000,000*l*. and 260,000,000*l*.; in 1887 it has fallen to below 160,000,000*l*. Where they once employed over 10*l*. per acre, they now scarcely employ 6*l*. The census returns of 1881 in a different way attest their impoverishment. The number of tenant farmers diminished between 1871 and 1881 by 10 per cent., while the great increase in the number of bailiffs shows that many are farming as servants land which they had formerly held as occupiers. Many of those who are still in occupation of land are only holding on by their eyelids in hope of better times, or protection. Up till the last year labourers had suffered least of all by agricultural depression. Their position was, and for those who are employed still is, immeasurably superior to their condition at the commencement of the century. Their cottages are improved, their wages higher, and the prices of all the necessaries of life lower; they are better housed, better clad, and better fed. But as arable land is converted to pasture, and farmers are hard pressed by unremunerative prices, numbers are necessarily thrown out of work, employed half-time, or crowd into towns to meet an exodus into the country of starving artisans; their El Dorado proves to be the workhouse or worse. The landlord's income is precarious, the farmer's fixed rent an improvident speculation, the labourer's wages an uncertain remuneration. With existing conditions all classes, but especially those engaged in agriculture, are necessarily dissatisfied.

Before considering the many remedies proposed, it may be said that, though State interests override the interests of individuals: though the cultivation and occupation of the soil are matters of national concern; though the limitation in the quantity of land attaches a fancy value to its acquisition and renders its possession a monopoly—no true distinction on the score of ownership can be drawn between real and personal property. Money invested in land and money invested in the funds are equally the fruits of industry, equally entitled to protection. Rights, legally acquired under existing land laws, cannot be disturbed without destroying that security which is the vital breath of nations. Sudden changes, subversive of the social system, rather aggravate than cure existing evils. Freedom of contract is a sounder principle than State interference, and voluntary action more satisfactory than compulsion. Whatever are the remedies applied, they must be consistent with established rights and recognised economic laws. On the one side, the accumulation of large estates in few hands is admittedly an evil; on the other, the mixture of large, middle-sized, and small holdings is economically and socially the most advantageous organisation. But, unless legislation is ill-considered and revolutionary, no general change can be immediately effected in the occupation or even the cultivation of the soil. Wise reform will only affect existing conditions by degrees; it will pave the way for, but not effect, radical change; it will create no artificial class by the stroke of a pen. Relief from agricultural depression must be sought, not in the manufacture of a peasant proprietary by suppression of landlords, but in the restoration of confidence and the consequent attraction of more capital into land, the extinction of all hindrances to the development of high farming, the removal of every obstacle to the wider distribution of landed interests, and above all, the revival of paralysed energies.

Crude panaceas are in vogue at the present day; wild theories are promulgated for the redistribution of English land. In the days of her commercial and agricultural supremacy, England might safely ignore such demands for change. An ever-increasing prosperity postponed the shock of antagonistic interests. But now, when disastrous seasons and foreign competition paralyse the energies of agriculturists, when commerce ceases to expand with sufficient rapidity to employ a growing population, land questions are not merely considered with curiosity, but the exclusive privileges of the few are discussed with deepening eagerness. The assailants of property may be noisy out of all proportion to their numbers; their confidence may rather proceed from ignorance than from the calm of reasoned conviction; they may have given no proof, tested by success, that their schemes are feasible; they may forget that the first and worst sufferers by economic blunders are the poor; but it is idle to ignore the danger of an agitation which has already scared away capital from the land, and renders chronic the enfeebled condition of agriculture. It is easy to distinguish the historical and economical aspects of Irish from English land questions; yet the exceptional legislation which has been deemed necessary for the Irish tenantry has already borne fruit in England. The cry is raised, and assiduously encouraged by political leaders, that landlords are a parasitical growth, a remnant of feudalism, a class that reaps what others sow. The misconception is industriously fostered that England is a solitary exception to the universal rule of European landholding. It is maintained with increasing vehemence that God made the land for the people, that land is an *ager publicus*, which the State has granted to landlords to administer, but which she may at pleasure resume. Men quote with approval Mirabeau's retort to the objection that he could not sell the landed property of the Church—'Not sell it! then I will give it.'

CHAPTER XII.

PEASANT PROPRIETORS.

THE chief social and theoretical remedy which is proposed for the existing agricultural distress is the forced growth of a peasant proprietary. The peasant proprietor is the spoilt child of theorists; his artificial creation by the stroke of a pen is the favourite panacea of a large section of land reformers. Towards this end, in one shape or another, all theoretical reforms appear to tend. No one will deny that the spontaneous increase of small owners is socially and politically valuable, or that the aggregation of large properties in a few hands is a source of political and social danger. ' Latifundia perdidere Italiam ; ' and it is quite possible that land monopoly may prove the ruin of England. The happiness of a people depends on the distribution, not on the accumulation, of wealth ; the larger the proportion of those who enjoy a proprietary interest in the soil, the stronger is the guarantee afforded to the stability of the State. From an economic point of view it may be doubted whether peasant proprietors are profitable ; but the enquiry whether a large or small farm produces most per acre yields in importance to the question—Which contributes most to the sum total of national prosperity ?

It is useless to appeal in favour of peasant proprietors to the instances quoted by Mill. His authorities belong to an extinct condition of society. At the present day means of communication are easy; agriculture has ceased to be self-sufficing, and has become dependent on manufacture; machinery has been introduced into all farming operations; foreign competition has to be faced. Reports of agricultural enquiries abroad prove that the Continental peasantry are not more capable of competing with prairie farmers and rich, if not virgin, soils than are our English tenantry. The Agricultural Congress at Nancy, which concluded its session in the last week of August 1886, practically decided that ' une seule ressource reste donc aux cultivateurs qui veulent éviter la ruine, c'est d'élever les rendements de leurs récoltes.' In other words, high farming is the recommendation of the congress.

No country and no system of farming has entirely escaped the present depression. Peasant proprietors have suffered less than tenant farmers, only because they employ no hired labour and grow corn, not for sale, but for their own consumption. For tenant farmers the agricultural crisis is hardly less serious in France than it is in England. The proof lies on every side. Forced sales of stock and rural bankruptcies are numerous; disputes are rife respecting claims to unexhausted improvements; farms are difficult to let, rents are falling, population migrates into the towns, land decreases in value. It no longer pays to grow wheat; flockmasters get nothing for their wool; American pork undersells French produce; the florist of Angers complains of his Belgian rival; the madder of Vaucluse is beaten out of the field by indigo. Wages are rising in a falling market; labour is not only scarce and dear, but it has deteriorated in quality. The younger generation is not, it is said, like the old; lads go off to seek fortunes in towns, or cannot endure, after the gaiety

K

of barrack life, the monotony of the country. Girls will not work like their mothers, but become dressmakers or shopgirls. In France, as in England, politico-economical questions are chained to the car of party politics; no one dares to investigate the principles which regulate commercial dealings. In France, as well as in England, a new privileged class has been created, that of the *rentier*, who escapes the taxation which crushes the agriculturist. As in England, so in France, through railway rates are said to favour the foreigner; and in both countries the cry grows louder that the cheapest loaf becomes the dearest when no one has money to buy it. If French peasants and tenant farmers have suffered less than their English brethren, it is because the land has never been called upon to produce two gentlemen's incomes, and because large employers of labour are never ashamed of the blouse and the sabot. In Germany, again, the business of farming is in a most depressed condition. A United States consul of great experience reports that farming properties in districts which are remote from large cities, and where the consumption of milk and other perishable produce is small, may be purchased at fifty per cent. of their former value. Farmers who bought land at the high prices of 1871–74, have sunk half the capital thus invested; those who raised the purchase-money on mortgage have suffered still more. The cause of this downward tendency is the low price of corn and cattle. Increased import duties have not directly benefited farmers. It is only under the new tariff law, which provides that a portion of the income derived from income duties shall be paid over to district authorities, and credited against their bills for local taxation, that they gain by the taxes on produce. A programme was adopted by a farmers' meeting at Cassel in 1883, which might have been laid before an English Chamber of Agriculture. The following are some of the measures which were decided upon as vitally necessary to the existence of farmers:—

(1) The diminution of their outgoings by economy in administration, increased liability of personalty, a revision of stamp duties and other charges on land transfer, a tax on stock exchange transactions, an increase in indirect taxation.

(2) The increase of their receipts by protective duties on foreign produce, suppression of middlemen, readjustment of railway rates which favour the foreigner, reintroduction of domestic industries.

(3) The extinction of the land tax; the abolition of the law of succession, which drives peasants to contract debts in order to keep estates together and provide portions for younger children; the provision of cheap loans; and the adoption of a double standard of coinage.

Acre for acre, the English system produces more than the foreign. What reason is there to suppose that the raw agricultural labourer of England, suddenly planted on a cottier farm, will extract more from the soil than his Continental rival, who is favoured by a genial climate, centuries of training, and acquired habits of industry and thrift? The heavy rainfall and low temperature of this country narrowly limit the number of agricutural products which are suited to the farming of peasant proprietors, and even confine cereals to a limited area. Under such circumstances it is impossible that peasant proprietors can flourish universally in Britain. Nor in districts most adapted to their existence can their capital command those artificial manures which, to the exhausted fertility of an old country, have become a necessity.

This statement is strongly confirmed by the conditions of agriculture in France. Variety is at once the charm and the solid advantage of France. It is by her diversities of soil and climate that her peasant proprietary thrives. By the same diversity she is protected against foreign competition or adverse seasons. As in England the relations of landlord and tenant farmer constitute practically the only system of land tenure, and corn-growing and cattle-feeding her only agricultural industry, so her districts are purely agricultural or purely manufacturing. It is not so in France, and too much stress can hardly be laid on the contrast. On the one hand, her land tenures are more flexible and more elastic, and her modes of cultivation more diversified, so that all her eggs are not stored in a single basket; on the other hand, agriculture and manufacture are not separated into distinct districts. The squalid haunts of English trade are surrounded at the best by blackened wastes; in French Flanders dense population and high farming advance hand in hand. At the doors of factories, at the brink of coal-pits, is some of the best cultivated land in the world, land which affords recreation and profit to thousands of artisans. The importance of this feature in its bearing on the happiness of the industrial population and on the alleged pulverisation of the French soil can hardly be exaggerated. But even in this favoured country there are certain conditions which are necessary for the existence of a peasant proprietary.

The departments in which large properties are rarest are the following :—Gers, Charente, Haute-Loire, Manche, Lot, in which only 6 to 10 per cent. of the properties exceed 300 acres; and Charente-Inférieure, Rhône, Tarn-et-Garonne, and Seine. It is impossible to assign any general reasons for the relatively large number of peasant proprietors in these departments. In each different locality much depends on the character of the soil and climate, the special crops, the rate of agricultural wages. Thus, for instance, in Manche, with its unrivalled pastures, its ready markets for eggs, poultry, and butter, its fruit orchards, and its domestic industries, peasant proprietors flourish. Owing to the amount of grass and to the decrease of population, but little agricultural employment is provided. Consequently wages are very high, and self-farming is profitable. The same remarks apply to the neighbourhood of Paris, where the rural population is attracted into the city, and where market-garden produce commands a ready sale. In Rhône, again, where manufacturing industries abound which give employment to thousands of peasant proprietors, tenant-farming is unprofitable, while at the same time the market is good, and the peasant supplements his earnings in the muslin works of Tarare or some of the numerous manufactories of Givors. So, lastly, Charente-Inférieure is well suited to a peasant proprietary. Its soil varies between the reclaimed marshlands of La Rochelle and Rochefort to the valleys and gently undulating plains of Saintes, the well-wooded district of St. Jean d'Angely, or the heathy ground of Jonzac. Peasant proprietors, who number considerably more than half of the adult male rural population, are to be found in the richest districts, where, besides the vine and the ordinary cereals, hemp, flax, fruits, and garden vegetables are grown in great abundance. There is also a large trade carried on in horses. One farmer breeds the colts, the other buys them at six or eight months and sells them at two or two and a half years old. Lastly every farmhouse has its still for the manufacture of spirits; large quantities of oil are extracted from walnuts; and the paper-works on the river Touve employ thousands of artisans, who are also small landowners.

In purely agricultural districts, where hired labour is cheap, or in mountainous and barren tracts, peasant proprietors do not thrive. On the other hand, the system of small farms worked by their owners succeeds wherever population is dense, labour dear, manufacturing industries abundant, and markets good for garden stuff, dairy produce, or poultry. The absence or presence of peasant proprietors depends on certain conditions of success, without which no peasant proprietor is eager to buy the land. They will not thrive wherever they are planted; a fact which is often overlooked by theorists who point to the French peasant as a proof that owners of land will make gardens out of deserts. The fact is, no French peasant makes the attempt where it appears useless. If he can command some specially fertilising substance like the seaweed which the Breton peasant collects, or if he enjoys exceptional advantages of climate like that of Roscoff, his industry and energy know no limits, and he will in a few years transform a wild coast into a *ceinture dorée*. But it is not inland, on barren moors of heath, ling, broom, and stunted pine, that he thrives or even exists. A closer review of French farming than space permits would prove the point that the presence or absence of peasant proprietorship depends on the presence or absence of some essential conditions of success.[1]

The excessive subdivision of the soil is often urged against the system in France. But the objection is based

[1] See 'Rural France,' *Edinburgh Review*, October, 1887.

rather on the presumed results than the actual effect of the *partage forcé*; customs have sprung up which so far evade the law as to prevent *morcellement* becoming pulverisation. Greater objections may be urged against the operation of a law which subdivides the soil on mechanical rules without reference to demand and supply, which splits up estates into minutely scattered parcels, wasting both the soil and the time of the owner, and breeding perpetual litigation. Another formidable danger is the amount of the French peasant's debt. No one is more possessed by the demon of property, more maddened by the *soif du sillon*, or more seduced by the fascinations of *angulus iste*. He raises money, not for improvements, but for additional purchases; he increases his debt with blind recklessness, borrowing often at 7 per cent. from the local Rigou, and becomes proprietor only in name. Yet the mortgages on landed property in France do not amount to half the sum with which land in England is encumbered. In some parts of France the mortgage debt is said to be 80 per cent. of the value of the land, but the general average is only 15 per cent. Balzac's portrait of 'Courtecaisse' is less favourable than Michelet's graphic picture. Perhaps the true condition of the modern peasant lies midway between the two. In actual command of the luxuries of life, the creation of a class of small owners in England would lower the standard of comfort. The French peasant is worse housed and worse fed than the English labourer. His cottage is generally a single room with a mud floor, in which he, his family, and his livestock live, eat, sleep, work, and die; in cold weather he defies all sanitary laws, and makes his room a tank of stagnant air. From morning to night his toil is excessive and prolonged; female labour is the rule; children are continuously employed.

Progress and education are alike difficult; the rural population often remains ignorant, narrow-minded, jealous, and obstructive.

Holiday writers seem to believe that the French peasant always enjoys summer weather. If Englishmen spend a winter in the country, it is probably in the sunny south. It is not thus that they can understand the melancholy *timbre* in the voice of the Auvergnat, or the wail of his 'Il faut travailler pour vivre.' No one who has read the 'Satires Picardes' of Hector Crinon, the 'laboureur, poète et sculpteur' of Péronne, can doubt the hardships of peasant life in France. The peasant working in the fields, as Crinon describes him, eats nothing but bread—hard, green, and mouldy—with a beard as long as that of a sapper. The food sticks in his throat, but he has nothing to wash it down. Drenched to the skin with the showers that sweep over the treeless plains, cut to the bone with the bitter cold, exhausted by a long day's work, he finds nothing ready for his refreshment when he returns home. No fire has been lighted; the water for his soup is still at the bottom of the well; it must be drawn up, the pot put on, and the fire kindled. His soup, when he gets it, is only water with the chill taken off, in which float a few raw vegetables. Small farmers are the first in the barn in the winter, the first in the fields in the summer, and the last to leave their work. They only rest in the grave. The sleeping fox catches no hen, and the gain is so small that labour is unremitting. As the ass that earns rarely eats the oats, so the peasant fats fowls for his richer neighbours. 'Pour tout régal nous n'avons que de la flammiche,' a thick dough cake baked on the hearth. For meat he eats once a year, at the 'fête de Pâques,' a small piece of tough, skinny cow beef. At other times his food is cabbage or sorrel soup. His only drink is water. Easier, exclaims the poet, is the lot of the hired labourer. In Brittany many of the peasants live on porridge made of buckwheat without milk, potatoes, rye bread, and buckwheat pancakes without butter. If they are a little better off, they add milk and salt butter, and pork and cabbage two or three times a week. In Berri, Marche, Limousin, Auvergne, and the Cevennes, chestnuts are the staple diet of the rural population converted into a sort of porridge or peste and eaten hot. The fate of the peasant in his old age is often cruel. So long as the old man has not signed the deed of partition, he has the best seat by the fire ; no morsel is too choice for him. The moment it is signed, he is regarded as a burden ; he is sent out to beg with ragged clothes ; the sooner he dies the better. In fact, the French peasant is seldom far from the border-line of starvation ; all the product is consumed on the spot ; money is scarce, and famine periodical if not frequent. He is rarely well off unless he has other means of support. Many peasants in Belgium combine agricultural with other agricultural pursuits ; many in France are agricultural labourers for hire, and eke out their subsistence, as in the Alpes Maritimes, by *moneta forestiere* ; in Hérault they are day labourers who till their own plots of land, or, as their patois expresses it, '*font l'impéraou*' out of working hours ; in Hautes-Pyrénées they hire themselves out for daily wages ; in Tarn-et-Garonne the *pagés*, as the peasants are called, work in harvest times as *estivandiers* and *solutiers* ; in Auvergne the ground is tilled by old men, women, and children, while the able-bodied men work in large towns all the summer as porters and water-carriers ; so, too, the Limousin supplements the scanty produce of his land by wages earned in summer months as a bricklayer or stonemason. Yet, on the whole, the French peasant is less hopeless and more independent than the English labourer; he possesses greater weight in the social scale. Arthur Young was no friend to peasant proprietors, but he says of those in the Isle of Axholme: 'Though they work like negroes, they are very happy respecting their mode of existence.' The lot of the French peasant is indisputably hard, his fare meagre, his cottage filthy, his standard of life and education often lamentably low. On the other hand, a peasant proprietary increases the number of those who have something to lose and nothing to gain by revolution, encourages habits of thrift and industry, gives the owner of land, however small his plot, a stake in the country, and a vested interest which guarantees his discharge of the duties of a citizen. Combined with the *partage forcé*, it checks population, for 'la plupart des Normands n'ont pas lu Malthus, mais ils pratiquent instinctivement ses conseils.'

No one will deny that the system of peasant proprietors is socially advantageous. It affords a training to the rural population for which we in England have found no substitute. It checks the centralisation of pauperism, the overgrowth of population, and the migration into towns. The element of stability which it contributes to the State is more valuable to the French than ourselves. There the towns are inflammable as touchwood, while the country ignites more slowly. Yet even here it is useful to have a class of slow-thinking men, who will answer political firebrands with 'Cela est bien, mais il faut cultiver notre jardin.' But, while conceding the advantages of a peasant proprietary, it is impossible to ignore the inseparable difficulties which beset its establishment in England. The poverty and misery or the wealth and happiness of French peasants are often exaggerated in the interests of politicians or of theorists. The small owner is not superior to the ordinary conditions of agricultural success. He will not thrive wherever he is planted, or live on land which starves a rabbit. The chief conditions of his prosperity do not exist in England. We have no commons, no domestic industries, no union of agriculture with manufacture, no special crops for which his minute labour is peculiarly adapted. Some of these conditions can be created; but it is well to bear in mind what is entailed in the establishment of a peasant proprietary, as well as to recognise the duties which such a system throws upon the State.

Finally the example of France is often quoted to prove that a happy and contented peasant proprietary may be established by legislation. The illustration is unfortunate. In the fourteenth century peasant proprietors were numerous in the country, and on the whole increased continuously. In 1697, as Bois-Guillebert states in his 'Détail,' famine compelled them to sell the land which they had painfully acquired in the two preceding centuries. But this check was only temporary. Forbonnais points out that in 1750 impoverished landlords sold their lands to their tenants. Necker states that there were in his time 'une immensité' of peasant proprietors. Doniol ('Histoire des Classes rurales') says that before the Revolution a quarter of the soil had passed into their hands. Arthur Young goes further when he states that in 1787 a third of the land was tilled by peasant owners. The returns on which the land tax of 1790 was based show that, in many districts, the number of proprietors then amounted to two-thirds of the landowning population. It is a travesty of history to assert that the peasant proprietary of France was created by legislation, inasmuch as it was firmly established under the same land laws which existed in this country.

On general grounds the proposition can hardly be disputed that an increase in the number of those who enjoy proprietary interests in the land is socially and politically, if not economically, advantageous. But the increase must be obtained by evolution, not revolution. For immediate relief of agricultural distress it is folly to look to peasant proprietorship. None of its advantages can be secured unless its growth is spontaneous. Habits of thrift, industry, and sobriety are formed by centuries of custom and training—they will not spring up like mushrooms in a single night. State legislation opposed to natural laws is as effective as the Pope's bull against a comet. The disappearance of the class in England and its prevalence abroad result from gradual, well-ascertained causes. No argument for its artificial creation can be drawn from agrarian legislation on the Continent, while in every European country it only exists side by side with landlordism. If it can be shown that the difficulty and expense of the transfer of land obstruct the natural growth of peasant proprietors, let the obstruction be removed. Its removal is on other grounds desirable. But the destruction of large estates and the creation of a class of small owners is a more than doubtful experiment of the legislature. Peasant proprietorship cannot be revived without a return to an extinct social system. Reduce population by one-half, revive domestic industries, return commons and wastes to their former barrenness, make the farmer independent of manufacture—in a word, restore the conditions of self-sufficing agriculture, and the peasant proprietor may still thrive. Under the present conditions of production, when crops must be sold as commodities for money, it is only under exceptional circumstances that the peasant owner maintains his ground.

CHAPTER XIII.

LANDLORDS A NATURAL GROWTH.

The case against nationalisation of land might be rested on the impracticable nature of the object for which it is demanded. If the legislative introduction of a peasant proprietary is condemned as impossible, the broad features of the existing cultivation by landlords, tenant farmers, and wage-earning labourers must remain unchanged. But defenders of this system are challenged by the oft-repeated statement that landlords in this country are a parasitic growth. Although the State purchase, or nationalisation, of land is chiefly demanded for the creation of peasant proprietors, time will not be wasted by an attempt to prove the futility of this statement, which is continually used as a rhetorical point.

In France the system of peasant owners and tenant farmers exists side by side, and is the outcome of natural causes and economic laws. France offers no parallel to the commercial exigencies which in England during the fifteenth and sixteenth centuries required the home production of wool, and evicted crowds of small farmers from the land to make room for the shepherd, his dog, and his flock. So, again, the population of France remained stationary, while that of England increased at the rate of geometrical progression; the one country, confronted by the practical problem of making bread and meat for the million, concentrated her energies on the wholesale production of corn and cattle; the other, opposed by no such difficulty, developed a different system of land tenure and of farming. The effect of the French movement was to tighten the peasant's grasp upon the land, of the English to tear it from his clutch.

In Belgium, as in France, the relations of landlord and tenant exist side by side with a peasant proprietary. In both countries the peasant owners are the growth of natural laws. In Belgium the largest portion of the land and the most productive and fertile districts are held by tenant farmers. The 'Pays de Waes' is not cultivated by small owners, but by tenants, who have for their landlords the little tradesmen of the towns. The poorest soils, such as the Campine or Luxembourg, are tilled by peasant proprietors. But even in the Campine the farmer ekes out his agricultural earnings by travelling over Europe as a pedlar in human hair.

Both the objects and results of agrarian legislation in Germany have been misinterpreted by English land agitators. Stein and his successors did not expropriate the landlords, or deprive them of their land to create a peasant proprietary. Before 1807 land in Prussia was divided, like society, into three castes; peasant land could not be exchanged for burgher land, or burgher land for noble. The old Teutonic communities occupied the greater part of the land, but the ownership was vested in the feudal barons. Peasants could not acquire more than the *dominium utile*; the *dominium directum* belonged to the landlord. They were really serfs, fixed to the soil, irremovable from the manor, holding their land by money rents and personal services. They enjoyed common rights among themselves and usufructuary rights over the demesne. Thus, though the soil was divided into a number of individual properties, freehold ownership was practically unknown. The objects and results of Prussian agrarian legislation were to emancipate the peasant from serfdom, release him from the manorial land, and abolish his personal services, to consolidate intersected estates and extinguish common rights. Landlords received as compensation for the release of their serfs a portion of the peasant lands; the peasant retained as freehold a diminished portion of the soil which he had occupied. The Legislature in fact effected a compromise by an interchange of interests. Prussia remains to this day an example of that union of small, middle-sized, and large properties which is economically and socially the most advantageous organisation.

As with Prussia, so with other states in Germany. Between 1817 and 1848, in Baden, Württemberg, Bavaria, and Hesse, the serfdom of the peasants was abolished by redemption of feudal services; common rights were extinguished, or so regulated as no longer to retard agricultural progress; absolute individual ownership was substituted for common occupation by members of agrarian communities; landlords emerged from the transaction with an increased private estate, and peasants with a diminished but freehold property.

The same legislation has produced with some varieties the same results both in Austria and in Russia. Nor was the legislation which is in Denmark associated with the name of Hansen and 'the peasant's friends' of a more revolutionary character. Landlords abandoned their fiscal immunities and feudal rights, but retained their land. Each estate is now divided into demesne and peasant lands. Over his demesne the landlord's rights are unfettered; he leases it to tenants by contracts which the State does not seek to control. But he may not increase this portion from the Böndergaard or peasant lands. The Böndergaard is occupied by peasants who rent from the landlord the land which they cultivate. When leases expire, the landlord is bound to offer the farm at a fair rent. If no tenant accepts the farm, he may parcel it out among other peasant farmers, or let it in lots to the hired labourers, or absorb it in the demesne on giving an equivalent, or sell it to the peasant tenants. To encourage him in this latter course, he is allowed to annex to the demesne one-tenth of the peasant farm thus put up for sale.

Throughout the Continent landlordism exists side by side with a peasant proprietary; in no country has the State expropriated the landlords; in none has the experiment been tried of an artificial creation of small owners. At the most the State has superintended and assisted the passage from primitive communism and mediæval usufruct to individual ownership. All Teutonic nations started from the same agricultural basis; in all feudalism was a universal feature; in all the same conflict was waged between the manor and the mark; in all there has been the same transition from common to allodial property. In no country has the land been nationalised; in all proprietary rights are acquired by private individuals; the same system is at work in each, but the results are not identical. Both in England and on the Continent rights of ownership and of usufruct were once vested in different persons. Lords of the manor were lords of the soil, but their profitable enjoyment of every portion except their demesne was limited by the usufructuary rights enjoyed by their tenants. When the primitive germs and natural laws of social development are thus identical, it might be expected that results should prove analogous. If England appears to form an exception to rules of development which have elsewhere prevailed, the exception is rather apparent than real. The change which took place on the Continent within living memory commenced in England four centuries ago, and was practically completed before 1800. Its causes and progress have been already traced in considerable detail.[1] On the Continent the land problem was solved by the light of the French Revolution; in England it was determined while the spirit of feudalism still predominated. Yet in Germany in 1810 the interests of the 'Halb-Bauern' were as much overlooked as those of cottagers in England during the sixteenth and eighteenth centuries. What England lost in one direction by the disappearance of a peasant proprietary she gained in another by that early start in the race of commercial prosperity which necessitated the extinction of small proprietors. The higher class of artisans represents the yeoman farmer, and its creation is the direct result of our land system. Neither nations nor individuals can eat their cake as well as keep it. Without large farms, capital, and increased production, it would have been impossible for England to feed her growing population, or to attain her commercial prosperity. No such economic necessity affected the agriculture of the Continent; no industrial changes as yet revolutionised the conditions of foreign society. Buffon's maxim, 'A côté d'un pain il naît un homme,' still held good on the Continent, when, in England, population trode on the heels of production, and when peasants were no longer born to the bread on which they lived, but were suddenly required to furnish food for

[1] See Chapters II., III., VII., and IX.

vast centres of manufacturing industry. Abroad population remained stationary; the habits of the people continued to be agricultural; manufacturing classes were comparatively unknown. Consequently, on the Continent, farming retained its self-sufficing character, and the agrarian communities, which belonged to primitive conditions of society, outlived the decay of feudalism.

In England the security, if not the profit, of the investment, together with the social and political advantages which once attached to the possession of land, stimulated capitalists to lay field to field, and those yeomen who still owned the soil either consulted their pecuniary interests by selling their estates, or were compelled by the widespread ruin of the first half of the present century to relax their hold upon the land. The result is that the whole number of landowners, properly so called, in England and Wales scarcely exceeds at the present time 170,000 persons. No one contends that such a condition of things is sound or healthy. But the difficulty of resisting the natural tendency to accumulate land is forcibly illustrated by the report of a Land Commission recently published in the United States. Statistics show that, in a country where estates in fee tail are obsolete or abolished by law, where there is no feudal tenure, no primogeniture, no privileged class—in a country, finally, where the transfer of land is simple, easy, and cheap—large estates and large farms have become the rule. The United States contain more tenant farmers than any other country in the world, and, where this class exists, those who do the drudgery do not own the land. Land monopoly is becoming the system of America.

The course of agricultural history in England has on the whole been governed by natural economic laws; its present condition is the result of gradual well-ascertained causes. But the record of the growth of large estates is not so free from the taint of oppression that landlords can appeal with entire confidence to their moral title-deeds. The paucity of their numbers, and the exceptional nature of their position and property, should add no element of insecurity to their possessions; yet they warn landlords to think less of their rights than their duties; they render it essential that no individual should fall below the highest standard of the class. It is inconceivable that any serious attack upon legal rights of property should be sanctioned by the law-abiding English nation. No more fatal blow could be struck at that national credit upon which our very existence depends. There is nothing in the examples of foreign legislation, there is still less in the history of the growth of English landed property, to justify the State in violently forcing back or putting forward the clock of social progress, in defying the natural laws of agricultural development, in arbitrarily replacing the peasantry of the country in a position which the majority abandoned nearly four centuries ago, and for the surrender of which compensation was, in most cases, offered and accepted. Even if State interference were in theory so justified, practical experience does not invariably encourage a repetition of the experiment. Foreign precedents cannot be accepted when favourable and rejected when adverse. In Greece the rent to the State was from the first repudiated; in Belgium the tenants always regarded themselves as State pensioners. Nor is the failure confined to foreign countries. At Snigs End and Minster Lovell the experiment was tried after the Chartist movement. It cannot be said to have succeeded. If it is to be repeated on a large scale, we may once more witness the spectacle of tillers of the soil setting up perches for rabbits to roost upon. If economic laws, precedents, history, experience, national justice, and national security still weigh for anything with the legislature, the conversion of the State into a land agency for the immediate and artificial creation of a peasant proprietary may be dismissed to the limbo of crude panaceas and unpractical theories.

Nor should it be forgotten, in the interest of landlords, that all the improvements in English agriculture, which have given us, speaking generally, an undisputed supremacy in the art of farming, have been effected by private capital and individual enterprise. In these days of competition, agriculture must advance or retrograde. Peasant proprietors cannot conduct expensive experiments or invest money in the improvement of stock. If the State creates a class of small owners, it must be at the same time prepared to assume the expenses which have hitherto fallen on private individuals. In France, for instance, where a peasant proprietary exists, the State stands in the place of the landlords. Where properties are large State interference is rarely necessary, because enlightened self-interest generally coincides with public policy. But among a mass of ignorant, small owners, minute, isolated policies prevail, and the State alone regards larger interests. In the eighteenth century, the existence, not merely the commerce, of England imperatively demanded large holdings, owned by capitalist landlords, and let to capitalist tenants. By this means only, when no foreign produce supplemented native resources, could the soil supply food for its vast population. France has felt no such overwhelming pressure of population; no inexorable law of demand and supply has divorced her peasantry from the soil. In England, for public purposes, the State favoured the growth of a small class of capitalist landlords. In France the State sacrificed the few to the many, and promoted the increase of small owners standing on the border-line of pauperism. In England the State has left agricultural improvement to private enterprise; in France she supplies out of the pockets of the taxpayers the capital and direction in which her land system is deficient. If the present system is abolished in England, the State must not only undertake the expenditure of the landlord, but make the outlay of the tenant farmer. Peasant proprietors are, in fact, costly exotics, which, in their present surroundings, can only be reared with a certain loss to the community in the general productiveness of the land, a deterioration in their own standard of comfort, and a perpetual expense to the taxpayer.

A glance at some of the leading features of the French system of State aid to agriculture will bring home the difficulty of creating a peasant proprietary to the breeches-pockets, if not the consciences, of legislators.

Elementary agriculture is taught in primary schools, where children learn to distinguish between plants, grasses, and soils; often a plot of ground is attached to the school which serves as an experimental farm. The school teachers are supplied with training in the subject by departmental professors, who, under the direction of the Minister of Education, give courses of lectures in the *écoles normales* The rest of the system of agricultural education falls under the department of the Minister of Agriculture. Three classes of schools are provided:—(1) the *fermes-écoles*; (2) the *écoles pratiques*; (3) the *écoles nationales*. The *fermes-écoles* are numerous and useful; among them are those of Trois-Croix, near Rennes; St.-Gauthier, at Domfront; St.-Michel (Nièvre); Nolhac (Haute-Loire).

Many of these primary agricultural schools were founded by private enterprise after the Restoration, but in October, 1848, they were recognised as part of the administrative system of the State. Lads enter these schools as apprentices, not as pupils. They must not be over sixteen at the time of entrance; they are fed and treated as labourers; they go through a course of two or three years, and at the end leave the school with a certificate which qualifies them to act as bailiffs. If they show decided aptitude, they may obtain a bursary at one of the *écoles nationales*. The yearly cost of each farm pupil to the State is 10*l.*; the State also defrays the expenses of the salary of the director and his assistants. The director obtains the labour of the pupil for nothing, and manages the farm for his own profit and at his own risk. The *écoles pratiques* are assisted and superintended by the State. It was intended that there should be one school in each of the twelve regions into which France is agriculturally divided. These agricultural high schools are designed for the sons of the wealthier class of cultivators. The cost is from 400 francs to 500 francs a year. The pupils learn practical agriculture and the elements of physics, chemistry, natural history, botany, veterinary science, and stock-breeding. They have not proved particularly successful; the best known is that of Merchines (Meuse). The three *écoles nationales* are placed in the centres of three districts of France. They are Grignon, near Versailles (Ile de France); Grand Jouan, near Nozay (Loire-Inférieure); Montpellier (Hérault), formerly La Saulsaie (Ain). All three schools were founded before the Second Empire—Grignon in 1827, Grand Jouan in 1832, La Saulsaie in 1840. The course of instruction at Grignon lasts two and a half years; and each year is divided into two terms, the first from October to March 15, the second from March 15 to August. All the pupils are obliged to pass the entrance examination, unless they have previously taken the degree of Bachelier ès-Sciences. They may be either *externes* or *internes*. The *externes* pay 200 francs a year for their lectures; the *internes* pay from 1,000 francs to 1,200 francs for their *pension* and lectures. There are bursaries in each of the three colleges, which are filled up in open competition among the pupils of the farm schools. The Institut Agronomique, which crowns the fabric, forms a faculty of agriculture.

Besides these schools in the general practice and science of agriculture, there are special schools, such as the sheep farm at Rambouillet, the gardening establishment at Versailles, the school of drainage and irrigation at Lézardeau, near Quimperlé, the three veterinary schools of Lyons, Alfort, and Toulouse, and the *écoles de dressage* like that near Caen. In 1879 departmental professors were appointed, whose duties are twofold. Under the direction of the Minister of Education, they lecture at the normal schools to pupils who are being trained as schoolmasters; under the instructions of the Minister of Agriculture, they hold conferences with the agriculturists, teachers, and proprietors of each canton, perambulate all the country villages to observe agricultural processes, keep in touch the various local societies, and spread the knowledge of improvements. By the law of June 16, 1879, each department is to be provided with a professor, and their agricultural duties were minutely defined in a circular of M. Tirard in 1881.

Agricultural shows and competitions as well as horse-races are encouraged by the State. The great central show is held at Paris; but, for the promotion of provincial competitions, the whole country is divided into twelve regions, Algiers forming a thirteenth. These *concours régionaux* are under the direction of the State, which gives the prizes and pays the expenses of the judges. Agricultural societies have been formed under State patronage for the departments, the arrondissements, and even for the cantons. Veterinary science is a subject to which the State pays great attention. A veterinary officer is attached to each arrondissement, who has passed through the four years' course at one of the three veterinary schools, and has received the diploma entitling him to practise. His powers are considerable. All the foreign livestock is subjected to a veterinary examination at one of the points at which it is permitted to be imported, and only sound animals enter the country. Internally, the existing law contains most stringent provisions for the slaughter of infected cattle. State indemnities are granted to owners of slaughtered animals. The State interests itself in the breeding of horses, cattle, and sheep. The Ministry of Agriculture contains, for instance, a Directeur des Haras, who has under him inspectors general and inspectors. At the Haras du Pin there is a free school, in which is taught every detail connected with the management of horses. There are twenty-one depôts of the great Haras de Pompadour; and more than 2,500 stallions are placed at the disposal of the owners of mares.

Nor is the State aid confined to education and the improvement in livestock. Each arrondissement has its Ingénieur des Ponts et Chaussées, who assists proprietors in all drainage operations. In each arrondissement again there is the *agent royer*, who inspects the roads of the district in his care. There are three different classes of roads, the *chemin vicinal, départemental*, and *national*. The first class is kept in repair by the Communes, the second by the Department, the third by the State. It is the duty of the road overseer to assess the expenses of the repairs.

Lastly, the State assists works of irrigation, reclamation, and similar improvements, indirectly through the Crédit Foncier, and directly with subventions and loans. It has facilitated means of transport, subventioned the erection of bridges in place of the old ferries, assisted canals, railways, and roads. It has aided in works of irrigation like those of Verdon, near Aix, St. Martory (Haute-Garonne), Lagoin (Basses-Pyrénées), La Bourne, near Valence. It has helped to improve barren wastes by such means as winter submersions in the valleys of the Durance, the Arc, and the Isère. It has attempted to replant the forests, and so check the ruinous floods so common in the mountainous districts of the Alps. It has assisted in the reclamation of La Sologne, the barren tract of heath and furze or sandy wastes diversified with marshy ponds, which formerly belonged to the Orléanais, and now makes up part of the Departments of the Loir-et-Cher, the Cher, and the Loiret. Thirty years ago this district was a desolate thinly populated plain, soppy as a sponge in winter, dry as a cinder in the summer, and so unhealthy that the average length of human life was only twenty-seven years, inhabited by a stunted race whose stupidity passed into the proverbial saying of ' un niais de Sologne.' The State set on foot drainage works, cleaned out the watercourses, introduced marl, planted pines, and set an example which has been followed by many proprietors. So, too, it has aided to drain the district of the Dombes (Ain), where grass alternates with water and cattle with fish, and to bring into cultivation the *landes* of Gascony by pine plantations.

Are English taxpayers prepared to pay several millions every year in order to try an experiment which, economically at least, is of doubtful utility, and would probably result in establishing as the real proprietor, not the agricultural labourer, but the city money-lender?

CHAPTER XIV.

DISTRIBUTION OF LAND.

If the State acquisition of the land and its arbitrary redistribution among the class of peasant proprietors be rejected as an extravagant and impossible plan, the broad features of the existing system of land ownership, occupation, and cultivation must remain unchanged. What are the conditions of that system?

The total acreage [1] of England and Wales under all kinds of crops, bare fallow, and grass was, in 1887, 27,753,207 acres.

The New Domesday Book [2] shows that there are 972,836 proprietors of land in England and Wales, holding between them 33,013,510 acres. These figures may be thus analysed:—

Class of Owners	Number of Owners	Acreage of their lands
Owning over 50,000 acres . . .	4	376,500
,, between 50,000 and 5,000 acres.	870	8,990,500
,, ,, 5,000 ,, 1,000 ,,	4,535	9,328,500
,, ,, 1,000 ,, 100 ,,	37,116	10,145,000
,, ,, 100 ,, 10 ,,	98,479	3,541,700
,, ,, 10 ,, 1 ,,	121,983	478,680
Under one acre	703,289	151,170

But the returns in the New Domesday are incorrect

[1] Appendix XI. gives the statistical returns of the crops of England and Wales for 1867, 1877, and 1887, and, for purposes of comparison, four other estimates of the dates respectively of 1688, 1771, 1808, and 1827.

[2] Moved for by Lord Derby in the House of Lords, February 1872. Compiled, 1874–5.

and misleading ; and the following analysis [1] gives a more reliable answer as to the conditions of land ownership in England and Wales :—

(1) 4,217 persons own, in estates of over 1,000 acres, 18,546,000 acres.
(2) 33,937 persons own, in estates of between 1,000 and 100 acres, 8,927,000 acres.
(3) 217,009 persons own, in estates of between 100 and 1 acres, 3,931,000 acres.
(4) 14,419 public bodies own 1,443,500 acres.
(5) 703,200 persons own, in holdings of under 1 acre, 151,000 acres.

But even this result leaves a false impression, if it is forgotten that it applies not merely to agricultural but to building land. The number of owners of agricultural land

Number, Acreage, Average Size, and Number of Horses and Livestock

NUMBER OF AGRICULTURAL HOLDINGS	ENG-LAND	WALES	PROPORTIONAL No. per cent. in each class		ACREAGE cultural in each
	No.	No.	Eng.	Wales	England
*Of ¼ of an acre and under 1 acre	21,069	1,083	5·08	1·80	9,988
*Of 1 acre and not exceeding 5 acres	103,229	11,044	24·88	18·35	286,526
Above 5 acres ,, ,, 20 ,,	109,285	17,389	26·34	28·89	1,219,663
,, 20 ,, ,, ,, 50 ,,	61,146	12,326	14·74	20·48	2,042,370
,, 50 ,, ,, ,, 100 ,,	44,803	10,044	10·82	16·69	3,285,350
,, 100 ,, ,, ,, 300 ,,	59,180	7,844	14·26	13·03	10,285,988
,, 300 ,, ,, ,, 500 ,,	11,452	389	2·76	0·65	4,328,722
,, 500 ,, ,, ,, 1000 ,,	4,131	63	·99	·10	2,697,794
,, 1000 acres	565	8	·13	·01	735,138
Total	414,950	60,190	100·00	100·00	24,891,589

Compiled from the Agri-
* Probably many of these small holdings are also

[1] See *English Land and English Landlords*, by the Hon. G. Brodrick, London, 1881, 8vo ; and *The Great Landowners of Great Britain and Ireland*, by John Bateman, 4th edition, London, 1883, 8vo.

is far smaller. Thus 4,217 persons own half the land of England and Wales; and an amount exceeding the cultivated area of the country, or over 28 million acres, is the property of 38,000 persons.

English land laws, prior to 1882, combined with social and economic causes to lessen the number and increase the size of landed properties. At the same time small farms decreased in number, as they were consolidated and thrown together to economise management and utilise machinery. The census for 1881 gives the number of tenant farmers at 223,943. But a fuller answer to the question—'How is the land occupied?' will be supplied by the following table. Though the average size of holdings in England and Wales is only 53 acres, yet 19 millions out of the 27 million cultivated acres, or rather more than

on each Class of Agricultural Holding in England and Wales in 1885.

of agri- holding class	AVERAGE SIZE of holding in each class		No. of HORSES in each class of holding		No. of CATTLE in each class of holding		No. of SHEEP in each class of holding		No. of PIGS in each class of holding
Wales	Eng.	Wales	England	Wales	England	Wales	England	Wales	England and Wales
530	½	½	—	—	—	—	—	—	—
34,532	2¾	3¼	21,259	1,837	85,910	13,955	85,730	21,947	155,048
200,169	11¼	11½	68.250	9,327	383,574	69.253	385,248	166,102	303,474
420,482	33½	34	107.897	24,049	554,941	124,027	905,771	489,602	298,724
735,671	73¼	73¼	160,755	39,562	750,165	189,820	1,673,657	770.948	353.770
1,233.374	173¾	157¼	446.260	57,768	1,908,372	276,114	6.469.357	1,100.444	754,386
143,623	378	369¼	164,996	5,494	645,016	28,181	3,670.977	137,883	225,010
39,793	653	631¾	90,041	1,082	301.224	5,527	2,784,094	43,170	114,836
10,373	1301¼	1296½	19,410	242	60,343	1,214	792,620	12,262	21,504
2,818,547	60	46¾	1,078,868	139,461	4,689,545	708,091	16,766,854	2,742,358	2,226,752

cultural Returns of 1886.
included in the field allotments (see Appendix XIV.).

two-thirds, are occupied in holdings ranging from 100 acres to upwards of 1,000 acres. The land thus owned and occupied was in 1881 tilled by 870,798 agricultural labourers.[1]

These conditions may be contrasted with the analysis drawn up by Gregory King,[2] the Lancaster Herald, of the population of the country in 1688. King calculated the total number of families at 1,349,586. Of this total number more than three-fourths were directly connected with agriculture, and three-fifths of the agriculturists enjoyed proprietary interests in the soil. The figures of early statisticians cannot be implicitly relied on; but whatever allowance is made for errors, the contrast is startling enough. Up to the commencement of the eighteenth century it was rare to see 'one only master grasp the whole domain.'[3]

The most marked peculiarity of English land tenure is the small number of landlords, tenants, and labourers. At the present crisis this system has apparently collapsed, and failure is not unnaturally commonly attributed to its distinguishing feature. During the past fourteen years dis-

[1] In England and Wales, in the reign of Elizabeth, there were three million agriculturists to one million non-agriculturists. In the years of Protection 1801-41 the agriculturists were (1811) 35 per cent., (1821) 33 per cent., (1831) 28 per cent., (1841) 22 per cent. of the population. Now barely one-fifth of the population [26 millions, 1881] are engaged in agriculture. In France, in 1851, the industrial classes numbered 83 per cent. of the total population, and of these 56 per cent. were engaged in agriculture. In 1876 the industrial population had risen to 90 per cent., and 53 per cent. were agriculturists.

[2] See Appendix VII. Census Returns, Table 1.

[3] In 1862 M. de Lavergne calculated that in France $37\frac{1}{2}$ million acres were owned by 50,000 owners, whose estates averaged 750 acres; $37\frac{1}{2}$ millions by 500,000 owners, whose estates averaged 75 acres; $37\frac{1}{2}$ millions by 5,000,000, who held properties averaging $7\frac{1}{2}$ acres. In other words, one-third of the land was held by 50,000 owners, one-third by 500,000, one-third by 5,000,000. The statement is too neat to be absolutely true. But it is remarkably confirmed by the most recent estimates. See *Edinburgh Review* (Oct. 1887), 'Rural France.'

tress has gradually increased in intensity, till it has ruined hundreds of landlords and tenant farmers. The stress of foreign competition falls with increasing force upon rents as the screw continues to tighten. With every turn of the screw the pressure becomes more intolerable for those landowners who are required to meet fixed charges from dwindling revenues. Their sufferings are none the less real because they are unexpressed. At a low estimate land has depreciated in letting value 35 per cent.; and a competent authority, Lord Derby, has computed the aggregate loss of the landlords at 300 millions sterling. The sufferings of tenant farmers rise more rapidly to the surface because the land is, as a rule, their only source of income. The last report of the Royal Agricultural Benevolent Institution affords significant proof of the reality of the distress. Upwards of 400 farmers, who had recently cultivated holdings varying from 100 to 1,000 acres, were applicants for relief. The same ruin now attacks the agricultural labourer. As the area of corn cultivation contracts, and land grows grass instead of grain, the economical transition means the destitution, if not the starvation, of thousands.

The facts are patent, but they do not necessarily result from any defect in the existing tenure or cultivation of the land. Their causes must be sought elsewhere. In the past, 'large landlords and large farmers won for England, directly or indirectly, the first place both in manufacture and agriculture. Nor is it only yesterday that they did good service to the State. Our system admits abuses and lacks elasticity; but capitalist landlords have proved the saviours, not the ruin, of farming. It is this class which to-day has saved England from the horrors which accompany distress in Ireland, and English landlords have, voluntarily and by private bargain, offered reductions which law has there enforced. In this country the worst cultivated and most highly rented soil, and the most beggarly farm buildings, are found on the estates of small investors. If the numbers of this latter class were larger, distress would be proportionately increased, and their wretched dependents might as well hope to suck honey from flint as to obtain generous consideration of their distress. The blow has fallen upon the wealthy classes, not upon those who in ignorance resort to agrarian outrage. Nor has the country failed to profit by the losses of individuals. Diminished rentals do not mean a corresponding increase in the wealth of foreign producers. The greater part of the 300 millions that landed proprietors have lost is distributed among the toiling millions of our great cities. Schedule D of the income tax,[1] which includes all trades and professions, proves that within the past ten years the number of incomes ranging from 150*l*. to 500*l*. a year has grown 21 per cent. The public servants and salaried employés of private houses of business have increased 50 per cent. Estates paying probate duty below 5,000*l*. are more numerous; the capital of registered companies shows an increase of 90 per cent., but, while the number of shareholders has risen, the average amount of their holdings has fallen; the number of insurance policies has grown steadily, but the sums insured are smaller; the number of depositors in savings banks has increased, and the deposits per head are less; the insurance companies of the poor have enormously extended their business. These facts minister cold comfort to impoverished landlords and ruined tenants,

[1] See presidential address of the Right Hon. G. J. Goschen before the Statistical Society, December 6, 1887.

but, in striking the balance of profit and loss, they cannot be overlooked.

Under other systems of land tenure than our own, ruin is widely spread. Everywhere the pressure of foreign competition is severely felt, but in other countries it is accompanied by demands for relief which it is impossible to resist and mischievous to concede. Advocates of a peasant proprietary belong, as a rule, to the party which is most deeply pledged to a Free Trade policy. Do they reflect that foreign experience shows their economical and agricultural theories to be opposed? The agricultural labourer has hitherto supported Free Trade; transform him into a small farmer, and you make him a Protectionist. From this, as well as from every other point of view, it is assuredly no time to hazard agrarian experiments, which can only succeed under exceptional combinations of favourable circumstances.

In many respects the existing relations of landlords, tenants, and agricultural labourers, might be advantageously modified. But the true lesson to be drawn from the small numbers directly interested in land is not that the existing system is to blame for the collapse, not that the three profits are necessarily doomed, but that the day has passed for legislation which favours a few producers at the expense of millions of consumers. In France one half, in England barely one fifth, of the total population are engaged in agriculture. The English landed interests waste their strength if they struggle for relief in the form of Protection, or the reduction of the tithe rent-charge. What chance have 38,000 landlords and 224,000 farmers of persuading twenty millions to pay $6d.$ for a loaf of bread which they can now purchase for $4\tfrac{1}{2}d.$? For every one who says bread is too cheap there are a hundred who find it too dear. Or what prospect has this same handful of persons of appropriating to their own use funds the reversion of which belongs, under remote and doubtful, but not impossible, contingencies, to the nation as a whole?

CHAPTER XV.

PROTECTION AND TITHE RENT-CHARGE.

HISTORICALLY[1] Protection is associated with a period of prolonged and unprecedented distress, with agricultural gambling and reckless speculation in land, with bankruptcy and insolvency of farmers, with the degradation and pauperism of agricultural labourers, with high prices and extravagant poor-rates, with incendiarism and starvation, with hunger made and perpetuated by law in the interests of a single industry. This was the price which the nation paid for artificial rents and artificial prices.

There once lived a philosopher, who, seeing that he had scratched out both his eyes in a quickset hedge, determined
> To jump into a bramble bush
> And scratch them in again.

His example is urged by Protectionists, not only upon the nursery, but upon the nation generally.

A black mark is set against Protection in the memory of consumers in this country; the system itself is also discredited by comparative failure on the Continent. It is established in France and Germany;[2] but import duties do not enable farmers to grow wheat at a profit. In Germany, as has been said, farmers have only gained by

[1] See Chapter IX.
[2] See Appendix XII., Return of prices of wheat in France, Belgium, and Prussia.

Protection, because the Government applies the revenue which it yields to the reduction of local burdens on farming industries. From France comes the same tale. France had always preserved an import duty of 60 centimes the quintal on foreign wheat, and of 1 fr. 20 c. on foreign flour. In December, 1884, the Chamber of Deputies decided to propose import duties not only on wheat and flour, but on oats, rye, barley, and malt, which had been hitherto imported free. In spite of strong protests, the policy of Protection was finally adopted in 1885. The duty on foreign wheat was fixed at 5*s.* 3*d.* the quarter, and 25 francs per head was charged on all foreign cattle. M. Tirard, the present Premier, was then Minister of Finance, and the Ministry promised increased duties if agriculture did not improve. The pledge has been kept; the duty on foreign wheat was raised to 8*s.* 9*d.* in 1887, and other duties in proportion. It may be added that France annually imports eight million quarters of grain. The recently published reports by English Consuls at French ports show that 5*s.* 3*d.* per quarter was an inadequate duty. At Bordeaux duties on foreign cattle have not raised the prices of live stock, which, within the last two years, fell from 6 to 8 per cent., and the same remark applies to cereals. Near La Rochelle corn does not pay, live stock sells cheaper at each successive fair, markets are overstocked with fruit and vegetables. Peasant owners must either sell their land or be supported by the nation. They will undoubtedly choose the latter alternative, and the next elections will be decided on the cry for increased protection. In the Brest district rents are unpunctually paid, and peasant proprietors are falling hopelessly into debt. Round Havre import duties have not raised the price of cereals.

In the neighbourhood of Boulogne and Dunkirk prices both of corn and cattle have fallen. On the other hand, the important grain trade of Marseilles is suffering severely from the Protectionist policy. The obvious result of Protection is to decrease both exports and imports of agricultural produce; but the example of France shows that import duties have not raised the prices of wheat and beef, which are lower than when the duties were first imposed. The fault is that the duty is not large enough, and it may be confidently anticipated that it will be shortly raised from 8s. 9d. to at least 12s. a quarter.[1]

The result of English and foreign experience on the subject of Protection is universally this. Import duties ruin the grain trade of seaport towns, but they do not necessarily raise the home price of wheat, because they stimulate over-production at home. In England from 1820–48, in France and Germany from 1885 to 1887, wheat did not rise, but rather fell, in consequence of the exclusion of foreign competition. Farmers cut their own throats by increasing their breadths of corn cultivation. Hence, if protection is advocated as a remedy for low prices, it fails to produce the desired result, and the cry is raised for higher duties. It is probable that nothing short of a duty of 20s. a quarter would raise home prices to the point at which wheat would become profitable; and if bread rose to 6½d., this price means an income tax of at least 1s. a week on the wages of labour.

Everyone now regrets that Mr. Gladstone, in 1869, took off the 1s. duty on corn, which did not keep out a single quarter of wheat or raise the price of bread a

[1] In Germany the demand of agriculturists for increased Protection seriously embarrasses the political action of the Government. Austria and Hungary export quantities of wheat and flour to Germany, which the agrarian party desire to exclude by doubling the existing duty.

farthing; in the seventeen years that have since elapsed, this economic pedantry has cost the nation nearly twelve million pounds; and once taken off it cannot be put on again. It is not denied that import duties, if they are high enough, would benefit farmers, or that the stimulus which they would give to arable farming would indirectly prove advantageous to agricultural labourers. But wheat cannot, it is said, be grown at a profit under 40s. Is an import duty of 20s. likely to be obtained, or, if granted, is it large enough to succeed? Both questions must be answered in the negative. Fair traders are not likely to embarrass the question of taxing manufactured articles with the unpopular demand for the taxation of raw necessaries of life. Bread is the exclusive food of thousands; its cheapness cannot be diminished in the face of trade depression; it is the very last article which any Government can venture to tax, for the charge falls on the very poor. Agriculturists will only prove the catspaws of manufacturers if they swell the cry for Fair Trade. It is useless to ask for what, in all human probability, can never be granted. The consumers, and not the producers, of bread and meat now govern public opinion. The landed interests would, it is submitted, be wiser to concentrate all their strength upon obtaining pecuniary relief from foreign competition, not by raising the price of bread and meat, but by shifting a portion of the load of taxation which burdens real property to the shoulders of personalty. The effect of an import duty is to counterbalance existing taxes upon land; if those taxes themselves are lightened, the same object is effected in a less objectionable manner.

Tithe rent-charge difficulties are less obviously, but not less vitally, affected by the numerical inferiority of the landed interests. Fifty years ago agricultural depression raised an agitation against tithes. It was said, with great force, that tithes upon produce discouraged and retarded agricultural progress at a moment when the rapid growth of population rendered it necessary to develope to the full all the resources of the soil. One among many of its evil effects was to prevent the ploughing up of pasture land. A Parliament of landlords listened favourably to the cry. The gross tenth of the annual produce of titheable land on the average, taken from 1829 to 1835, was 6,756,105*l*. But the sum at which it was commuted was 4,053,663*l*. In other words, 40 per cent. of the gross tenth went at once into the pockets of the landlords. Besides this, they also received all that portion of the increased value of the produce of the land which, prior to 1836, would have fallen to the Church, and which Sir J. Caird, in 1877, estimated, at two million pounds a year. Tithe rent-charge stood still while rentals rose; it was in 1836 as 4 millions to 33 millions (or more probably 28 millions); in 1877 it was $4\frac{1}{2}$ millions to 51 millions. Thus the gain which landowners received from the Tithe Commutation Act of 1836 must be measured by many millions.

In 1887, as in 1836, under the pressure of agricultural distress, the cry against tithe rent-charge is renewed. But times and tempers are entirely changed. Landed interests no longer rule supreme in Parliament, and it cannot now be said that the charge retards and discourages agricultural progress, for it falls on the land and not on the produce. The agitation takes the shape of a demand for its revaluation, that is to say, its reduction. It is said that tithe rent-charge has become a disproportionate burden, and must be readjusted, or, without circumlocution, must be cut down to relieve landlords and tenants. In the first place, the Act of 1836 was designed to fix proportions not between rent-charges and the value of the land out of which they issued, but between rent-charges and their purchasing power in coin, to commute tithe of produce in kind for variable money payments charged upon the land, and maintain existing relations between values of titheable produce and prices of living. So far as the Act has failed, it has failed because it has not guarded the interests of tithe-owners. In the second place, even if the real issue was whether the tithe rent-charge is disproportionate to the value of land and ought to be readjusted, the factors in the question are the relations which the charge bears to the rentals of 1829–35 and 1887, not those which it bore to the rentals of 1870–80. Those who bought land fifteen years ago purchased unprofitable bargains, and undoubtedly the tithe rent-charge has not decreased proportionately to their rentals. But this fact, though it may elicit sympathy, is beside the mark. The question is—does the tithe rent-charge at $3\frac{1}{2}$ millions bear a relation to the rental of 1887 disproportionate to that which it bore at four millions to the rental of 1836 ? The answer can only be in the negative. Assume that rentals in 1887 have fallen to the figure at which they stood in 1836, and no one can pretend that they have fallen below twenty-eight millions, there still remains a considerable margin in favour of the tithe-owner.[1]

[1] Sir James Caird takes 33 millions as the amount of rental in 1836. If this figure had been arrived at by Sir James himself, it would command acceptance upon his authority. But it appears that Sir James adopted it from the *Encyclopædia Britannica* (Letter to the *Times*, July 22, 1879), and the estimate is, for two reasons, probably extravagant. The gross annual value of the produce of the land in 1829–35

Even supposing landowners could prove their case against the tithe rent-charge, a glance at the nature of the charge shows how hopeless is their expectation that the nation will submit to its reduction. Tithes form part

averaged 101,000,000*l.* If 33 millions was at that time the rental, the produce only amounts to three rents. Four rents is a more reasonable allowance, and this would bring the rental of 1836 to 25 millions. Again, Schedule B of the Income Tax, 1814-15, gives the rental of England and Wales at 34,028,655*l.* But these are the war rentals. There was no Income Tax from 1816 to 1842; but the evidence given before Sir James Graham's Select Committee on Agriculture in 1833 shows that rents were undergoing a reduction of from 20 to 30 per cent. They continued to fall for the next five years. If in 1836 the rental was 25 millions, it would show a reduction of 25 per cent.; 33 millions only allows a reduction of 3 per cent., which is contrary to the evidence before the Select Committee. Lastly, in 1845, a careful inquiry into the valuation of land for taxing purposes shows that it had not even then materially increased in value since 1815. (See Parl. Papers, 1846, vol. xl. page 14). For these reasons it is impossible to put the rental of 1836 higher than 28 millions. The tithe rent-charge has been reduced 12½ per cent. since 1836. Therefore, unless landlords are prepared to prove that their rentals amount in 1887 to only 24½ millions, they cannot assert that the relation which the rent-charge bears to rents in 1887 is disproportionate to that which it bore to rent in 1836. It is perhaps worth while to notice that a pamphleteer in 1767, who advocates the commutation of tithe, states that it then amounted to between a fourth and a third of the rent. He puts the rental of England and Wales at 16 millions, and the tithe, at its lowest computation, at 4½ millions. (*Political Speculations on the Dearness of Provisions*, Part II., 1767.) Another writer (*Three Letters to a Member of the House of Commons, from a Country Farmer*, 1766) demands the abolition of tithes in kind, and asks that the existing charge should be commuted at a 'portion of the fair rent—say an 8th, a 7th, a 6th, or a 5th.' This advanced reformer never contemplated that for a considerable portion of the last half-century the tithe would not amount to a tenth of the rent. Arthur Young calculates tithe at 3*s.* 6*d.* an acre; to this he adds a further sum for the gathering. He estimates the rental of the land of England at 22,400,000*l.* and the tithe at 7,000,000*l.* (*Eastern Counties*: London, 1771, vol. iv. p. 459.) Yet landlords and farmers complain that they have lost by the Tithe Commutation Act of 1836. See also 'The Tithe Question,' *Edinburgh Review*, January, 1888.

of a fund vested in the clergy to promote the spiritual interests of the nation, and are, as the law now stands, inalienable, so long as religion is recognised to be a vital element in the national welfare. But subject to this life-interest of the Church, the nation claims the revenue in reversion. It is the duty of the State to preserve intact the corpus of the property. Upon this point Church and State are united; the present interests of the first, the prospectively possible interests of the second are identical. Sections of the community desire to divert the fund to secular purposes; but though those who seek to secularise the charge are actuated by antagonistic motives, they are agreed that the fund shall not be reduced.

Doubtless the landed interests might benefit by the appropriation of tithes to the relief of local taxation. But so far as landlords and tenants have joined in the anti-tithe agitation, they have demanded its reduction, not its secularisation. They therefore ask the very thing which the clergy, the secularists, and the Nonconformists, and indeed the whole body of the nation, are interested in refusing. No class benefit can be obtained except at the expense of the community; no relief can be extended to landlords without a corresponding diminution of the fund now dedicated to religious purposes, but under certain contingencies, available for education or similar objects. It is the obvious interest both of the Church and the State that whatever profits are derived from dealing with the charge should be secured for national purposes. If the four millions of money alienated from the Church at the Reformation and in 1836 were still available for national objects, the sting would be gone from the present agitation against tithes. Till now each successive change has impoverished the clergy and enriched the landlords; but while the Church is weakened, no portion of the sum has hitherto been set aside to meet the cry that there are other national purposes besides those of religion. Is this fatal course to be again pursued at the present crisis? Is it at all likely that a handful of the community can repeat their financial triumphs at the Reformation and in 1836, in opposition not only to the life interests of the clergy but the reversionary interests of the nation? If landlords or farmers agitate against tithe in the hope that it will be reduced, they will be inevitably disappointed. They are in fact only the stalking-horses of those who desire to appropriate the funds to secular objects.

Some change in the charge is doubtless imminent. The first proposal leaves the incidence where it now rests, but alters the calculation. Thus the septennial averages give the tithe-owner for every 100*l*. of tithe rent-charge 87*l*. 8*s*. 10*d*.; the prices of the year 1886 would have given him only 75*l*. 1*s*. 5½*d*. If the charge were computed in 1888 according to the preceding six years, and that for 1889 according to a quinquennial average, the charge of 1893, if the length of the averages were thus annually reduced, would be the prices of 1892. But there is no reason to suppose that so slight a change would reconcile tenants to the continuance of their liability; and if the concession is only the first of a series, there is absolutely no ground for thus mulcting the clergy.

A second proposal changes the incidence and does not alter the calculation. It makes tithe rent-charge altogether a landlord's outgoing, and insists that all land shall be rented tithe free. But the proposed change hardly pretends to be final; the spiritual interests of the nation will still be prejudiced, though the clergyman becomes the tithe proctor of the landlord instead of the evicting bailiff of the tenant farmer; and, lastly, if 5 per cent. compensation is granted to the landlords by the legislature, the national reversioner can never again claim the whole of the tithe rent-charge. It irrevocably surrenders to individuals, for doubtful benefits, 5 per cent. of a property which belongs to the whole body of the clergy and laity.

These considerations seem fatal to any legislation which only proposes either to continue the present liability of occupiers or to render the charge an owner's outgoing. The Government Bill of 1887 erred, as it seems, in not going far enough. So long as the principle of voluntary redemption by landlords is adopted, the scheme must be necessarily impaled on the horns of a dilemma. If the terms are made easy, the scheme may work, but it works at the cost of clerical and national interests. If the terms are disadvantageous, clerical and national interests are preserved, but the scheme is stillborn and a dead letter. The terms offered in the recent Bill rightly protected religious life tenancies and national reversions. But the result was that only trustees, colleges, and other bodies, whose powers of investment are limited, could have profitably redeemed the charge. Apart from a landlord's unwillingness to store all his eggs in a rickety basket, the proffered terms would have tempted no one who could command more than 3 per cent. for his money. So long, also, as agitation can be brought to bear upon a small body of tithe-owners, tithe-payers will hold back for better terms of redemption. Convince agitators that the interest of the tithe-owner and the nation is in fact one, and you convince them of the hopelessness of delay. The only principle upon which a scheme of redemption can be made immediately operative, without enriching individuals from the corpus of a property which belongs to the clergy and the State, is to show that the life-tenant *and* the reversioner are the parties with whom the bargain must be struck.

Redemption, therefore, appears to be the final solution of the difficulty.

The first step towards the extinction of the charge is for the State to undertake its collection, and compel tithe-paying tenants to deduct the charge from the rent. Assume, by way of illustration only, that the State guarantees to the clergy a net 60 per cent. of the 100*l.* charge regularly paid, free of rates, taxes, and costs of collection. At present values this would leave the State a margin of $27\frac{1}{2}$ per cent., out of which to pay the necessary outgoings. In the hands of the clergy there must be deducted from the gross value of the tithe, besides 15 per cent. for rates and taxes, 10 per cent. for arrears, remissions, abatements, and costs of collection. In the hands of the State this last percentage would be reduced to $2\frac{1}{2}$ per cent., and thus the State would have 10 per cent. in hand to meet further falls in the averages, and compensate, in special cases, the losses incurred by landlords pending new arrangements with their tenants, or by the clergy through diminution of income. But the margin would be rapidly freed from liability in respect of these two last payments. Thus protected, the State could well afford to wait a turn in the tide, and escape a ruinous sale in a falling market.

All schemes of redemption, whether compulsory or voluntary, proceed on the basis of State co-operation. The State raises a loan at 3 per cent. and lends at 5 per cent. The difference at compound interest pays off principal and interest within a fixed period. The amount of the State loan, the extent of the advance to landlords, the rate of interest charged, are mainly determined by the rate of years' purchase at which the charge is capitalised. It is the interest of the State to demand thirty years' purchase, of the landlord to offer fifteen. Between the two rates lie the possible compromises. But the basis upon which the charge is generally valued for redemption seems false in principle. A uniform rate of purchase based upon the *gross* value of the charge, subject to the deduction of the *average* necessary outgoings, would press hardly on individuals. Rates vary in every parish. Thus in A the rates are 7s. 6d., in B 5s., in C 2s. 6d. The *average* outgoing in these three parishes is 5s. in the pound, and this deducted from the gross value of a hundred pound tithe rent-charge leaves 75l. as the sum to be redeemed. Assume, for the sake of illustration only, that twenty years' purchase is a fair rate at which to capitalise the charge, and in A, B, and C the charge is redeemed for the same capitalised sum of 1,500l. But observe the different values of the purchase. The withdrawal of the tithe rent-charge from the amount of rateable property in each parish necessitates a readjustment of the assessment upon the remaining property. Practically speaking, landowners will be additionally burdened by the amount now borne by the tithe rent-charge. Therefore, in A parish the annual value of the purchased charge is 62l. 10s., in B 75l., in C 87l. 10s. In other words, the landowner in A buys a very bad, in B a fair, in C a very good bargain. The most equitable method would be to calculate not the *average* but the *actual* outgoings, and to purchase the charge at its *net* value. Under these circumstances the charge would be redeemed in A at 1,250l., in B at 1,500l., in C at 1,750l.[1]

[1] If the outgoings are similarly capitalised at twenty years' purchase, it will seem that the sum in each parish is actually the same. Thus in

This calculation shows the important bearing of rates upon the question of tithe redemption, and indicates the direction in which, if anywhere, landlords and tenants must look to gain by the State collection of the tithe rent-charge. Redemption may be compulsory and immediate, in which case landlords would borrow from the State at 5 per cent. the sum required for redemption, and in less than fifty years would have paid off principal and interest and extinguished the charge. But the terms would be necessarily governed by the miserable state of the present market. Church and State must be content not only to make a wretched bargain, but to see the value of the property rise for the benefit of individuals rather than of the community. Suppose, on the other hand, as has been suggested throughout, that the State undertakes the collection of the tithe, and, protected against possible loss by a considerable margin, waits for better times, and that redemption is voluntary and gradual. What then? It is in the highest degree improbable that land, which is limited in quantity, should permanently lose its value in the midst of a growing population, and the selling value of the rent-charge will benefit by any rise in the value of the property out of which it issues. If, again, agricultural depression should prove in some degree a question of currency, a readjustment of our financial conditions by depreciation of gold or appreciation of silver would restore agricultural industries to health and advance the value of the tithe. If, again, the country were to embark on a policy of Protection, the value of the charge would rise immediately, if not permanently. If, again, as the populations of foreign countries

A, B and C, respectively, the capitalised outgoings are 750$l.$, 500$l.$, and 250$l.$, and the respective prices paid are in A 1,250l + 750$l.$ = 2,000$l.$; in B 1,500$l.$ + 500$l.$ = 2,000$l.$; in C 1,750$l.$ + 250$l.$ = 2,000$l.$

increase, the surplus production which now floods our markets were consumed in the land of its growth, the tithe rent-charge would once more approach par value. Even its present value is unduly depreciated by the alleged insecurity of the tithe-owner's tenure; it is worth far more if not only the life tenant but the reversioner guarantee the title. Even to those who hold no optimistic views of the immediate future of farming, the sale of property of the nature of the tithe rent-charge, even though a purchaser is found by compulsion, appears little short of financial suicide. If these improvements in the value of the charge appear too distant or too problematical, it cannot be disputed that the readjustment of local burdens is a measure of the immediate future. Local taxation is the weight which really crushes English farming; relief has been long promised and long deferred; it cannot now be long postponed. But the immediate result of any readjustment of the load will be to enhance the net value of the rent-charge. If the State holds the charge, the benefit of this certain rise will be secured; the national fund, and not any private individual, will benefit; and, until religion is voted to be noxious or obsolete, the increased money will continue as now to be sacred to religious trusts. At the same time, so long as the State collects the fund, it can afford to be generous with the additional value its own action creates. The larger the reduction of local rates, the greater the gain upon the tithe rent-charge, and the larger the sum which might be devoted to such objects as the establishment of a system of land transfer by registration, the equipment of an efficient State department of agriculture, or scientific and technical education in farming.

CHAPTER XVI.

LEGISLATIVE AID; LAND LAWS, LAND TRANSFER, EDUCATION, RAILWAY RATES.

IF the nationalisation of land is rejected as an impossible plan; if rural society is not to be reconstructed on the ruins of the landlord system; if farmers must combat foreign competition with no other weapons than those of resolute, capable men; if Protection, condemned by history and discredited by recent failure, is placed beyond the reach of agriculturists; if a reduction of tithes is scarcely less hopeless because the reversion of the fund belongs to the community at large—what, it may be asked, becomes of the Land Question? It is reduced to its practical meaning; and that practical meaning varies, apart from peasant proprietors, Protection, and abolition of tithes, with the respective needs of owners, occupiers, and cultivators. Landlords may possibly hint that production is hindered because farmers have adopted extravagant standards of living, and neglect their business. Farmers, perhaps, blame landlords, and attribute depression to high rents, restrictions upon cropping, land laws, and want of security for tenants' improvements. Both will probably agree that the seasons have been adverse, that land is exorbitantly taxed, that railway rates favour foreign producers, that hired labour is scarce, dear, and bad. The agricultural labourer has his own special grievances. He complains that there is no rung in the social ladder on which he can place his foot; that his wages do not permit him to save; that, though unable to supplement them from other sources, he depends entirely upon them; that it matters little whether he scamps his work or does it honestly, whether he attempts to save or calls for another pot of beer, for the workhouse is his inevitable end. The general public may, perhaps, include among these and other causes of depression, the sense of insecurity which scares away capital from the land; dimly comprehended currency questions, to which, like the Gulf Stream, all that is inexplicable may be attributed; the want of elasticity and variety in farming practices; the lack of sufficient capital, adequate knowledge, energy, and business enterprise, among both landlords and farmers.

These are the practical meanings of the Land Question. Some of them can only be adequately discussed by experienced agriculturists, and upon such it may appear presumptuous to touch. But, without any desire to teach farmers their business, it is impossible not to observe in every country district many points in which the general standard falls hopelessly below the practice of the few. Many of the causes of agricultural distress can be controlled by farmers themselves; others, like the seasons, defy human calculation. Some, on the other hand, can only be removed by legislative action.

This chapter will be confined to this latter class, and to such subjects as the reform of the land laws, the provision for scientific agricultural education, the equipment of a ministerial department of Agriculture, the revision of railway rates.

Insecurity lies at the root of the present conditions of agriculture. Foreign competition, following upon disastrous seasons, produced the present collapse: it has been perpetuated by want of confidence. So long as wild proposals for compulsory redistribution of property received the support of prominent politicians, no landlord would expend money on improvements, no capitalist, large or small, would invest in the purchase of land, no tenant would accept a lease, no labourer would put his heart into his work. While the intentions of the Legislature remained dubious and threatening, land continued to be unsaleable and half-farmed. Behind all legislative changes lurked the ominous question of confiscation. Land may be treated as private property, held so as not to prejudice the public welfare, but not to be taken from owners without fair compensation; or it may be distinguished from private property, and the principles which guard private property held inapplicable to land. On which line was land legislation to proceed? Wild talk about State-ownership, ransom, and natural rights, societies to nationalise the land, heroic remedies of illogical half-disciples of Mr. George might be in themselves of little importance. But when the air was filled with vague threats, the attitude of ministers remained studiously neutral. Agitators complained of conditions which they themselves rendered chronic. Meanwhile the continued insecurity was rapidly producing results which threatened the subversion of rural society. Fortunately the example has been given that a patriotic fusion of political parties for the promotion of national interests is yet possible in party government. That restoration of confidence, which is the indispensable preliminary to agricultural revival, seems already to have begun, and to bear fruit in renewed energy.

Arguments urged against the artificial creation of a peasant proprietary scarcely apply to their natural growth. Economically States gain more by agricultural factories than by small farms conducted as domestic industries. Socially the advantages of a class of peasant owners are indisputably great. The rural economy of the nation would benefit by the diffusion of land ownership, and farming offers no exception to the rule that two strings to the bow are better than one. If legislation is only invoked to remove artificial aids to the aggregation of large estates, the process will not foster that sense of insecurity which has paralysed the energies of landlords, and rendered chronic the enfeebled state of agriculture. Already signs appear of a tendency towards the multiplication of small tenant-farmers, if not of small owners. Small holdings obstructed progress so long as capital was required for the reclamation, enclosure, or drainage of land. But at the present day this argument loses much of its force. So again, while England depended for grain on home supplies, corn could be produced more economically on large farms. Now, when prices render its home production unremunerative, and foreign supplies are adequate to our wants, another argument for large farms is at least modified. Small farmers, content with small profits, depending on gardens, livestock, and dairies, commanding the unpaid labour of their own families, may make both ends meet, where larger capitalists go through the Court. If agriculture is tending in this direction, legislation must remove all hindrances to its natural course; landlords are sufficiently alive to their own interests to do the rest. The risk of forcing streams into artificial channels is increased by the arguments which have been urged, from an economic point of view, against the creation in this country of peasant proprietors. In the uncertainty of their success under the changed conditions of modern agriculture, it is madness for the State to dictate, by positive legislation, the direction of their advance.

Many advantages undeniably flow from an increase in the number of proprietors of the soil, and where men do not become owners of small tenant farmers. But the creation of either class must remain a matter of individual enterprise. No State can afford costly experiments on a large scale, the success of which is doubtful.

Whether land is farmed high or low, by large or small farmers, by peasant owners or capitalist tenants, it is socially and politically expedient that legislation should remove all artificial obstacles to the acquisition of small interests in land, or the development of high farming, which hitherto has never obtained a fair chance of displaying its capabilities. In either case the preliminaries are the same, a reform of the land laws, and a scientific and practical agricultural education.

The object of land law reform is twofold: the extinction of all hindrances to the full development of landed property, and the simplification of the transfer of land. To the first head belong such changes as the abolition of primogeniture and entail, and other changes which assimilate the laws of real and personal property. The declaration of the spirit of the law in favour of primogeniture appears, from the rarity of intestacy, to be a matter of slight importance. It is different with the other objects of land law reform. Before 1882 the land was held by a series of life tenants, each of whom in turn, so soon as they arrived at the age of so-called discretion, deprived themselves irrevocably of the free use of their estates. Thus life tenants were hampered with restrictions upon the development of their property, burdened with encumbrances, unable and unwilling to spend money on improvements. Lord Cairns's Settled Land Act made one gigantic stride in the right direction; impending legislation makes a second.

Lord Halsbury's Bill, which will probably be reintroduced in the ensuing session, abolishes primogeniture and entail, but leaves untouched the power of testamentary disposition and of settlement. Taken in conjunction with Lord Cairns's Act, it relegates this side of land law reform to the limbo of obsolete grievances. Short of abolishing settlements altogether, it is difficult to see what additional freedom can be given to life tenants, unless, indeed, the power of creating life estates were limited to their creation in favour of children.

The second object of land law reform is to cheapen and facilitate the transfer of real property. Examinations of title are costly, tedious, and insecure : mountainous piles of unintelligible deeds, lengthy abstracts, heavy law charges, and blistered titles characterise the existing system. It is said that the transfer of land cannot be cheapened or facilitated until it is freed from the complicated titles which settlements encourage. The heroic remedy is therefore suggested to abolish settlements. If this course were adopted, indefeasible titles might be safely conferred by registration ; without this preliminary step, it is doubtless hazardous to guarantee registered possessory titles, even when, after due notice, they remain unchallenged. This risk is less than lawyers make it appear. Legal conservatism may go too far. National interests would suffer from the loss of the power to prevent property accumulated by thrift from being squandered by extravagance. But if lawyers insist too strongly on the injustice of guaranteeing titles by registration, they peril the existence of settlements. A cheap and easy method of transfer is imperatively demanded. Among European nations the want is almost universally supplied; England is nearly the solitary exception. It may be impossible to combine land registration with secret conveyances and equitable mortgages, though the example of Australia proves the contrary; but there can be no valid reason why all conveyances should not be public, or why informal mortgages should continue to exist. Unless titles are guaranteed by registration, registries become merely records of dealing with land, or additional epitomes of titles which lawyers are compelled to search. The mere establishment of a registry of deeds is a retrogression. What is required is a public and compulsory system of land registration, based upon careful cadastration, which shall pass the estate by the official act of the registrar. Some cases of hardship may admittedly occur in the first establishment of a land registry; yet the number and importance of these are exaggerated. Adequate means for introducing the new system are already provided by the register of the Land Tax Commission. The intricacy, expenses, insecurity, and delays of the existing mode of land transfer necessarily check the circulation of land, and lessen its value as the basis of credit. To small capitalists, the class which all land reformers desire to encourage, the cost of conveyance presents a formidable obstacle. Deeds are not only expensive, but to ignorant persons terrible. Small investors cannot afford the luxury, and, if they could, they shrink from the terrors of the unknown. The market might be glutted with land, but till the present system of examination of title and execution of deeds and conveyances is abolished, purchasers of the class of peasant proprietors cannot, and will not, come forward. The Settled Land Act of 1882 gave tenants for life powers to sell, but it could not make land saleable. The difficulty is, not how to increase the quantity of land for sale, but how to double the number of purchasers. There is plenty of land in the market, but there are few buyers, because, among other reasons, land is an inconvenient form of property, awkward to deal with, and therefore tempting only to the rich. The result of such a system is that the majority of persons in this country have no sympathy with ownership of land, and neither feel respect for, nor desire to secure, the sacredness of real property.

The difficulties of introducing land transfer by means of registration are undoubtedly great. They are courageously met in Lord Halsbury's Land Transfer Bill of 1887. The Lord Chancellor proposes to render transfer by registration universal, to bring estates gradually under the Act through the agencies of local registries in districts from time to time declared, to invalidate all dealings with land by sales, mortgages, conveyances, or settlements, except through the machinery of registration, and to establish a guarantee fund for the compensation of aggrieved purchasers. The details of the Bill will be better understood if the proposal is compared, both in its introduction and its working, with systems of land transfer already in operation.

In the Australian colonies the system has been in force since it was introduced into South Australia thirty years ago by Sir R. Torrens. Upon the Torrens Act Lord Westbury and Lord Cairns based their legislation of 1862 and 1875, and on it the Prussian legislation of 1872 is founded. All land alienated by the Crown subsequently to 1858 was brought under the Act compulsorily, and the title of the owner was the Registry; land previously alienated was registered voluntarily. In the latter case, the applicant submits his title to examiners, who report to the registrar upon the clearness of the title and of the description of the parcels. Notices of the application are then issued, and if no objection is alleged within a certain period, duplicate certificates of title are drawn up, one of which is placed on the Registry, the other handed to the owner. Applicants in undisturbed possession, or enjoying good holding titles, are registered. It is not necessary to show such absolute titles as will satisfy punctilious conveyancers, or can be enforced upon unwilling purchasers. Registrars do not demand strict proof, but admit qualified, possessory, and *primâ facie* claims. Error is guarded against by a guarantee fund. Cases of fraud or mistake hardly ever occur; in 999 cases out of 1,000, the title proves sufficient. If the registered owner mortgages his land, he retains his certificate of ownership, but it is endorsed with the charge. Thus, while he cannot deceive second mortgagees, he retains the power of additionally charging his land. He can, if he likes, effect equitable mortgages by lodging his certificate of ownership with a creditor, who issues a *caveat* to the registrar, forbidding him to register any further dealing with the estate till some named period has expired after notice is given. The land is then marked in the Registry with a red cross; and the notice given to equitable mortgagees of the intention to effect additional charges enables them to secure priority. Both settlement and entails exist in Australia, and are effected by registration. In these cases the life-owner is registered as such, and the folio of absolute ownership is closed. Each owner who places himself on the register, or succeeds to land by inheritance or by will, subscribes ½$d.$ in the pound to a Guarantee Fund, out of which, in cases of fraud or error, aggrieved purchasers or rightful owners are indemnified. No money is paid out of the fund to the first registered owner; but it enables him to offer the estate to purchasers with the guarantee behind his back. Purchasers are not entitled to compensation until they have exhausted all possible remedies against fraudulent vendors. In cases of error, the rightful owner is compensated, not placed in possession. This system has been in operation for many years in the Australian colonies. Up to 1886 only four titles have been cancelled, and only 2,000*l.* has been paid away in compensation. The aggregate amount of the Guarantee Fund is over 200,000*l.*

The Prussian system[1] was adopted in May, 1872, and has since been applied in many of the German States. It proceeds on the same lines as the Torrens Act. In Prussia registries of deeds in which all mortgages were registered existed in every market town, and also a cadastral survey in which estates were defined. On these bases the law worked. Full titles of ownership of land

[1] The subject is likely to prove of such importance that some of the best and most recent authorities are quoted below for the benefit of those who care to pursue it further.

(a) *For the introduction of the system.*
  (i.) Lehrbuch des preuss. Privatrechts, von Heinrich Dernberg, 3. Aufl. vol. i. p. 450 et seqq., sections 190–199.
  (ii.) Handbuch des deutschen Privatrechts, von Otto Stobbe, vol. ii., sections 94–95.

(b) *For the system itself.*
  (i.) Die preussischen Grundbuch- und Hypotheken-Gesetze, von H. Werner (1873) (quoted by Mr. Brickdale).
  (ii.) Das preussische Grundbuch-Recht, von H. Bahlmann (quoted by Mr. Scott).
  (iii.) Reports on Saxe-Coburg Land System and Prussian Land Transfer Laws, by Mr. Scott of the British Embassy at Berlin. Parliamentary Papers, Commercial Papers, part i. 1882, and Report, 1887.
  (iv.) Annuaire de la législation étrangère, Paris, 1873. Art. par M. Paul Gide.
  (v.) Law Quarterly Review, vol. iv. p. 63 et seqq. Jan. 1888. Article by Mr. C. F. Brickdale.

can only be acquired by registration; all charges on real property are invalid, until they are registered in the 'Grundbuch,' or Land Register, of the commune, arrondissement, or other territorial unit. No property acquired by will or inheritance can be alienated or charged until the new owner registers his title, and for this purpose he produces an official certificate of probate. Persons in possession of land when the Act came into operation were required to register their titles on the 'Grundbücher' of their districts. Mere possession for forty-four years, or possessory titles of ten years' duration, with *primâ facie* evidence that such had a legal commencement, were accepted; lesser titles required stricter proof. Like the Torrens Act, the Prussian law provides an insurance fund.

The foundation was already laid in Prussia for the introduction of registration, and in Australia titles were scarcely old enough to be complicated: but although some additional difficulties impede the establishment of this system in this country, the titles which are to be registered here will, if entails are abolished, be simpler than in Prussia or Australia. Lord Halsbury's Bill, though in some points it necessarily creates dissatisfaction, makes the first attempt to simplify land transfer which offers real prospects of success. To be placed on the register little more is probably required than guaranteed titles. The gradual establishment of the system may be necessary on the score of expense, but it is an undoubted blot upon the Bill. By the temporary employment of local solicitors, who are generally familiar with the titles by which the neighbouring land is held, the process of registration might be simultaneously and inexpensively effected, especially if only marketable titles are required for the first step in the proceeding. The exclusion of rightful owners in cases of error appears cruel; but it is less hard than our existing system, which confiscates the invested capital of innocent and *bonâ fide* purchasers. The guarantee should, it is submitted, be paid at once to aggrieved purchasers, and the registrars should, in their names, enforce all their remedies against fraudulent vendors. It is greatly to be hoped that a Bill, the advantages of which are so numerous, will be speedily passed.

The system is not new in this country, but as old as the Norman Conquest. Registrars resemble Stewards of Copyhold Courts, to whom the old estate is surrendered and by whom the new one is granted. Titles cease to be derivative, and rest upon the last entry in the registry; examinations, abstracts, deeds disappear; landowners can carry their certificates of ownership in their waistcoat pockets. Since mortgagees need not receive the legal estate, or 'sit upon their deeds,' mortgages are effected with the utmost ease for such small sums as $5l.$ or $10l.$, and foreclosure becomes a simple inexpensive process. Consequently charges will be effected at cheaper rates, and second mortgages will not be dearer than first. Land transfer by registration saves 90 per cent. in expense, prevents any possible litigation, is completed in a quarter of an hour, and is so simple a process that men of ordinary intelligence can safely transact their own business. No class is more interested in the removal of legal cobwebs than the English landlords. Recent experience of landowning has not been favourable; future prospects are gloomy. They have been severely taught the danger of storing all their eggs in one basket, especially when the bottom has fallen out. Many must be anxious to sell.

Whatever renders a commodity more marketable and more manageable adds to its value. The best chance of obtaining a reasonable price for land is to remove the fetters which restrain its transfer. From every point of view a reform of the land laws in the direction we have indicated would be a social and economical gain, but it is quite possible that increased facilities of transfer may encourage the consolidation as much as the diffusion of property.

If rents are permanently reduced, landlords must become their own agents. If increased production affords the remedy for agricultural collapse, scientific training is required by the tenant farmer. If the soil is to be tilled in small holdings, or by a peasant proprietary, preparation must be made to educate them for the task. Thus, from every point of view, education becomes an indispensable condition in the future of agriculture. In England little provision is made to supply the want. Our manufacturers woke from their dreams of industrial supremacy to find that technical schools on the Continent had in a few years counterbalanced the advantages this country had gained from an early start. It is not impossible that our agriculturists may, from the same cause, find themselves left behind in the race. Continental Europe is rich in the supply of teaching adapted to the wants of every class. Even Ireland possesses sixty tax-supported farm schools. In Great Britain the State subscribes a grant towards the teaching of agriculture in the Science and Art Department of Kensington[1] and contributes 150*l*. a year to the

[1] Kensington is a curious place for an agricultural department. Within the last year the number of students has increased by 25 per cent. In 1885 there were eight; in 1886 there were twelve agricultural pupils. The Australian Colonies have recently increased facilities for agricultural education. In Victoria, for instance, a central college is to

endowment of a professorial chair at Edinburgh; private enterprise provides Cirencester, Downton, and Aspatria; agricultural societies offer examinations and prizes; and farming is taught in some of the country schools. Scotland, as usual, leads the van of education. Edinburgh University has recently formulated an exhaustive scheme for examinations in agricultural science. The examinations established by the Surveyors' Institute for land agents attract an increasing number of candidates. Night schools for teaching scientific agriculture have been at work for three years with considerable success in Aberdeenshire and Forfarshire. But, if the country is on the eve of an agricultural revolution so great as the creation of a peasant proprietary, or even the multiplication of small holdings, something more is required than isolated efforts. A glance at the means provided in some of the principal European states may bring home to us our relative deficiencies, and urge the country to inaugurate a new departure.

A sketch has already been given of the French system. France has an organised system of education which works with great efficiency, and to which it annually devotes 70,000*l*. It is designed to encourage men of science to experiment in chemistry and machinery, to afford practical as well as theoretical instruction to landed proprietors, agents, and farmers, to train up intelligent peasant proprietors and labourers. For these objects there are four grades of schools. In most of the departments model farms, or *fermes exemplaires*, are established for farm labourers; provincial schools are carried on for bailiffs

be founded at Melbourne, and a new farm school is to be established at Longerenong. It is expected that the existing farm school at Dookie will show a profit for 1887.

and farmers, as well as higher grade schools, like Grignon, for landed proprietors and estate agents; and finally the Institut Agronomique supplies every appliance that is required for scientific investigation. There are besides special schools, and veterinary schools at Alfort, Lyons, and Toulouse. In many of the primary schools agriculture is taught, and to some of the normal schools land is attached for practical teaching: each department already is, or shortly will be, pervaded by a peripatetic professor.

In the Austrian Empire the school of Krumman was founded so far back as 1799. There are now, scattered through the country, three superior, four middle-class, and seven lower agricultural schools; there are also several special establishments in which instruction is afforded in such branches as shepherding, bee-keeping, grape and orchard management.

The dairy schools of Denmark have already enabled Danish farmers to rival English produce in London markets. Belgium, Italy, Norway, Saxony, Sweden, are all more amply provided with means of general education in agriculture than England. As France has her Institut National Agronomique, Germany has her Institute; the Agricultural Sections of Jena, Poppelsdorf, Bonn, or Göttingen correspond to Grignon and the *écoles nationales;* the Landwirthschaftschulen to the *écoles pratiques*, the Ackerbauschulen to the *fermes écoles.* In Prussia more than thirty institutions teach the practice and theory of agriculture; Möglin, founded in 1806 by Thaer, the Arthur Young of Germany, offers education of the highest class; Annaberg trains peasant farmers and bailiffs; in twelve primary schools agricultural pupils act as hired servants, and do the work of the model farms; itinerant teachers are paid by the Government to travel from village to village. There are also thirteen special schools in which such subjects as meadow culture, flax dressing, and gardening are taught.[1]

Württemberg is especially well provided with means of agricultural education. Besides the Royal Institution of Hohenheim, there are three school farms, an agricultural chair at Tübingen, and a veterinary school at Stuttgard. On many large farms there are apprenticed pupils preparing for Hohenheim. Voluntary winter schools, obligatory evening schools, and lecture meetings enable farmers to keep pace with the latest scientific discoveries. Practical agriculturists, in the pay of the State, visit the different districts, discuss special branches of farming, and co-operate with local associations in experiments and improvements. In all these countries admirable means exist for diffusing agricultural knowledge, and bringing home to the smallest farmers the best modes of cultivation. Scientific instruction is given in a practical form, and in a shape which is easily comprehended.

Almost every nation on the Continent is better provided with means of agricultural education than England, and a Committee of the Royal Agricultural Society is now

---

[1] After the emancipation of the serfs, Russia recognised the urgent need of spreading among the mass a rational knowledge of agriculture. She has her agricultural museums, her three grades of primary, secondary, and higher education, as well as special schools adapted to the wants of different districts. Bavaria, besides large institutions at Weihenstephan near Munich, Lichtenhof, and Schleissheim, has agricultural sections in all the technical schools. Hesse possesses an agricultural college at Darmstadt, open to young farmers from November 1 to March 31. Courses are given for the benefit of national schoolmasters; botany, physics, and chemistry are taught in the national schools; *wanderlehrer* impart instruction in the villages, visiting their circuits every year, so as to be able to note improvement.

investigating our deficiencies. The course is often too ambitious and laid out on too large a scale; but every tiller of the soil has the opportunity of learning the principles of his art, and of using to the utmost advantage the materials at his command. In every other department of human knowledge, where practice depends upon science, the shortest road to success is the mastery of general principles; in other words, theoretical investigation. The truth of this fact, as applied to agriculture, is ignored by the State in England. The art is carried to considerable perfection, but the science is neglected. Our farmers are skilful in the practice of received principles; they despise the general laws on which those principles depend; to them agriculture is only a collection of accepted precepts. Science has turned many traditions upside down; it may have a similar revolution in store for farming. The principles of scientific agriculture must be explored by men of science, and applied by men of practice; but a better understanding between the two can only be obtained by education. Every farmer does not require the highest scientific training; but, even in his isolated experiments, some knowledge of physics, chemistry, botany, or geology is useful, if it only teaches him what to avoid, and how to apply the results of the work of others. Doctors' boys do not qualify as practitioners by delivering medicines; nor do tillers of the soil become farmers by learning a traditional round.

Landlords require education as much as any of the classes which are interested in the cultivation of the soil. They alone have, to some extent, the means of supplying their want. In the future many must manage their own properties. Even if they can afford the luxury of an agent, it seems absurd to surrender to others the practical control of their estates. From this point of view it might be advantageous to introduce applied agricultural chemistry into the Science Schools of Oxford and Cambridge. At Oxford Mr. Primrose McConnell has taught agriculture with marked success to the selected candidates for the Indian Civil Service.

To occupiers and cultivators of the soil, the value of agricultural education needs no demonstration. Unlike the landlords, their wants in this respect are inadequately, or not at all supplied. One feature, at least, in the continental system of education imperatively requires introduction into England. Account-keeping is as essential for farmers as for tradesmen. Chalkmarks on backs of doors or scattered notes in memorandum books will never show farmers how they stand, or in what special department they are losing money. On the Continent book-keeping forms a prominent feature of agricultural education. Pupils write journals of everything done on the farm, make particular notes of special work done and of the workmen employed, keep cashbooks of payments, sales, accounts with the house, and accounts of separate departments. If the way is to be paved for the growth of a peasant tenantry or proprietary, farm accounts should become a feature in all the rural schools of England.

Farmers, if rich enough, are to some extent able to gratify their children's wish for education in farming subjects. Experience shows that the wish is rare. Large sums of money have been voted by Congress to found agricultural schools for farmers' sons in America; but very few avail themselves of their exceptional advantages. Even for the wealthier classes of agriculturists much remains to be done. But no agricultural teaching of any sort is provided for labourers. And it is here that the greatest need is felt. In rural districts boys lose practical training to gain the three R's, and acquire in the process a distaste for farming occupations. Thus farmers suffer in two ways: they pay men's wages for boys' work, and labour is less efficient. Elementary education in the first principles of agriculture would go far to mitigate these evils. At the present day children in rural schools learn to read from books which are useless; their object lessons are polar bears or creatures with which they are equally unfamiliar; the natural history of horses, cattle, sheep, pigs, and poultry, or insects and birds, is entirely neglected; they know more of glacial action than they do of air and water; their minds are stuffed with historical facts, but of the nature of soils, seeds, grasses, or trees they are probably entirely ignorant. If after passing a certain standard, say the third, they received technical education in the work of their future lives, practically illustrated from a few acres attached, as is often the case on the Continent, to the school itself, they would be better equipped as labourers, and would take intelligent interest in work which to them is now dreary routine.

Hitherto agricultural progress has, in this country, depended entirely upon private enterprise. But as agriculture grows more scientific and landlords more impoverished, the need of a State Department of Agriculture is urged upon Government with increased force. Something is already done in this direction, but much remains. The Agricultural Department of the Privy Council, which already commands the services of Professor Brown, has been recently strengthened by the appointment of Mr. Whitehead as agricultural adviser. State aid is also given to horse-breeding. The Government devoted 5,000*l.* for this purpose in 1888, and appointed a committee to frame a scheme for its distribution. They propose to offer twenty-two prizes, or 'Queen's Premiums,' of 200*l*. each, to thoroughbred stallions, in the hope of securing the service, at nominal fees of 2*l*., of first-class thoroughbred sires in every district in England. They are also considering the German and French systems of State *haras*, and the improvement of the old English strains fostered by the Cleveland, Hackney, and Coaching Horse Societies. It is also probable that the Committee upon Dairy Produce may suggest some technical education in butter and cheese making. In other directions the want of an Agricultural Department is severely felt, as, for example, to stamp out swine-fever and pleuro-pneumonia, and to give reliable analyses of artificial manures or reports upon seed samples. In this last direction technical education may supply farmers with the necessary knowledge, but meanwhile the loss is heavy.

State departments for agriculture already exist abroad.[1] Some account has been given of State aid to farming in France. It may be interesting to illustrate the practical working of that system. In the autumn of 1887 M. Barbe, Minister for Agriculture in the Rouvier administration, issued two circulars. In the first, which was addressed to the Prefects, he calls attention to the black rot, a new disease among vines in the Garonne district,

[1] Germany has a powerfully equipped Ministry of Agriculture for Agriculture, Domains, and Forests. In the United States the Central Department of Agriculture is divided into 12 branches, each presided over by a separate officer directly responsible to the Minister of Agriculture for the work of his division. Thus the Seed Division purchases, tests, examines, reports upon seeds, experiments in their cultivation, and ascertains the localities to which they are best suited. The other divisions are (2) Botany, including plants and grasses; (3) Mycology, which investigates diseases of trees and plants caused by fungi; (4) the Microscope; (5) Forestry; (6) Ornithology; (7) Mammology; (8) Pomology, for the assistance of fruit-growers; (9) Chemistry; (10) Entomology; (11) Veterinary Science; (12) Statistics.

notices certain insect pests which destroy farm crops, directs that farmers shall be invited to give notice of their attack, and requires Prefects and Professors to investigate the subject, and, if possible, devise the appropriate remedy. In the second circular, addressed to the departmental Professors of Agriculture, M. Barbe insists on the losses caused by bad seed, and directs his subordinates to call public attention to the Government Seed Trial Station, established three years ago at the office of the National Agricultural Institute in Paris. It may be added that the Institute, to which are attached experimental farms and laboratories at Joinville, inquires into methods of cultivation, examines and reports upon samples of seed which farmers propose to buy, or investigates the introduction of new varieties, and the amelioration of those already introduced. The Professors of the Institute, which is temporarily located in the Conservatoire des Arts et Métiers, include the best known specialists of the day, and its director, M. Eugene Risler, enjoys a European reputation as a scientific agriculturist.

Another point, in which legislation is urgently needed, is the revision of Railway Rates. The question is less simple than it at first sight appears. But the grievance of English farmers is real and substantial.

Three modes of rating have been proposed : (i.) equal mileage rates; (ii.) rates regulated by costs of conveyance; (iii.) differential rates. The third is the principle adopted in England.

Equal mileage rates are manifestly unfair, because it is reasonable to consider the costs of construction from point to point on the same line, the steepness of the gradients or other costs of service. It may be also conceded that consumers derive advantage from special through rates for long distances, and that it is only by their means that London draws fish from Hull, meat from Aberdeen, vegetables from Penzance, and sweeps a radius of 150 miles for her milk supply. But the inexpediency of charging on the *same* scale for long distances as for short does not make it fair to charge *higher* rates for short distances than for long. You cannot argue in the same breath that consumers gain by placing remote markets on the *same* footing as near, and by placing near markets on a *worse* footing than those which are remote.

But the case against through rates for foreign perishable produce is still stronger. Foreign produce may be brought to London partly by sea and partly by land, or wholly by sea. If goods are imperishable, if quick delivery is not essential to their good condition, if they do not suffer by delay in transit, foreign producers may choose either mode of conveyance. They naturally choose the cheapest. In this case, if low railway rates encourage foreigners to send their goods partly by land, English producers are little, and possibly not at all, injured. Their grievance would be formulated thus. Railway companies admit that they carry at a profit hops from Flushing to London for 25*s*.; therefore their profit must be enormous on the same weight of hops at 36*s*. 8*d*. from Sittingbourne to London. It is only by charging local producers high that they can so cheapen rates for foreigners as to secure their traffic. The answer would probably be: Kentish hop-growers pay more, because they can only employ land carriage; foreigners can send by sea, and it is this competition between two modes of conveyance that determines the cheapness of the rates.

But there is no such competition possible in the case of perishable produce, such as butter, fruit, vegetables, and fresh meat—the very commodities to which farmers are recommended, and peasant proprietors would be obliged, to turn their attention. Here time is of the essence; delay injures condition; quick transit is a necessity; and consequently there is no natural competition between sea and land carriage. If perishable produce was sent to London by sea, it could not compete in quality with English goods. When, therefore, foreign perishable produce is sent through to London at through rates, which are actually *less* than those charged to local growers, and in fast trains from which local growers are excluded, the English farmer is indisputably injured. Here is no natural competition between sea and land carriage, both of which are available to the foreigner, to cheapen the through rates, but only the artificial competition, created by rivalry between competing companies, each seeking, in the interests of their respective shareholders, to outbid the other and attract the traffic to their own lines. Here, then, British farmers pay the carriage bills of their foreign rivals. It is idle to plead the interests of the consumer; they would be equally consulted if companies paid smaller dividends, and they cannot be served at one and the same time by bringing remote markets to his door, and by driving near markets to a distance. Space is annihilated, but only if it is sufficiently great; food is cheapened, but only by bounties to foreign producers, and premiums on distance at the expense of proximity.

What is the remedy? Equal mileage rates are simple, but the simplicity is attained by the sacrifice of equity. Rates based on the cost of conveyance without reference to the value of the articles are financially unsound. A ton of sand would pay the same as a ton of copper, or a hundredweight of fresh beef as a hundredweight of potatoes. On the whole, differential rates, if fairly worked, are the most equitable system. But in no case should special import rates be actually lower for long than for short distances, and a different scale should be provided if the perishable character of the article precludes natural competition between land and sea carriage. The scale of rates should be published in a clear, intelligible form, and an appeal should lie to a Board of Control, whose decisions should bind the companies. Such Boards of Control are no novelties. In Holland, Belgium, and France the Government retains power to adjust rates in the public interest. In Prussia, and the German Empire generally, similar powers are vested in Conciliation Boards. It is true that in these countries railways were partly built by the State; but the common principle is that, if railways are primarily commercial undertakings, they are endowed with exceptional powers, because they are designed to develop, and not to cripple, the resources of the country.

CHAPTER XVII.

FISCAL RELIEF. PROTECTION PRICES AND PROTECTION TAXES, OR FREE TRADE TAXES AND FREE TRADE PRICES.

RESTORED confidence, larger powers of dealing with their land, increased practical and scientific knowledge, well-directed State assistance, revised railway rates, may infuse new life into landlords and tenants. But their special public grievance is the unfair incidence of local taxation. At the present moment agriculturists are oppressed by Protection taxes upon Free Trade prices. In the debates on the Repeal of the Corn Laws, both Sir Robert Peel and Lord John Russell argued that the removal of the burdens upon land must necessarily accompany the extinction of its immunities and privileges. So long as consumers of agricultural produce were heavily taxed through import duties for the benefit of producers, it was but reasonable that agricultural land should bear the largest share of the burden of rates. But from 1848 onwards that reason ceased to apply. Free Trade ought, in common justice, to go hand in hand with fair taxation. Yet legislators continue to burden agricultural land, as if the community was still burdened for its support. Rates are charged with innumerable items of national concern, inseparable from civilisation or social organisation; and existing arrangements exhibit a chaos of areas, districts, and local authorities, in which national and local purposes are confusedly intermingled. A comprehensive measure of local government is alleged to be the only ultimate remedy; but meanwhile the plea is made a subterfuge to evade that relief, the justice of which the proposed reform itself concedes.

Taxation of land mainly consists in (1) the Land Tax; (2) Local Taxes. It is often contended that landlords have evaded payment of the Land Tax by reducing it to insignificance. But, in the first place, the true representative of the Land Tax for national purposes is Schedule A of the Income Tax. In the second place, the evasion of payment is not by realty but by personalty. In its existing form the Land Tax dates from 1692, when a new assessment was made; but it undoubtedly represents a part of the ancient subsidies, scutages, hidages, and tallages. Present inequalities, increased by partial redemptions, sprang from the politics of the Revolution; the counties in which it was heaviest were most attached to the House of Stuart. The Land Tax, following the practice of the ancient subsidies, which it represents, originally applied to personalty as well as to realty, but the difficulty of assessing the former proved so great, that in 1833 the net receipts only amounted to 5,214*l*., and in that year an Act was passed abolishing its application to personalty. So far as the Land Tax is concerned, it is personalty, not realty, that has evaded payment. It is not, however, by abolition of the Land Tax, which at the best would afford but partial relief, that landlords should seek redress. The Land Tax is an old tax, subject to which estates in this country have all been acquired.

Local Taxation consists of old and new rates. The old rates were the following (1) Poor Rates, (2) County Rates, (3) Highway Rates, (4) Church Rates. To these must be added other rates which fell upon land, such as

Light and Watching Rates, Sewers Rates (not Metropolitan), Drainage and Inclosure Rates. The amounts of this last class are not separately returned in early reports on Local Taxation.

The four first-mentioned rates formed the chief items of Local Taxation. If, as it is believed, the value of agricultural land has fallen to about the value of 1815, it becomes not only historically, but practically, interesting to give the amount of Local Taxation so far as it can be made out in 1815, 1827, and 1841. The total amount, and, where practicable, the items, will be found set out in the note,[1] and in Appendix XIII. These years, it will be observed, are years in which it was reasonable that Local Taxation should fall heavily upon agricultural land, because, under the protective system, the community at large was heavily taxed for its support.

In 1848 England adopted a Free Trade Policy, but she did not readjust her Protection taxes. On the contrary, she has every year added to the burden upon agricultural land. In reason, if agriculturists have no Protection, they ought to have fair taxation; in fact, they have neither. Personalty or building land eats its cake in the form of Free Trade, and keeps it in the shape of relief from taxation. House property never had, and therefore never lost, the benefit of Protection; but it is in building land that the increased value of the soil now consists. The whole force of the double blow inflicted by the loss of

[1] The returns in early reports for any given year supply the item of one rate, another supplies a second, but 1827 is the first year in which all four are given. In 1803 and 1814 Poor Rate was 5,348,205*l.* and 8,388,974*l.*; in 1792, County Rate was 218,215*l.*; in 1803, 317,977*l.*; in 1814, 573,504*l.* Highway Rates averaged for the three years 1811–12–13, 1,407,200*l.*; in 1827, Church Rates were 564,388*l.* For other details, see Appendix XIII.

Protection and by increased taxation without commensurate increase in value, has fallen upon agricultural land, and it is agricultural land alone that requires relief. As a curious comment upon the existing crisis in England, it may be noted that when, in 1884, the proposed protective duties were referred to a French committee of deputies, an amendment was moved and carried, remitting the whole of the Land Tax, except that portion which was assessed on vineyards and building land; but the Chamber and the Senate preferred Protection. In England justice imperatively demands the remission of taxation on agricultural land. Such a measure is due of right to agriculturists as the necessary consequence of Free Trade; it was promised in 1848; it is virtually conceded in every Treasury subvention; it is implied in the repeated answer that landlords must wait for Local Government Reform; it has been accepted by several resolutions of the House of Commons; it has been recommended by recent commissions on agriculture.

In 1815 the rental of England and Wales was 36,000,000*l*.; in 1878 it was 51,000,000*l*. But at least 35 or 40 per cent. reduction has been made in 1887. At this moment rents are certainly no higher, possibly they are lower than in 1815. Again, in 1815 foreign corn was excluded under 80*s*. a quarter, and the duty acted as an income tax on the wages of consumers to enable producers to bear the charges upon land. In 1887 there is no import duty, and no tax paid by the community for the benefit of the producer. Again, in 1815 agricultural land paid an enormous proportion of poor rate, because ratepayers contributed to the farmer's labour bill; but in 1834 the Poor Law system was totally changed, and farmers now pay wages from their own pockets. Are, then, local burdens readjusted? Are they lightened? On the contrary, they are enormously increased. Agricultural land is assessed at 82 per cent. of the gross income, while railways, mines, and houses, which alone enjoy the so-called unearned increment, escape respectively at 31, 42, and 77 per cent. Once this was just, now it is flagrantly unjust. New charges have been thrown upon agricultural land: as local burdens, education rates are glaring anomalies; ratepayers have lost their tolls and the whole maintenance of highways falls upon the landed interests, though it is the brewer or the coal merchant who makes the profitable use of roads. If landlords and tenants invest capital in improvements, or borrow money and similarly apply it, they are assessed upon the improvements. If they invest in the funds they escape, as does the mortgagee who holds a charge upon the land. Is it then surprising that farming improvements, in these hard times, are not effected? Traders, fundholders, manufacturers enjoy a regulated system of poor law, security of life and property, and wellkept roads for nothing; owners and occupiers of land at the cost of millions. Not only are new charges thrown upon agricultural land, and old means of assistance withdrawn, but, item by item, with the exception of church rate, every one of the old charges[1] is increased, and this upon what is possibly a lower income than that of 1815, when Protection prevailed, and when the Poor Law acted as a wages fund. Mr. Goschen, in the conclusion of his report on Local Taxation,[2] says of 1868, 'An historical retrospect seems to prove that, as regards the burdens on land, they are not heavier than they have been at various periods of this century.' But, with all deference to his eminent

[1] See Appendix XIII., Local Taxation.
[2] Parliamentary Accounts and Papers, 1870, vol. lv.

authority, his historical retrospect is only an historical squint if it fails to notice the two most prominent features of early local taxation—first, that, as regards rates generally, agricultural land was heavily burdened because it enjoyed, so to speak, a drawback in protective duties; secondly, that, as regards poor rates in particular, agricultural land was heavily burdened because, prior to 1834, the administration of the Poor Law taxed the community to pay the farmer's labour bill. The two reasons for the burden are now gone, but not the load; rather it is, in the past twenty years, enormously increased. The climax of injustice has been reached within the last ten years, when distress has increased rates by more than a third. Agricultural depression raises the value of realised personalty, because it cheapens the cost of food, but it proportionately lowers the value of agricultural land. The property which profits by depression escapes scot free from the burden of local taxation, which falls more heavily upon agricultural land as its value declines.

It would not suffice to show, even if it were possible, that the burden of local taxation is the same in 1888 as in 1841.[1] The following comparison between the figures of the four old rates in 1841 and 1885 shows that it is higher by $3\frac{1}{2}$ millions. In both cases the Metropolitan expenditure under the heads of Poor Law Authorities and Churchwardens (church rates) is included :—

[1] This date is chosen in preference to 1827, because the new Poor Law had then come into operation, while Protection still continued. In other words, that year is the simplest of the two detailed returns in the period of Protection, because one great factor which previously swelled rates in the interests of agricultural land is eliminated.

Rates	1841	1885
	£	£
Poor Rates	5,690,151	8,350,354
County Rates	963,223	2,008,048
Highway Rates	1,169,891	1,589,995
Church Rates	506,812	9,468
Totals	8,330,077	11,957,865

To this comparison must be added the facts that, in 1841, turnpike tolls amounted to 1,348,084*l.*; that of the old rates, Sewers Rates, Drainage, Embankment, and Conservancy Rates, and Burial Board Rates are all increased; that a new rate falling wholly upon the land, the Rural Sanitary Rate, amounts to 313,724*l.*; and that the School Board Rate, partly urban, partly rural, has risen to 1,320,923*l.*[1]

Since 1815 the total sum levied by local rates has risen from 8 millions to more than 26 millions in 1885. By far the largest share of the increased burden falls upon towns, and the Treasury subventions must also be considered (3,773,610*l.* in 1885). But it will hardly be disputed that not less than 2 millions of additional taxes have fallen upon rural districts, in which the value of property has, if anything, decreased, which now derive less direct benefits from a large portion of the expenditure than heretofore, and which no longer enjoy the compensating advantages of the protective system. In strict justice, if the principle was carried out upon which land was originally burdened, the agricultural interests are entitled to be placed, with regard to local taxation, in a better position than they enjoyed in 1815, when the total amount raised by rates was 8 millions instead of 26 millions. Their present position is that of

[1] For the detailed comparison of the rates in 1841 and 1885, see Appendix XIII.

Protection taxes and Free Trade prices; they are, therefore, abundantly justified in demanding either Protection prices or Free Trade taxes.

It will be admitted on all sides that Local Government Reform is necessary. Local organisations growing up haphazard, and created from hand to mouth, are needlessly complicated, and the spread of population intensifies their ineffectiveness. The mischief is brought home to ratepayers by the astounding growth of local debt. Between 1868 and 1885 local rates, exclusive of tolls, dues, and rents, rose from 16 to 26 millions, while during the same period Imperial taxation, excluding the Post Office, and miscellaneous receipts, only increased from 48,570,000*l.* in 1868 to 53,223,000*l.* in 1885. During the ten years ending in 1884 the liabilities of the local authorities, in respect of outstanding loans, rose from 93 to 165 millions, and at the present moment the local debt is little less than a fourth of the National Debt. This enormous burden accumulates unchecked, if not encouraged, by its interested administrators. Ratepayers, aghast at the amount of their indebtedness, cannot see, much less control, its growth, their pockets are emptied on every side by local bodies, each invested with large powers to tax or borrow They cannot, at the same moment, keep an eye on quarter sessions, vestries, burial boards, sanitary boards, poor law guardians, parish overseers, drainage or sewers commissioners. Thus this burden grows day by day, uncontrolled by any central body, affecting different areas in different degrees, each portion administered by different authorities, elected on different methods, exercising their respective powers over intermingled areas which are not conterminous, and enjoying a practical anarchy and collective irresponsibility. A strong central body with consolidated powers, is imperatively needed to enforce economy, promote efficiency, and exercise control over conveniently-sized and well-arranged districts.

But administrative reform ought not to hinder financial relief. Excessive taxation and its wasteful distribution are two distinct abuses capable of separate removal. Whatever portion of local taxation is reduced for agriculturists must be necessarily transferred to some other form of property. Nor would it be difficult to establish a local taxation income-tax, and use existing returns to assess realised personalty. But if this method of supplying the deficiency is rejected, other alternatives exist. Subventions from general taxation are clumsy expedients, but the State supervision which they carry with them, if reform of local government is postponed, becomes a valuable advantage. Another and simpler method of relief is afforded by the allocation of certain taxes, like the dog, gun, game, and carriage licenses, to local authorities.[1]

But the mode of financial relief hardly belongs to the present inquiry, which is not so much intended to suggest remedies as to insist upon the unfair incidence of protection taxes upon agricultural land. Here, and not in its incidence upon building-land, lies the inequality of the present system. Here, whatever increment has been gained is hardly earned, and here alone is relief urgently required.

It is often argued that the reduction of local rates exonerates property at the cost of labour, and quarters landlords upon the State. Though the reduction of local rates is primarily a landlord's question, because upon him

---

[1] Another financial measure which would indirectly confer substantial benefits upon agricultural land would be the reduction of 3 per cent. consols to 2½ per cent. By such a change capital would be necessarily attracted from consols to land, since both would then be placed upon much the same footing as remunerative investments.

P

falls three-fourths of the charge, yet the interests of farmers are not limited to the remaining fourth. They are strong enough to secure reduced rents as a consequence of remission. Again, the existing incidence of local taxation would necessarily prevent the growth of small owners, the spoilt children of those who use this argument against any reduction in the burden of rates. It is a novel mode of encouraging peasant proprietors to tax them more heavily than any other class in the community. Unless the soil is partially relieved from rates, the dreams of extreme land-reformers are impossible of realisation.

CHAPTER XVIII.

SELF-HELP NOT PROTECTION.

LEGISLATION and financial reform may, and, it is hoped, will, do something for agriculture; but it can, and must, do most for itself. State aid may be a good crutch; it is certainly a bad leg. The only certain and immediate assistance comes from self-help. When the situation is looked fairly in the face, foreign competition in corn is seen to be, for the present at least, a fixed quantity. If agriculturists expect foreign wheat supplies to cease, they may starve where they stand, like Horace's rustic waiting for the river to cease to flow. It is true that American or Indian grain production and population will some day run neck and neck; but few of the present generation of men will live to see that agricultural millennium. It is so inherently improbable that import duties on wheat will ever be imposed, that farmers only follow the will-o'-the-wisp of Protection to be lured still deeper into the Slough of Despond. Agriculturists must therefore revise their practical ideas. if they cannot, in this respect, revise the fiscal system. From other sources relief will be but infinitesimal.

Where, then, are agriculturists to look for a livelihood? In 1886 the total value of imports of agricultural produce[1] amounts, in round figures, to 113 millions of pounds. Of this total value, 62½ millions consisted either of grain, not

[1] See Appendix VIII., Values of Imports of Agricultural Produce.

including Indian corn (35 millions), or of articles which either cannot be produced at all or cannot be grown advantageously in this country (27½ millions). The remaining 50¼ millions consists, for the most part, of produce which not only might be produced in this country, but, if railway rates were readjusted, could be produced with equal advantage nowhere else. Excluding salt and preserved meat, cheese, margarine, and lard, which are not perishable, and therefore could be conveyed here by sea, we annually import from abroad perishable produce, such as livestock, fresh meat, butter, eggs, fruit, and vegetables, of the enormous value of 30,600,000*l*. This sum, which exceeds the total value of the imported wheat by 4½ millions, can be produced at home under superior advantages of proximity.

Our foreign meat supply arrives alive or dead. In the first case, English farmers suffer constant risk from imported contagious disease. Against this influx of living beef and mutton, if not unduly favoured by railway rates, English farmers can and must contend. But imported livestock should not be suffered to spread infection among the flocks and herds of this country. In France veterinary officers belonging to the Agricultural Department are stationed at all the ports of entry, armed with full powers to exclude or slaughter foreign livestock. In the Netherlands the vigorous action of the Ministry of Agriculture has stamped out pleuro-pneumonia. Why should not a similar practice prevail in England? So long as contagious diseases are not shut out, British farmers fight foreign meat-producers with one hand tied behind their backs. Railway rates tie up the other. Under no natural system of competition could 30 million pounds' worth of perishable produce be thrown upon the London markets in equal condition to English goods. If once the protective rates were revised, which now exclude home growers from home markets, English farmers would turn for profit to fresh perishable produce; and if they do so, there is an additional 6 millions of imported bacon, hams, and cheese, in the best qualities of which they might defy foreign competition. This $36\frac{1}{2}$ millions probably amounts to more than the rental of farms in England and Wales in 1887.

History proves that farming has twice before changed its front. In the sixteenth century farmers turned from the plough to pasture; in the eighteenth and nineteenth centuries they reverted to tillage. Now, at the close of the nineteenth century, livestock and dairy-farming must supersede corn as the farmer's sheet-anchor. Changes of front in the faces of watchful rivals are dangerous manœuvres, attended with risk and loss; but the sooner they are effected the better. There are signs that the new departure has in fact commenced; and its inevitable result, the decreased demand for agricultural labour, is lamentably manifest. The area of corn cultivation has decreased by 618,000 acres upon the area in 1875-7; on the other hand, more land is under rotation grasses, clovers, and permanent pasture, or fruit orchards and market gardens.

Under changed conditions, agriculture begins to show faint symptoms of revival, which the scarcity of winter food, compensated as it was by abundant pasture up to December, has failed to check. Every county can produce instances of shrewd, industrious, persevering men who now farm with profit by adapting low-rented land to new requirements, by economy of labour and personal supervision. Holdings have been reduced in size, and the proportions of arable and pasture are better adapted to varied and diversified husbandry. Land once more yields a profit; the unoccupied area is less in 1887 by 18,533 acres than it was in 1881; agricultural-implement makers report an increased demand for their goods. The invention of new dairy implements and processes, the study of foreign systems, the importation of American experts, the establishment of milk factories and creameries, the formation of associations and unions among milk-producers, testify to the growing importance of dairy-farming.

The country, then, appears prepared to enter upon a great agricultural change. But without cordial co-operation between owners and occupiers no new departure can succeed. Both profit by getting the utmost from the land; and the real question for both parties to consider is, How can even-handed justice best be meted out to their respective interests? Landlords dislike to surrender control over their estates, and farmers dislike to risk capital on insecure tenures. Something may be said for both positions. But unless landlords find the whole capital, farmers have justice on their side.

Parties to contracts must, as a general rule, protect their own interests; but though farmers are now able to drive a bargain, their position is in some respects peculiar. The profession of a farmer is seldom lucrative, and he embarks in it everything that he has. He follows the most hereditary of callings; he cannot transfer himself and his money to other trades; he is as helpless as generations of farming can make him. It is the consciousness of this fact that drives him into ruinous competition for land. He may lose money on his farm, but he cannot readily throw up his holding, especially if he has a family. It is often better for him to suffer an annual loss than to risk the auction sale which closes his occupation. He has little incentive to improvement; he cannot patent his agricultural processes; till recently his landlord often appropriated in the shape of increased rent the results of his enterprise. He has no benefit of fancy prices for his produce; he cannot wait his market, for his goods suffer in the keeping; he is deprived by railway rates of the natural protection afforded by distance; he is subjected, without the favour of fashion, to the barest competition; his scanty profits are intercepted by middlemen, who stand between him and the producer.

On the other hand, if agricultural produce all round has decreased in value by 25 per cent., rents have fallen from 30 to 40 per cent., while seed corn, cake, manure, or store cattle and sheep are cheaper in proportion. Much, too, has of late been done for farmers. The Game Laws,[1] which, for more than a century bred bitter feelings, have been modified. The law of distress, which, by giving artificial security to landlords, often raised rents above their natural level, is limited in its range. The old legal maxim ' *Quicquid plantatur solo accedit solo* ' is at least shaken. The present Government has removed some of the inequality of taxation by allowing farmers to declare their actual income under Schedule D. It has also protected them against adulterated produce, which robbed their dairy-farms of legitimate profits,[2] or their purchases in cake of half their value.[3] But such remedies only touch

[1] Game is no new grievance. In 1774, Arthur Young (*Political Arithmetic*, p. 204) speaks of the number of hares as ruinous to farming. In 1830 a pamphleteer, writing as Agricola, begs landlords to abandon their 'contemptible place-hunting battues,' the proceeds of which are 'destined for the London poulterer,' and speaks of the 'nursery of game' as 'the stepping-stone to a sinecure.'

[2] *The Margarine Act.* But it may be doubted whether the Act will effect its object. Perhaps the best legislative protection against the admixture with butter would have been to require it to be coloured red or pink.

[3] *The Merchandise Trade Marks Act.*

the fringe of the farmer's difficulties. His real grievance against the landlord is the absence of security for unexhausted improvements under a lease. Ownership affords the strongest encouragement to agricultural progress. On large estates it cannot be combined with occupation; the relations of landlord and tenant must necessarily be maintained. Tenants of the class of *chevaliers* of agricultural industries are easily found, who cultivate the soil as lodgers, skim and rob the land, and reduce farming to leave to an exact science. But how can improving farmers be induced to hire land? Three plans have been proposed. The first is to create peasant proprietors; the second is to recognise that dual ownership which is involved in tenant-right; the third, and most feasible proposition, is to secure to the tenant in the fullest degree the benefit of the improvements which he effects. English farmers have no claim to fixity of tenure; but they may fairly ask, and are entitled to obtain, absolute security for their outlay.

With high farming, tenant-right, in some form or other, became an absolute necessity; but the Legislature proved slow to recognise the change in agricultural conditions. Although the need of maintaining the fertility of the soil increased every year, modern tenants possessed no more security for outlay than medieval farmers who never put a sixpence into the soil. How compensation should be given is a much-debated question. Holdings acquire additional value in three ways: first, by permanent improvements effected by the landlord; secondly, by artificial manures which produce a temporary increase in the fertility of the soil; thirdly, by a course of skilful farming, the effects of which last for years, but are capable of exhaustion. No question arises on the first head, and very little on the second; the real difficulty begins with the third. If tenants, by skill and liberality, have increased the letting or marketable value of land, they are entitled to compensation for whatever increase remains when landlords seek to change the conditions of a tenancy. Thus, even on the third head, difficulty only arises when, at the expiration of a lease, a notice to quit is given, or the rent is raised. In order to ascertain the value of the tenant's improvements, two plans are proposed—open sale in the market, and valuation with arbitration. The first is the free sale of tenant-right; the second is the principle adopted in the Agricultural Holdings Acts of 1875 and 1883. One fatal objection may be urged against the first plan. The incoming tenant buys the improvements; in other words, he enters upon the farm with his capital reduced, if not exhausted. Farmers, in fact, cut a stick for their own backs. On other grounds the three F's, with the attendant tutelage of a land court, are not only historically indefensible, but unnecessary and unfair to English landlords.

To quitting tenants, the principle of reference and arbitration, adopted in the Agricultural Holdings Acts of 1875 and 1883, affords adequate security. The latter Act is compulsory, and therefore escapes the danger which made the first inoperative. But its provisions are cumbersome, and its schedules of improvement minute but inadequate. It gives no security to sitting tenants against a rise of rent based upon their improvements. If they refuse the rise, their alternative is to quit. The choice is unfair; the losses on a sale preparatory to quitting a farm often amount to ruin; countless considerations besides those of business induce tenants to consent to a rise which they cannot afford. The advantage taken of this dilemma negatived the intended results of the Irish Land Act of

1870, and was made the excuse for the three F's of 1883. For the present time in England, the parts are reversed; land competes for tenants, not tenants for land. But it will not always remain so, and tenant farmers have now the opportunity of, as it were, legislating for themselves. Ample security might be given by a very simple bill, dealing with the principle of compensation, the mode of its assessment, and the manner of its payment. The broad principle is, that when changes in the condition of a tenancy are proposed, tenants are entitled to compensation for any additions which their skill and capital have made to the letting value of the land : landlords are entitled to similar compensation for any diminution caused by niggardly or negligent farming. The value of the addition must be calculated by reference to experts and arbitration, and the amount limited to seven years' purchase, the period within which it would generally be exhausted. Lastly, in the case of quitting tenants the compensation thus estimated and capitalised should be paid by or to landlords on the surrender of the farm ; in the case of sitting tenants the compensation should either be paid by the landlord in a capitalised sum, or be for seven years deducted from the increased rent. A measure constructed upon these lines would give tenants every necessary security and inducement for skilful and liberal farm management.

But even if compensation were thus secured, many agreements are objectionable on account both of their contents and their omissions. Restrictions upon cropping or sales of produce belong to bygone conditions of farming, and fail to achieve their objects. If it is necessary to guard against the impoverishment of the land in the interests of the owner or the incoming tenant, the best protection, next to the interests of the occupier himself, will be to prescribe the annual quantity of manure, and the course of the latter year's cultivation. To the class of omissions belongs the want of a sliding scale to adjust rents to the rise or fall of prices. Without such a scale a fall in the value of agricultural produce places tenants under leases at the mercy of landlords. The following system is, it is believed, adopted on Lord Tollemache's estates; and although difficulties may arise in working out the percentages of the rise and fall, the fairness of the principle admits of no dispute.

Average price of three crops.	Rise or fall upon the rents.
s. d.	
44 0	Rise of 25 per cent.
41 6	,, 20 ,,
39 0	,, 15 ,,
36 0	,, 10 ,,
34 0	,, 5 ,,
Standard 31 6	
29 0	Fall of 5 ,,
26 0	,, 10 ,,
24 0	,, 15 ,,
21 6	,, 20 ,,
19 0	,, 25 ,,

Upon this system, assuming the rent on which the standard is obtained to be 1l. an acre, if prices reach 44s. the rent only rises to 25s. an acre. On the other hand, if prices fall to 19s. the rent falls to 15s. The scale for the fall is less equitable than the scale for the rise. If prices fell so low as the two last figures, the surplus profit for rent would be a minus quantity. But though particular percentages might always be disputed, the principle of sliding scales and fluctuating rents is at once so reasonable and practicable, that its adoption would go far to remove those natural objections to leases which spring from fear of falling prices and fixed outgoings. Mutual confidence between landlord and tenant, just agreements, security for outlay, freedom of and in contract, sliding scales for rent, would remove the principal hindrances which scare away improving tenants. Farms at present rentals may, it is believed, be made to pay. Undoubtedly if farmers slumber in their empty corn-bins dreaming of Protection, they will be worn out before things wear round. But capable men of energy and enterprise, wide awake to every chance of profit—men who in personal expenses cut their coats to their cloth, who thoroughly understand and keep the master's eye upon their business—can, and do, make farming answer. They have, in many respects, rarely occupied a more favourable position; they have a choice of holdings and their own terms. But profits do not lie in the old ways, nor are fortunes to be expected. Profits lie in pennies saved rather than in pennies made—in careful planning, skilled management, economy of working expenses, minute attention to detail. Many losses might be prevented or controlled if farmers more often remembered that no part of their holdings better repays tillage than their heads.

Profitable farming has been revolutionised by the annihilation of time and space, and the reduction of freights of ocean transit which steam and trade-depression have together effected. But agriculture, like some heavy body which has reached a high rate of speed, cannot be pulled up abruptly. The machinery has ceased to drive it forward, but the way that is still upon it carries it in the direction of wheat. Yet the mass shows signs of breaking off into different directions. Low farming takes the place of high because it is safer. Holdings are reduced in size— a change which may prove advantageous to agricultural labourers; breadths of arable land are diminished, and farms better proportioned for mixed farming. Dairying, livestock breeding, rearing, and fatting, are the most remunerative forms in which tenant farmers can employ their capital. Nor is it only to this or that side of the country that mixed farming is suited. It is sometimes said that one district grows wheat, another dairies, according to the value of the soil. But the example of France is not required to prove that stock may be bred and reared, and cheese and butter made, on arable land. Dairying is more a question of markets than of soil. It is true that the butter made in the rich pastures of Gournay and Isigny fetches from 2s. 6d. to 3s. 6d. a pound in the Paris markets; but much of that which competes in English markets is produced on cultivated lands by the yield of tares, clover, roots, rye, and oats. Varied husbandry pays on light, shallow soils which will not produce a permanent grass. It employs more labour than land which is laid down permanently to grass. It also saves expenses both of men and horses, because it diminishes the area under the plough, by substituting for three-fourths of the arable portion a three or four years' lea, which may be grazed or cut for hay. The system of rotation and temporary grass which it adopts costs less in seeds than permanent pasture, and may be reconverted to tillage whenever necessary. It restores the fertility of arable soil, because it gives time for the vegetable matter to accumulate. It supplies fodder-crops, which in dry seasons, like 1887, are the saving of stock-breeders and dairymen. It secures more profits from breeders and dealers, because more stock is reared at home and fewer 'stores' are purchased. It minimises the risk of contagious disease, because it lessens the number of cattle which travel through the country; and not only is home-bred stock less liable to disease, but it is better suited to the soil and climate. It enables farmers to compete with foreigners in those forms of produce in which proximity gives them natural advantages. It is, in fact, peculiarly adapted to the growth of beef, mutton, veal, butter, milk, and pork—articles in which home markets enjoy a natural monopoly, and the imported value of which annually exceeds 20 millions. It increases the proportion of livestock, and thus assists farmers to consume at home produce which they cannot sell at a profit. Better prices are realised in milk and butter than were made thirty years ago. Prime qualities of English hard cheese maintain their prices; there is an increasing demand for soft cheese of the Coulommiers type; buttermilk commands a ready sale among confectioners. If half-and-half cheese like Brie, or skim-milk cheese like Gervais, both famous in Paris, command no sale; if separated milk is not, as in the North, bought to mix with porridge, skim-milk may be used to rear calves and pigs with peculiar advantage. Shorthorns, as is well known, take kindly to rearing by hand; and the excessive fatness which depreciates the price of maize-fed American 'hog-products' is best counteracted by nitrogenous food, like milk mixed with pea-meal or barley.

Where markets are convenient, the milk trade is easy and remunerative; but farmers have hitherto given away their profits to be reaped by middlemen. One of many signs that they are awakening to the importance of the trade is seen in their alliances to determine the prices of the districts. Co-operation in the sale of produce is sorely needed. It is probable that that uniformity which places Normandy at the head of the butter trade can only be secured in factories. If so, let us have them. But it is certain that if English cheese and butter are to compete at all with foreign goods, they must, before all things, be above suspicion for purity. In a war of 'wrinkles' we should go to the wall, and genuineness is our only strength. Bogus butter mixed with margarine, or bogus cheese made up with hog's lard, would kill the industry. So, too, if it is to compete with success, English butter must be well and uniformly made, carefully packed, and sent to market in attractive condition. Slovenly systems result in strong taste and low prices. These necessary elements have of late brought into prominence milk-factories and creameries. The danger of the system, unless it is conducted by and for farmers, is that it may establish another race of middle-men.

If tenant-farmers could but clear their eyes of the dust of Protection, their outlook is by no means dismal. They enjoy a climate which is admirably adapted for diversified farming; they have at their very doors an insatiable market; they command the best breeds of live animals; the diminished value of agricultural produce is met by a corresponding fall in rents and the costs of production; labour is cheap, abundant, and, when good, the best in the world. They have before them examples, in every county, of men of their own class who have conquered circumstances, and who are at the present moment making money in their profession. All that is required is a frank recognition, both by landlords and tenants, of the changed conditions under which farming can be made to pay; on the one side, fair rents and proper homesteads for the manufacture of meat and dairy produce; on the other, revived energy, scientific practices, and more direct relations between producers and consumers.

CHAPTER XIX.

AGRICULTURAL LABOURERS.

STANDING as agricultural labourers do on the brink of pauperism, the slightest slip downwards carries them over the verge. But the most cheering symptom in rural distress at present, as contrasted with the past, is that hired labourers have been the last, and not the first, to suffer by depression. Looking back to the period of protection from 1790 to 1840, their condition was deplorable, a disgrace to civilisation generally, and to landlords and farmers in particular. Between 1770 and 1850 the average rent of arable land had more than doubled, while wages increased by one-eighth, the rent of cottages rose by a half, and the commons, by which the labourer had improved his income, were enclosed—rarely, indeed, without compensation, but generally without any permanent equivalent. The old Poor Law degraded peasants to parish pensioners, checked the circulation of labour, deteriorated its efficiency by fixing pay with reference to wants rather than services, encouraged the growth of a surplus population by rewarding the most productive couples. The standard of life from 1800 to 1834 sank to the lowest possible scale; in the South and West wages paid by employers fell to 3s. to 4s. per week, augmented by parochial relief from the pockets of those who had no need of labour; and insufficient food has left its mark in the physical degeneracy of the peasantry. Herded together in cottages which, by their imperfect arrangements, violated every sanitary law, generated all kinds of disease, and rendered modesty an unimaginable thing; driven to a distance from their work in order to create model villages, and congregated in 'open' parishes, where they were subjected to the extortions of house-building speculators; compelled by insufficient wages to expose their wives to the degradation of field labour, and to send their children to work as soon as they could crawl—the peasant had little cause in the past to be enthusiastic for the land laws, the corn laws, and parochial relief. Disorganised by his divorce from the soil, demoralised by the poor law, degraded by insufficient money wages, lodged worse than the animals, oppressed by the high price of necessaries, the labourer would have been more than human had he not risen in an insurrection which could only be quelled by force. He had already carried patience beyond the limit where it ceases to be a virtue.

The relative improvement in the present condition of the agricultural labourer is enormous. Landlords have spared no pains to improve his moral and material position. Labourers are comfortably lodged, and few are without land in the shape of field or cottage gardens; the agricultural gang, public or private, is at an end; fewer women and young children work in the fields; the abuses of the truck system have been reduced. They enjoy comforts to which twenty years ago they were strangers: they are better housed, better fed, better clad; their work is lighter, and their wages, tested by the purchasing power of money, higher than they have been for centuries. But slow-witted as Hodge proverbially is, his memory is singularly tenacious. Deeply hidden in the recesses of his intricate mind lurk vague theories of lost rights, and more distinct traditions of past wrongs. He forgets that his present condition, in its substance, results from the natural operation of economic laws; he only remembers the occasions on which its unfortunate accidents have been aggravated for the benefit of landlords or of farmers.

Speaking generally, the worst aspects of peasant life at the present moment are the decreasing demands for agricultural labour, the absence of any reasonable prospect of emerging from the condition of hired service, and the pauper allowance which rewards the most industrious career. Some readjustment between the demand and supply for labour, some social ladder, and some better provision against old age are the true needs of the agricultural poor. So far from relieving the glut of labour, the new departure in the practice of farming will still further congest the market. Economical management and increased breadths of grass, whether permanent or temporary, mean a reduction of working expenses, which will take the form, not of less wages, but of less employment. Emigration affords the only outlet for the excess of the labour supply. But, putting this aside for the moment, do the agricultural changes which appear imminent afford no hope of partial remedy?

Everything points to a great reduction in the size of holdings, and closer relations between the labour and the land. Capital, in the shape of money, is being withdrawn from farming; large tenants are scarce, large farms hard to let. Capitalists worth from 5,000*l*. to 10,000*l*. will not invest in a trade which now means daily drudgery or pecuniary loss. Others, who have lost half their capital, would be glad to lose half their land, and desire to concentrate their money on narrower areas. Large farms go begging, when smaller holdings create competition. Thus the demand for land increases in extent as it diminishes in intensity; and the same fact has been already noted as the characteristic of social progress.[1] If agriculture for the time discards steam ploughs, it may find that spades are trumps. Easy-going farmers, bred in the traditions of cornlaw prices, are yielding to smaller men who, by sheer hard work, will force the land to pay.

Small peasant tenancies of 15 acres, in these days of small profits, offer a better chance of success than co-operative farms, where Jack is as good as his master, and one idler drags down the rest. Small tenants, who make no outlay for labour, are indefatigable in their industry. If they soil their cattle, as every peasant does in France, they can keep three cows on land which, if grazed, would barely keep two. Calves, pigs, poultry, are within the reach of the humblest. Bigger men might also find breeding mares a profitable investment, especially if the Government provided good sires at easy rates. In France eggs are collected by *cocotiers* who travel the districts: a similar plan would enable the English peasant tenant to compete for a share in the 2,881,000*l.* which the country annually pays for foreign eggs. If a butter-making factory or a market for milk were at hand, his success would be as certain as anything can be in farming.

But the most industrious tenants require money capital with which to start. How is it to be provided? On the Continent the Prussian land-banks have proved useful agencies for the purpose. But, with the English dislike to State interference, '*caisses de crédit Raffeisen*' may prove more popular. Societies of landlords form syndicates, and issue 3 per cent. bonds on the security of their

[1] See page 160.

land. The money thus raised is advanced to farmers at easy rates, from $3\frac{1}{2}$ to 4 per cent. The system was started by M. Raffeisen in Neuwied on the Rhine, and, wherever it has spread, has proved successful. It is, however, essential that the circle within which each bank operates should be narrow, so that the members of the syndicate may be accurately informed of the position of would-be borrowers.[1] One great feature of French agriculture during the recent depression is the increase of *métayage*. Many agricultural writers admit that, on this system, landlords and tenants have got most from the land, and suffered least from falling prices; some have even called it the land system of the future. The theory of *métayage* is admirable, and its working has been completely revolutionised since it was condemned by Arthur Young and Mill. Landlords and tenants combine to stock a farm ; the tenant tills the soil, and manages the live stock under the direction of the landlord; the profits are divided as the interest on their respective capitals. *Métayage* applies co-operation directly and simply to agricultural industries ; it forms an association of capital with labour, of practice with science ; it brings to bear upon both partners the strongest motives of self-interest. It affords every variety of tenure, from the *maître-valet* who contributes nothing but his labour, or the *personniers*, companies of *maître-valets* working under the

[1] In some cases syndicates have been allowed to issue paper money against their cash in hand. The Prussian Land Bills of Exchange considerably increase powers of borrowing on real property. This negotiable mortgage (*Grundschuld*) may be made payable to order, and, if endorsed in blank, passes by mere delivery ; and the holder for value can always enforce his claim against the estate. The power to transfer whenever the holder wishes increases the value of land as a security, and is easily obtained if a land registration system were once established in the country.

supervision of their leader, the *bourrat*, to the *métayen* who brings 100*l*. into the partnership.[1]

It may, therefore, prove that, in the future, some large percentage of discharged labour will be settled on small holdings. On larger farms economies will take the form rather of reduced numbers than of reduced wages. The best men will probably be regularly employed at present rates; but nothing can, it is feared, secure permanent wages for industrious but unskilful labourers, still less for idle, drinking loafers, who are only servants on Saturday nights.

Different rates of wages have always existed, and may be illustrated from the scales fixed by justices of the peace in the seventeenth century.[2] So, too, it was the habitual practice of farmers, at the commencement of the present century and previously to the general adoption of turnips and artificial grasses, to dismiss half their labourers in the winter months. The new and deplorable result of necessary changes in agricultural practices is not merely reduction of wages, or even temporary loss of work, but the sheer impossibility for a considerable section of the rural community to find work in the Old World.

There are, then, three classes of agricultural labourers, who will be differently affected by the new departure which seems imminent: those who themselves settle on small holdings, those who find employment on large farms, and those who are discharged. If the tendencies of Eng-

---

[1] For further details see 'Rural France,' *Edinburgh Review*, October 1887, pp. 312–15.

[1] *E.g.*, in 1610, in Rutland, three classes of labourers are distinguished. 'A superior servant in husbandrie which can eire, sow, mow, thresh, make a rick, thacke and hedge the same, and can kill a sheep, hog, and calfe,' obtained 2*l*. 10*s*. a year with food; a common servant, 2*l*.; a 'meane servant,' 1*l*. 9*s*.

lish farming are rightly interpreted, the change will supply
to the first two classes that social ladder, those means of
making independent provision for old age, and that stimulus
to energy, which their condition has hitherto lacked. The
marked deterioration in the quality of English labour is
partly due to hopelessness, partly to the educational needs
of the day, partly to want of varied experience. The first
cause may be removed by the stimulus afforded by small
farms or allotments, by new sources of livelihood or new
adjuncts to wages; the second may be mitigated by technical teaching in village schools; for the third it is perhaps
hopeless to look for the extended revival of the bothy system
of the north, which under a slightly different form prevailed
at no distant period throughout the country. Farmers and
their men once lived together and ate together; but the
relations of the agricultural classes are altered. The reports of the Agricultural Commissions at the beginning of
the century show that the practice of lodging and feeding
farm servants died out because farmers' wives were 'too
fine to keep house.' But such a practice benefits farmers,
because, when prices are low, they need not sell large
quantities of produce to realise money wages; and, in times
of scarcity, labourers obtain a larger money value in the
shape of food than they could buy for themselves. The
farmer had constantly on the premises a large staff of
labour: labour was more efficient; boys, boarded and
lodged in farmhouses, learned all kinds of work, turned
their hands, like Mr. Arch, to everything, and, like him,
were perhaps worth 24s. a week to their employer. Above
all, the system checked early and improvident marriages.
The discomforts of a lodger in an overcrowded cottage
blind the agricultural labourer to all prudential considerations; he marries before he has time to save; for the next

few years his life is an arduous struggle, which generally brings him on the parish. To the peasant the bothy system offers the same advantages which clubs afford to a different class. It enables him to wait in comfort till he has saved money. In some parts of France and in the north of England the hind's house is a frequent appendage to a farm. Labourers are hired for the year, and barracked on the spot in homesteads presided over by married labourers. They are better fed, and enjoy many comforts which they must forego when married. If such a system could be revived, labourers would not be driven to improvident marriages; they might save money before they start in life; they would be better trained to various kinds of work; they would acquire the money and the skill to make the most of allotments.

Sound policy and justice alike required that allotments should become universal. The most satisfactory and effective method of extending the system is the voluntary action of landlords; but to apathy or selfishness compulsion is rightly applied. Few cases remain in which the want is not supplied, and the question seems to be rapidly passing into an urban phase.[1] The last session of Parliament, it may be added, secured compensation to allotment tenants for unexhausted improvements. Socially allotments stimulate thrift in early youth; they make labourers independent, train them to habits of industry, occupy their leisure, enable them to provide for old age. Agriculturally they counteract the prejudicial effects of education on the practical efficiency of labour by making boys and girls knowledgeable in agricultural matters; they prevent agricultural labour from migrating to the towns. Economically they occupy the leisure time of labourers, and reclaim the

[1] See Appendix XIV., 'Allotments.'

drunkard, the idler, and the poacher; they relieve the rates, and, if a cow is kept, improve the health of the nation by supplying children with milk. Commercially they pay where the size is not too great to occupy more than the leisure time of the labourer, where the position is readily accessible, and where the rent is fair and paid direct to the landlord.

England and Wales, at the present moment, contain 807,608 agricultural labourers, farm servants, and cottagers. The table in Appendix XIV. shows that of this number 102,774 persons have potato-grounds or cow-runs; and that there are 387,574 field and 257,482 garden allotments. Thus more than three-fourths of the agricultural labourers occupy land in one form or another. The field allotments are for the most part conveniently placed, since, out of 387,000, 318,000 lie within half a mile of the cottages. A considerable number of those labourers who do not possess allotments are lodgers, or sons living at home with their parents. It is therefore strictly true that allotments are almost universal in rural districts.

The Table of Allotments has been drawn so as to show the districts in which they preponderate. It is intended for comparison with the Table of Wages,[1] which has been similarly drawn. Comparatively few allotments exist in grazing districts, where wages are relatively high; they are most numerous in the corn counties, where wages are relatively low. 'It will be seen that the average weekly wages of agricultural labourers were estimated in 1771 by Arthur Young at 7s. 5½d.; in 1824 they had risen to 9s. 7½d.; in 1881, to 14s. 5d. Thus not only do labourers enjoy better cottages than heretofore, as well as a system of allotments which is almost universal, but their nominal

[1] See Appendix XV., 'Agricultural Wages.'

wages have risen within the last half-century by nearly five shillings. Nor is this all. It will be seen, from a glance at Appendix XVI.,[1] Table 2, that, within the last fifty years, their real wages have increased to an almost equal extent. Every item, except butter and butcher's meat, costs less, while the 4-lb. loaf has fallen from 1*s.* 4*d.* to 4½*d.* The condition of agricultural labourers may be, and ought to be, improved in directions already indicated, and it seems almost incredible that in the whole of England and Wales there should still be only 9,466 of the total number who have the opportunity of keeping a cow. But the advance which they have made in material prosperity is enormous, especially if it is remembered that their earnings, though primarily consisting of weekly wages, are largely supplemented by payments for task-work, piece-work, and allowances; that, if employed at all, they are employed more continuously than in former times; and that though coal varies too widely in price in different districts to admit of any average being taken, yet not only firing, but all articles of clothing, are far cheaper in 1887 than in 1824.

On the other hand, many articles of clothing which were formerly made at home are now bought, and the very large additions to the weekly earnings of the family which were made by the wife and children are, to a great extent, withdrawn. Wages from 1871 to 1873 rose far higher than the figures shown in 1881, and further reductions have taken place within the last six years. But it seems probable that the average fall upon the wages of 1881 is not more than 1*s.* a week, and this loss is partially covered by the increased purchasing power of wages.

It is, then, evident that agricultural labourers in full

[1] See Appendix XVI., Prices of Provisions, &c.

employment are, at the present moment, better off than any of the classes directly interested in agriculture. If small tenancies, as a consequence of the impending changes in farming, were placed within their reach, their prospects would be brighter than they have been for a century, their narrow horizon wider, their opportunity greater of rising in the social scale, their chance of independence better. The reverse of the picture is black. A large displacement of labour is imminent, which will further overstock the market. For this excess of supply there seems no remedy but emigration. The German labour colonies have succeeded among the unemployed, and their introduction into Russia has relieved the distress of the 180,000 peasant proprietors who in bad times have thrown up their holdings.[1] But the system aims at little more than temporary relief; it affords no such prospects of permanent independence as are offered by State-directed colonisation, which plants well-assorted groups of emigrants on the vacant lands of our colonial empire. The Old World offers no advantages comparable to those, for instance, of the village settlements of New Zealand. The Government sells land in small lots at 1*l*. the acre, or lets 20 acres for the same sum, and advances loans at 5 per cent. to enable buyers or tenants to build houses or clear land. The colonies have the vacant land; England, the surplus population. The need of outlet is urgent, and every day increases its pressure. Private enterprise cannot bring together colonial land and English labour on a scale large

[1] The first of these labour colonies (*Arbeiter-Kolonie*) was established in 1882 at Wilhelmsdorf in Westphalia. There are now (1887) sixteen, most of which are managed by 'House Fathers,' who are 'Brothers of the Inner Mission' trained at Hamburg and Berlin. As temporary expedients they are interesting, because successful, experiments.

enough to prove effective. But private money would be, it is believed, subscribed in abundance if the Home Government framed, and negotiated with the colonies, a scheme to relieve that congestion of the labour markets which is the most pressing evil of the nineteenth century.

CHAPTER XX.

CONCLUSION.

It only remains to sum up the conclusions which have been formed.

The history of agriculture in this country traces the English system of land tenure to commercial or social exigencies which did not affect Continental nations. To these natural differences, rather than to artificial causes, is due the contrast in respect of land-ownership which England and the Continent present. What England lost in one direction she gained in another; she sacrificed the yeoman to the artisan.

Historically no substantial foundation exists for the cry that the English peasant proprietary was forcibly divorced from the soil. Still less does the history of any foreign country support the theory that the class can be created by the stroke of a pen. Nor can agricultural depression be attributed to our system of land-ownership. Whatever social and political advantages belong to a peasant proprietary, Continental experience shows that it is little less exposed to agricultural depression or foreign competition than the class of tenant farmers, and that its standard of farming can only be raised or maintained by a large outlay of public money, which in England is borne by private individuals.

The collapse of English agriculture must therefore be traced to other causes than conditions of land tenure. It commenced with inclement seasons, but it now springs from low prices arising out of foreign competition, cheap freights, over-production, and the increased purchasing power of gold. Where is the remedy to be sought?

Not in violent changes in conditions of land tenure; throughout the present crisis capitalist landlords have proved the saviours of the industry, and not an incubus on the soil. The paucity of their numbers should add no element of insecurity to their property, but it narrowly limits the range of practicable measures for their relief. As a remedy for low prices Protection fails. Continental experience shows conclusively that moderate import duties do not enable wheat to be grown at a profit. Even if Protection offered a remedy, it is unlikely to be applied. For every one man who says that bread is too cheap, there are a hundred who say it is too dear. Nor, again, is the remedy to be found in the reduction of the tithe rent-charge. Apart from the injustice of the demand, those interested in its existing application, and those desirous of its diversion to secular objects, are united to preserve the *corpus* of the property intact. Moreover, subject to the life interest of the Church, inviolable so long as religion is recognised to be a vital element in the well-being of society, the nation claims the reversion; and therefore it is a prime duty of the State to guard the property with jealous care.

If, then, the remedy is not nationalisation of the land, nor Protection, nor the reduction of the tithe rent-charge, what is it? Some of the causes of agricultural depression may be met by legislation, others spring from natural conditions which cannot be controlled; others may be removed or modified by agriculturists themselves.

To the first class belong such remedies as the following.

Land-law reform would increase the powers of life tenants to promote high farming, which hitherto has never enjoyed a fair chance of proving its capabilities. Increased facilities to transfer or charge land by the establishment of land registries would increase its value for sale or mortgage, and, even if they did not extend the number of proprietors, would remove all artificial hindrances to the natural growth of small owners. At present land lies so far beyond the general public that the masses have little respect for, or desire to guard, the sanctity of real property. Financial reform demands the readjustment of local taxation, which, as a burden on agricultural land, has lost its original justification, and now imposes Protection taxes on Free Trade prices. In this connection it may be suggested that since the dead capital, in the form of realised personalty, preys upon the living capital employed in industry, and since the fall of prices increases the value of the first in proportion as it diminishes the value of the second, a reduction of the interest upon the National Debt from 3 per cent. to $2\frac{1}{2}$ is not inequitable, and would attract capital from consols to agricultural land by equalising the remunerative value of the investments. The extension of technical agricultural education, especially among labourers, and the efficient equipment of a Ministry of Agriculture, are so urgently needed as to be indispensable preliminaries to the successful growth of a peasant proprietary or a peasant tenancy. Finally, the present scale of differential railway charges excludes English farmers from home markets. Higher rates upon local traffic than for long distances, and artificial competition between rival companies where land and sea carriage are not equally available and where time is essential, place premiums on distance at the expense of proximity, protect foreign producers, and offer bounties to remote markets by placing home growers at an actual disadvantage in respect of costs of conveyance.

No legislation can transform those elements of agricultural depression which depend on natural causes. So far as the currency affects the question, the increased production of gold will, on the one side, diminish its purchasing power, and, on the other, restore its relative value to silver; while a decreased yield of the silver mines would deprive Indian corn producers of their advantages in the cost of production, and corn merchants of their speculations in rates of exchange. No other remedy, except the introduction of an international monetary standard, suggests itself for currency disturbances, though the issue of 1*l*. notes, payable to bearer on demand, might reduce the existing appreciation of gold, and, in the face of present prices, it might possibly prove good policy to suspend forced sales of silver on behalf of the Indian Government. Cheap freights immensely increase the stress of foreign competition. If trade revived, foreign goods would no longer arrive as ballast or for nominal charges, and hopeful signs are manifest that the long frost of commercial languor is breaking up. In the last quarter of 1887 everything rose; pig iron, coal, copper, tin, lead, wheat, barley, oats, rice, beef, mutton, cotton, jute, petroleum—all realised better prices.

But though legislative aid may mitigate artificial hindrances to agricultural revival, and though one of the natural causes which intensify the stress of foreign competition appears to be passing away, self-help affords the best aid to agriculturists. Too many farmers slumber in their empty corn-bins, dreaming of Protection. If they cannot revise the fiscal system, they can at least revise their practical ideas. The reduction of the size of holdings and of the breadths of corn cultivation seems to indicate that the country stands on the edge of a revolution in farming practices, such as characterised the sixteenth and eighteenth centuries. Small farms are easier to let than large holdings, more suited to reduced capitals, better adapted to new requirements. Agriculture, if it is to pay, has become a daily drudgery, which men who are worth 5,000*l.* are indisposed to undergo. Such a reduction in the size of holdings harmonises with the laws of progress which have been observed as characteristics in society and other industries. Although large farmers with sufficient skill and capital to adopt the best practices of the highest farming may hold their own, the problem of low prices appears to be best met by economical management, minute attention to details, and constant personal supervision. Diversified farming, which concentrates its efforts on stock breeding, rearing, and fattening, and the production of fresh perishable articles of food, can be pursued with profit upon small holdings, whether farms of 250 acres, or peasant tenancies of fifteen acres where no outlay is made for wages. Prices have undoubtedly fallen; but land, labour, stock, and all the materials of farming have fallen in proportion. Every county can produce instances of enterprising men who regard foreign competition in wheat as a fixed quantity, accept the new conditions, and force the land to pay at present prices. Agricultural depression, in the strict sense of the word, is over for those who are not lured by the will-o'-the-wisp of Protection deeper and further into the Slough of Despond.

If the change from tillage to pasture is unaccompanied by an extension of present holdings, the new departure which appears to be imminent must inevitably increase the amount of unemployed labour. If, on the other hand, it results in the multiplication of peasant holdings and in more direct relations between labour and land, a percentage of the displaced labour will become absorbed in small tenancies to the great advantage of rural society in general. Small farms supply those ladders of thrift, wider horizons, incentives to energy, and prospects of independence which are the great wants of their present condition. The best labourers may find employment upon the larger holdings. But for the rest, who are too unskilful or too numerous to secure permanent wages, the New World offers advantages for which the Old affords no parallel. The crisis is indisputably grave; revolutionary legislation is powerfully advocated, and the position of landlords completely isolated. Agricultural labourers possess the franchise at a stage in their civilisation which renders them an easy prey to unscrupulous agitators. The fatal germs of the Irish Land Act of 1881 have already borne fruit in the demands of the Farmers' Alliance, and in the land bills which have been successively put forward by English, Scotch, and Welsh farmers. At the first gleam of agricultural prosperity the cry for tenant-right will be renewed. Landlords have now the opportunity of removing legitimate grounds of discontent; of increasing the number of those who, as small occupiers, will be interested in the maintenance of landed interests; of reviving those cordial relations with their tenants which in times past made English agriculture the model and example for foreign nations; of striking from the hands of socialistic theorists weapons which are dangerous to the safety of society. The distinction between giving and giving up is vital. But here there is not even a question

R

of giving. Changes such as are suggested entail no surrender of rights, no sacrifice of pecuniary interests. On the contrary, they are dictated to landlords not merely by political prudence, but by commercial self-interest.

APPENDIX I.

A TABLE SHOWING THE AVERAGE PRICE OF WHEAT PER QUARTER FROM 1043 TO 1886.

A.D.	s.	d.	A.D.	s.	d.	A.D.	s.	d.
1043	5	0	1455	1	2	1649	80	0
1125	20	0	1460	8	0	1650	76	8
1196	13	4	1463	2	0	1651	73	4
1197	18	8	1486	24	0	1652	49	6
1237	3	4	1491	14	8	1653	35	6
1243	2	0	1494	4	0	1654	26	0
1246	16	0	1497	20	0	1655	33	4
1257	24	0	1499	4	0	1656	43	0
1258	16	0	1521	20	0	1657	46	8
1270	96s. to 128	0	1551	8	0	1658	65	0
1286	2s. 8d., but from a storm on July 20 it rose to 16	0	1557 Before harvest the price rose to	8 53	0 4	1659 1660 1661 1662 1663	66 56 70 74 57	0 6 0 0 0
1287	3	4	After harvest it fell to	5	0	1664	40	6
1288	1	6				1665	49	4
1294	16	0				1666	36	0
1315	20	0	1574	56	0	1667	36	0
1316	32	0	After harvest.	24	0	1668	40	0
1317	44	0				1669	44	4
1336	2	0	1587	64	0	1670	41	8
1349	2	0	1594	56	0	1671	42	0
1359	26	8	1595	53	4	1672	41	0
1361	2	0	1596	80	0	1673	46	8
1363	15	0	1597 80s. to	104	0	1674	68	8
1379	4	0	1641	57	1	1675	64	8
1387	2	0	1642	60	2	1676	38	0
1390	16	8	1643	59	10	1677	42	0
1401	16	0	1644	61	3	1678	59	0
1407	4	4	1645	51	3	1679	60	0
1416	16	0	1646	42	8	1680	45	0
1423	8	0	1647	63	8	1681	46	8
1434	26	8	1648	85	0	1682	44	0

Appendix I.—cont.

A.D.	s.	d.	A.D.	s.	d.	A.D.	s.	d.
1683	40	0	1729	46	10	1775	48	4
1684	44	0	1730	36	6	1776	38	2
1685	46	8	1731	32	10	1777	45	6
1686	31	0	1732	26	8	1778	42	0
1687	25	2	1733	28	4	1779	33	8
1688	46	0	1734	38	10	1780	35	8
1689	30	0	1735	43	0	1781	44	8
1690	34	8	1736	40	4	1782	47	10
1691	34	0	1737	38	0	1783	52	8
1692	46	8	1738	35	6	1784	48	10
1693	67	8	1739	38	6	1785	51	10
1694	64	0	1740	50	8	1786	38	10
1695	53	0	1741	46	8	1787	41	2
1696	71	0	1742	34	0	1788	45	0
1697	60	0	1743	24	10	1789	51	2
1698	68	4	1744	24	10	1790	54	9
1699	64	0	1745	27	6	1791	48	7
1700	40	6	1746	39	0	1792	43	0
1701	37	8	1747	34	10	1793	49	3
1702	29	6	1748	37	0	1794	52	3
1703	36	0	1749	37	0	1795	75	2
1704	46	6	1750	32	6	1796	78	7
1705	30	0	1751	38	6	1797	53	9
1706	26	0	1752	41	10	1798	51	10
1707	28	6	1753	44	8	1799	69	0
1708	41	6	1754	34	8	1800	113	10
1709	78	6	1755	33	10	1801	119	6
1710	78	0	1756	45	3	1802	69	10
1711	54	0	1757	60	0	1803	58	10
1712	46	4	1758	50	0	1804	62	3
1713	51	0	1759	39	10	1805	89	9
1714	50	4	1760	36	6	1806	79	1
1715	43	0	1761	30	3	1807	75	4
1716	48	0	1762	39	0	1808	81	4
1717	45	8	1763	40	9	1809	97	4
1718	38	10	1764	46	9	1810	106	5
1719	35	0	1765	48	0	1811	95	3
1720	37	0	1766	43	1	1812	126	6
1721	37	6	1767	47	4	1813	109	9
1722	36	0	1768	53	9	1814	74	4
1723	34	8	1769	40	7	1815	65	7
1724	37	0	1770	43	6	1816	78	6
1725	48	6	1771	47	2	1817	96	11
1726	46	0	1772	50	8	1818	86	3
1727	42	0	1773	51	0	1819	74	6
1728	54	6	1774	52	8	1820	67	10

Appendix I.—cont

A.D.	s.	d.	A.D.	s.	d.	A.D.	s.	d.
1821	56	1	1843	50	2	1865	41	0
1822	44	7	1844	51	3	1866	49	11
1823	53	4	1845	50	9	1867	64	5
1824	63	11	1846	54	9	1868	63	9
1825	68	6	1847	69	5	1869	48	2
1826	58	8	1848	50	6	1870	46	11
1827	58	6	1849	44	6	1871	56	8
1828	60	5	1850	40	4	1872	57	0
1829	66	3	1851	38	7	1873	58	8
1830	64	3	1852	41	0	1874	55	9
1831	66	4	1853	53	3	1875	45	1
1832	58	8	1854	72	7	1876	46	2
1833	52	11	1855	74	9	1877	56	9
1834	46	2	1856	69	2	1878	46	5
1835	39	4	1857	56	4	1879	43	10
1836	48	9	1858	44	2	1880	44	4
1837	55	10	1859	43	9	1881	45	4
1838	64	4	1860	53	3	1882	45	1
1839	70	6	1861	55	4	1883	41	7
1840	66	4	1862	55	5	1884	35	8
1841	64	5	1863	44	9	1885	41	2
1842	57	5	1864	40	2	1886	39	4

The prices down to 1652 are taken from Fleetwood's *Chronicon Pretiosum*; from 1653 to 1764 from Charles Smith's *Tracts on Corn Trade* (edit. 1804), pp. 125-7. These latter are unusually high, as they represent the prices of the best, and not the middling, wheat.

APPENDIX II.

LEGISLATION AGAINST PASTURE FARMS ON SOCIAL GROUNDS.

(a) In the 4th year of Henry VII. an Act was passed relating to the Isle of Wight, to prevent the mischief arising from throwing small holdings into one large farm. The Preamble recites :—

'Forasmuch as it is to the king, &c., great surety, and also the surety of this realm of England, that the Isle of Wight be well inhabited with English people, &c., the which isle is lately decayed of people, by reason that many towns and villages have been beaten down, and the Fields ditched, &c., and many dwelling-places, ferms, and ferm-holds taken into one man's hands, that of old time were wont to be in many several persons holds and hands, and many several households kept in them, and thereby much people multiplied, and the same isle thereby well inhabited ; the which now, by the occasion aforesaid, is desolate, and not inhabited, but occupied with beasts and cattle ; so that if hasty remedy be not provided, that isle cannot be kept and defended, but will be open and ready to the king's enemies, which God forbid :—For remedy whereof it is ordained,' &c.

(b) 4 Henry VII. c. 19 is more general. The Preamble recites as follows :—

'The king our sovereign lord having a singular pleasure above all things to avoid such enormities and mischiefs as be hurtful and prejudicial to the common weal of this his land, and his subjects of the same, remembereth that among other things great inconveniences daily do increase by desolation, and pulling down, and wilful waste of houses within this realm, and laying to pasture what customably have been used in tillage; whereby idleness, which is the ground and beginning of all mischiefs, daily doth increase. For where in some towns two hundred persons were occupied and lived of their lawful labours, now there are occupied two or three herdsmen, and the residue fall into idleness, that husbandrie, which is one of the greatest commodities of this realm, is greatly decayed, churches destroyed, the service of God withdrawn, the bodies there buried not prayed for, the patrons and curates wronged, the defence of this land, against our enemies outward, feebled and impaired, to the great displeasure of God, to the subversion of the policy and good rule of this land if remedy be not provided,' &c., &c.

APPENDIX III.

AGRICULTURAL WRITERS OF THE 16TH, 17TH, AND FIRST HALF OF THE 18TH CENTURIES.

The principal agricultural writers of England and Wales from 1500 to 1740 are given in the following list; but the list does not pretend to be exhaustive, nor are the editions to which the dates are affixed in all cases the first.

1523. Fitzherbert (Sir Anthony) *One of the Justices of the Court of Common Pleas.*
  1. Boke of Surveyeng. 1523, 4to.
  2. Boke of Husbandry. 1525, 4to.
1537. De Benese (Sir Richard)
  This Boke sheweth the maner of measurynge of all maner of land. Southwarke, 1537.
1573. Tusser (Thomas)
  Five hundredth points of good husbandry. London, 1573, 4to.
1574. Scot (Reginald)
  A perfite platforme of a Hoppe Garden and necessarie instructions for the making and mayntenaunce thereof. London, 1574, 4to.
  [This is the first treatise upon hops.]
1594. Plat, or Platt (Sir Hugh)
  The Jewell House of Art and Nature. London, 1594, 8vo.
1605. Mascall (Leonard)
  The Government of Cattell.
   Part I. The Government of oxen.
   Part II. The Government of horses.
   Part III. The ordering of sheep.
                London, 1605, 4to.

1607. Norden (John)
  The Surveyor's Dialogue. London, 1607, 8vo.
    &c., &c.
1610. Vaughan (Rowland)
  Most approved and long experienced Water Workes. Containing the manner of Winter and Summer drowning of Medow & pasture. London, 1610, 4to.
  [This is the first treatise on irrigation.]
1614. Markham (Gervase)
  1. The English Husbandman. London, 1614.
  2. Countrey Contentments, 2 parts. London, 1615, 4to.
  3. A Way to get Wealth, 6 parts. London, 1638.
  4. Complete Farriar. London, 1639, 8vo.
    &c., &c.
1639. Plattes (Gabriel)
  A discovery of Subterraneal Treasure.
  (Not Agricultural but Mineral Works.) London, 1639, 4to.
1649. Blith (Walter)
  The English Improver ; or, A new survey of husbandry. London, 1649, 4to.
  [This is the first explanation of the science of drainage.]
1650. Weston (Sir Richard)
  A Discourse of Husbandrie used in Brabant and Flanders. (Edited by S. Hartlib.) London, 1650, 4to.
  [This is the first attempt to explain the cultivation of turnips.]
1650. Hartlib (Samuel)
  1. A discourse of Husbandrie used in Brabant and Flanders. London, 1650, 4to.
  2. Samuel Hartlib his Legacie ; or an enlargement of the Discourse of Husbandry. London, 1651, 4to.
  3. A Design for plentie by an universall planting of fruit-trees. London, 1652, 4to.
  4. The Compleat Husbandman. London, 1659, 4to.
    &c., &c.

1656. Lee (Joseph) Rev.
  Ευταξια του Αγρου ; or, a vindication of a regulated inclosure. London, 1656, 4to.

1659. Speed (Adolphus)
  Adam out of Eden, or an abstract of divers excellent experiments touching the advancement of Husbandry. London, 1659, 8vo.

1661. Stevenson (Matthew)
  The Twelve Moneths ; or, a discourse of every action proper to each particular moneth. London, 1661, 4to.

1662. Miles (Abraham)
  The Countryman's Friend and no . . . Mountebank, but a rare method of Chirurgery and physick. London, 1662, 8vo.

1664. Forster (John), of Hanslop, Bucks.
  England's Happiness increased ; or a sure and easie remedy against all succeeding dear years ; by a plantation of the roots called potatoes. London, 1664, 4to.
  [This is the first treatise upon potatoes. The cultivation of the root was practically little known till the end of the eighteenth century, when it was zealously advocated by the Board of Agriculture.]

1669. Worlidge (John)
  Systema Agriculturæ ; the mystery of husbandry discovered. London, 1669, fol.

1670. Reeve (Gabriel)
  Directions left by a gentleman to his sons for the improvement of barren and heathy land in England and Wales. London, 1670, 4to.

1673. Smith (John) Captain, late a London merchant.
  England's Improvement revis'd in a Treatise of all manner of Husbandry and Trade by Land and Sea. London, 1673, 4to.

1677. Yarranton (Andrew)
  England's improvement by sea and land, 2 parts. London, 1677–81, 4to.

APPENDIX III.   251

1681. Houghton (John), F.R.S.
  1. A Collection of Letters for the improvement of Husbandry and Trade. London, 1681-3, 4to.
  2. An Account of the Acres and Houses with the Proportional Tax, &c., of each county in England and Wales. London, 1693, s. sh. fol.
1685. Moore (Sir Jonas)
  1. History of the Great Level of the Fennes. London, 1685, 8vo.
  2. England's Interest, or the Gentleman and Farmer's friend, 2nd edition. London, 1703, 12mo.
1697. Meager (Leonard)
  The Mystery of Husbandry; or, arable pasture and wood-land improved. To which is added the Countryman's Almanack. London, 1697, 12mo.
1708. Mortimer (John)
  The Whole Art of Husbandry, 2 parts. London, 1708, 8vo.
1717. Jacob (Giles)
  The Country Gentleman's Vade Mecum. London, 1717, 12mo.
1724. Bradley (Richard)
  1. A treatise concerning the manner of fallowing ground. 1724, 8vo.
  2. A collection for the improvement of husbandry. 1727, 8vo.
  3. A complete book of husbandry, &c. 1727, 8vo.
1731. Tull (Jethro), of Shalborn, near Hungerford, in Berkshire, was a man of great inventive genius as well as scientific attainments. He advocated deep cultivation, drilling seed, small sowings, hoeing turnips. He also invented a variety of implements, such as ploughs, hoes, drills, &c.
  The new horse-houghing husbandry. 1731, 4to.
1731. Ellis (William), of Little Gaddesden, Hertfordshire.
  1. The Practical Farmer. London, 1731, 8vo.
  2. Chilton and Vale Farming. London, 1733, 8vo.
  3. A complete system of Improvements. London, 1749, 8vo.
           &c., &c.

APPENDIX IV.

THE CORN LAWS.

The English corn laws at different times aimed at three principal objects :—(1) Abundance and low profits. (2) Revenue. (3) Encouragement of tillage and agriculture by raising prices to an artificial height.

(1) The first object was secured by absolute prohibition of exportation, which was the policy of the Legislature from the Norman Conquest to 1329, or by compulsory sales of produce for what it would fetch at the nearest market, and laws directed against engrossers or corn-dealers.

The first object was gradually exchanged for the third, and the necessity of maintaining the rural population [1] or strengthening the navy forms the transition stage between the prohibition of exports and protection. The laws against engrossing, &c., were modified in 1663, when internal corn-dealing was permitted, and repealed in 1773.

(2) The second object governed the legislation of 1660, but was speedily abandoned.

(3) Encouragement of tillage and agriculture was the object of the Legislature, with certain exceptions, from the fourteenth to the nineteenth century.

The following are the principal Acts relating to corn :—

Year	Statute	Provisions	Price of Wheat at date
			s. *d.*
1323	17 Ed. II. c. 3	Permitting importation of corn from Ireland into England.	7 5¾
1329	3 Ed. III.	Prohibiting importations of corn into England unless the prices of a quarter of wheat, rye, or barley exceeded respectively 6s. 8d., 4s., and 3s.	6 6⅝

---

[1] Compare Appendix II. (*a*) and (*b*).

Appendix IV.—cont.

Year	Statute	Provisions	Price of Wheat at date
			s. d.
1436	15 Hen. VI. c. 2	Permitting exportation of corn from England when a quarter of wheat, barley, and rye did not exceed respectively 6s. 8d., 3s., and 4s.	1 10 (Fleetwood). In modern money
1463	3 Ed. IV. c. 2	Prohibiting importation absolutely except when prices of home produce rose above the point at which exportation ceased.	3 8 (Dr. Smith)
1562	5 Eliz. c. 5	An Act for the Maintenance of the Navy permitted exports at and under the following prices per quarter:— Wheat, 10s.; rye, beans, and peas, 8s.; barley, 6s. 8d.	
1571	13 Eliz. c. 13	Act for the Encrease of Tyllage, permitting exportation of corn from particular districts, subject to payment of 1s. duty.	
1593	35 Eliz. c. 7	Permitting exportation, subject to tonnage and poundage of 2s. per quarter for wheat and proportionate duty for other grains, when wheat exceeded 20s., rye, etc. 13s. 4d., barley 12s.	18 4½
1660	12 Car. II. c. 4	Attempted to raise revenue by permitting imports and exports subject to high duties.	56 6
1663	15 Car. II. c. 7	An Act for the Encouragement of Trade— (i) Permitted engrossing, i.e. buying in one market to sell in another when wheat was at or under 48s., and other grain in proportion. (ii.) Took off the high duties on importation, and imposed an ad valorem duty in their stead. (iii.) Permitted exportation of wheat (subject to a reduced duty of 5s. 4d. per quarter) when wheat was at or under 48s., and other grain in proportion.	41 8
1670	2 Car. II. c. 13	Act for the Improvement of Tillage and the Breed of Cattle— (a) Permitted importation of wheat subject to a duty of 8s. per quarter when wheat was between 53s. 4d. and 80s., and 16s. per quarter when below 53s. 4d.	37 0½

Appendix IV.—cont.

Year	Statute	Provisions	Price of Wheat at date
			s. d.
1670	2 Car. II. c. 13	(*b*) Prohibited exportation when the home price of wheat was 53*s*. 4*d*. or above it. Other grain in proportion.	
1688[1]	1 Wm. & Mary, c. 12	Bounties were offered of 5*s*. on every exported quarter of wheat when the prices were at or below 48*s*. 2*s*.6*d*. per qr. of barley or malt ,, 24*s*. 3*s*. 6*d*. ,, rye, beans, or peas ,, 32*s*. 2*s*. 6*d*. ,, oats or oatmeal ,, 15*s*. Imports continued to be governed by the Act of 1670. This Act remained in force till 1773, but it was suspended during each of the following years:—1698, 1699, 1709, 1741, 1756, 1757, 1759, 1765-67, 1768-69, 1771, 1773	46 8
1757	30 Geo. II. c. 7	Imports allowed duty free till August 25, 1757.	60 0
1766	6 Geo. III. c. 3 & 4	Permitted importation of wheat, oats, and oatmeal from America duty free up to Michaelmas in that year.	43 1
1773	13 Geo. III. c. 43	Burke's Act— (1) Prohibited exports and abolished the bounty when the quarter of wheat was at or above 44*s*., of rye 28*s*., of barley 32*s*., of oats 14*s*.	51 0

[1] *Bounties paid upon Exports of Corn under* 1 *William & Mary from* 1697-1765.

Years	Wheat	Barley	Malt	Oatmeal	Rye	Amount of Bounties
	Quarters	Quarters	Quarters	Quarters	Quarters	£ *s. d.*
1697-1706	552,867	251,689	623,345	2,015	238,985	289,670 14 0
1706-1726	2,518,213	433,237	4,381,205	11,922	789,618	1,371,032 4 0
1726-1746	4,461,337	590,080	3,871,332	45,932	520,020	1,769,756 4 2
1746-1765	6,800,017	1,268,080	4,777,303	67,186	930,580	2,628,503 4 7
1697-1765	14,332,435	2,543,096	13,653,186	127,056	2,488,206	£6,058,962 6 9

Between 1765 and 1773 the law was almost continuously suspended. In 1773 Burke's Act was passed. In the next twenty-six years the imports of wheat (and of other grain in proportion) exceeded the exports. The following table shows the gradual decline of our export trade:—

```
1765-74 imports of wheat exceeded exports by 830,619 quarters
1775-84       ,,              ,,         ,,      605,747    ,,
1785-94       ,,              ,,         ,,      711,462    ,,
1795-99       ,,              ,,         ,,    2,349,830    ,,
```

Appendix IV.—cont.

Year	Statute	Provisions.	Price of Wheat at date
			s. *d.*
1773	13 Geo. III. c. 43	(2) Permitted exports and continued the bounty when prices were below the above limits. (3) Permitted imports of foreign grain at a duty of 6*d.* a quarter when home-grown wheat was at or above 48*s.*, and other grain in proportion. (4) Imposed the prohibitory duties of 12 Car. II. upon foreign produce imported below those prices. (5) Allowed foreign corn to be imported duty free for exportation.	
1791	31 Geo. III. c. 30	(1) Rearranged the scale of duties on imports, 6*d.* a quarter on wheat at or above 54*s.*, 2*s.* 6*d.* between 54*s.* and 50*s.*, 24*s.* 3*d.* below 50*s.* (2) Permitted wheat to be exported up to 46*s.* without bounty, and up to 44*s.* with bounty. (3) Provided proper registration of prices of grain.	48 7
1804	44 Geo. III. c. 53	Imposed higher duties on foreign imports, 6*d.* a quarter when home prices were at or above 66*s.*, 2*s.* 6*d.* between 66*s.* and 63*s.*, 24*s.* 3*d.* below 63*s.* It also permitted exports up to 54*s.*	62 3
1806	46 Geo. III. c. 97	Free export and import of corn permitted between Great Britain and Ireland.	79 1
1813	53 Geo. III. c. 33	The bounty was discontinued and unrestricted freedom of exportation allowed. Importation was permitted at the following duties for wheat :— 1*s.* a quarter at or above 80*s.*, and an increasing duty, with decreasing prices, till the duty on wheat imported at 64*s.* = 24*s.*	109 9
1815	55 Geo. III. c. 26	Mr. Robinson's Act, only passed under a protest from ten Peers, entered on the Journals of the House, prohibited the importation of foreign wheat till home prices stood at the following figures per quarter :— Wheat, 80*s.*; barley, 40*s.*; oats, 26*s.*;	65 7

Appendix IV.—cont.

Year	Statute	Provisions	Price of Wheat at date
			s. d.
1815	55 Geo. III. c. 26	rye, beans, and peas, 53s. British North American corn was admitted on a lower scale.	
1822	3 Geo. IV. c. 60	Another scale was fixed which was to come into force so soon as the limits stated by the Act of 1815 had been reached. Nominally a concession, the new Act increased Protection by loading corn with additional duties for the first three months after opening the ports.	44 7
1825		The home crop was so deficient that foreign wheat was admitted, irrespective of home prices, at a duty of 5s. per quarter.	68 6
1826		Foreign rye and oats were admitted at nominal prices.	58 8
1829	9 Geo. IV. c. 60	The sliding scale admitted foreign corn duty free, to be warehoused and consumed at home at the following scale of duties:— 25s. 8d. when home price was at or below 64s. 16s. 8d. ,, between 64s. and 69s. 1s. 0d. ,, at or above 73s. The system was found to encourage speculative trade.	66 3
1842	5 Vict. c. 14	Reduced the sliding scale, and admitted cattle and fresh provisions to be imported from abroad.	57 5
1843	6 & 7 Vict. c. 29	Reduced the duties on Canadian wheat to 1s. a quarter.	50 2
1846	9 & 10 Vict. c. 22	On and after February 1, 1849, foreign corn was admitted on the following scale:— (*a*) Wheat, barley, oats, rye, beans, peas, 1s. per quarter. (*b*) For meal of any of the same, 4½d. per cwt.	54 9
1869	32 Vict. c. 14, s. 4	Abolished these duties, which were in the nature of registration fees.	48 2

APPENDIX V.

ENCLOSURES.

The number of acres enclosed since 1700 probably exceeds 8¼ millions. The progress of the movement is shown below.

Reign or Date	No. of Bills	Acreage
Anne	3	1,439
George I.	16	17,960
George II.	226	318,778
George III.—		
(a) 1760–97	1,482	2,980,000
(b) 1797–1810	956	1,897,980
(c) 1810–20	771	1,410,930
1820–30	186	340,380
1830–40	129	236,070
1840–50	66	369,127
1850–86	—	about 800,000
Total, 186 years	3,835	8,372,662

The decline in the number of enclosures is apparently arrested in 1840–50; but 270,000 acres out of the total enclosed in that decade of years were enclosed under the General Act of 1845.

The agricultural statistics from 1866 to 1886 show an apparently large increase in acreage; but this is mainly due to fuller and more correct returns. It is also to be noticed that the area of agricultural land is being constantly diminished by the growth of towns, the increase of railways, roads, &c.

More than three-fourths of the total enclosures (6,288,910 acres) were made in the reign of George III.

APPENDIX VI.

QUESTIONS ATTACHED TO THE CIRCULAR LETTER OF THE BOARD OF AGRICULTURE (FEBRUARY 13, 1816).

1. ARE any farms in your neighbourhood unoccupied by tenants; and have landlords, in consequence, been obliged to take them into their own hands? Please to state the number of farms, and their size.

2. Have any tenants, within your knowledge, given notice to their landlords of quitting their farms at Lady-day, or any other period?

3. Have any farms been lately relet at an abatement of rent; and if so, what is the proportion of such abatement?

4. What circumstances, denoting the distress of the farmers, have come to your knowledge, which may not be included under the above queries?

5. Is the present distress greater on arable or on grass farms?

6. Have flock farms suffered equally with others?

7. Does the country in which you reside suffer from a diminished circulation of paper?

8. What is the state of the labouring poor; and what is the proportion of poor rates compared with the years 1811 and 1812?

9. What remedies occur to you for alleviating these difficulties?

APPENDIX VII. 259

TABLE 1.—*A Scheme of the Income and Expense of the several Families of England and Wales, calculated for the year 1688.*[1]

Number of families	Ranks, degrees, titles, and qualifications	Heads per family	Number of persons	Yearly income per family £ s.	Yearly income in general £	Yearly income per head £ s.	Yearly expense per head £ s. d.	Yearly increase per head £ s. d.	Yearly increase in general £
160	Temporal lords	40	6,400	3,200	512,000	80 0	70 0 0	10 0 0	64,000
26	Spiritual lords	20	520	1,300	33,800	65 0	45 0 0	20 0 0	10,400
800	Baronets	16	12,800	880	704,000	55 0	49 0 0	6 0 0	76,800
600	Knights	13	7,800	650	390,000	50 0	45 0 0	5 0 0	39,000
3,000	Esquires	10	30,000	450	1,200,000	45 0	41 0 0	4 0 0	120,000
12,000	Gentlemen	8	96,000	280	2,880,000	35 0	32 0 0	3 0 0	288,000
5,000	Persons in greater offices and places	8	40,000	240	1,200,000	30 0	26 0 0	4 0 0	160,000
5,000	Persons in lesser offices and places	6	30,000	120	600,000	20 0	17 0 0	3 0 0	90,000
2,000	Eminent merchants and traders by sea	8	16,000	400	800,000	50 0	37 0 0	13 0 0	208,000
8,000	Lesser merchants and traders by sea	6	48,000	198	1,600,000	33 0	27 0 0	6 0 0	288,000
10,000	Persons in the law	7	70,000	154	1,540,000	22 0	18 0 0	4 0 0	280,000
2,000	Eminent clergymen	6	12,000	72	144,000	12 0	10 0 0	2 0 0	24,000
8,000	Lesser clergymen	5	40,000	50	400,000	10 0	9 4 0	0 16 0	32,000
40,000	Freeholders of the better sort	7	280,000	91	3,640,000	13 0	11 15 0	1 5 0	350,000
120,000	Freeholders of the lesser sort	5½	660,000	55	6,600,000	10 0	9 10 0	0 10 0	330,000
150,000	Farmers	5	750,000	42 10	6,375,000	8 10	8 5 0	0 5 0	187,500
15,000	Persons in liberal arts and sciences	5	75,000	60	900,000	12 0	11 0 0	1 0 0	75,000
50,000	Shopkeepers and tradesmen	4½	225,000	45	2,250,000	10 0	9 0 0	1 0 0	225,000
60,000	Artisans and handicrafts	4	240,000	38	2,280,000	9 10	9 0 0	0 10 0	120,000
5,000	Naval officers	4	20,000	80	400,000	20 0	18 0 0	2 0 0	40,000
4,000	Military officers	4	16,000	60	240,000	15 0	14 0 0	1 0 0	16,000
500,586		5⅓	2,675,520	68 18	34,488,800	12 18	11 15 4	1 2 8	3,053,700
								Decrease	Decrease
50,000	Common seamen	3	150,000	20 0	1,000,000	7 0	7 10 0	0 10 0	75,000
364,000	Labouring people and out-servants	3½	1,275,000	15 0	5,460,000	4 10	4 12 0	0 2 0	127,500
400,000	Cottagers and paupers	3¼	1,300,000	6 10	2,000,000	2 0	2 5 0	0 5 0	325,000
35,000	Common soldiers	2	70,000	14 0	490,000	7 0	7 10 0	0 10 0	35,000
849,000	Vagrants; as gipsies, thieves, beggars, &c.		2,795,000 30,000	10 10	8,950,000 60,000	3 5 3 2	3 9 0 3 4 0	0 4 0 0 2 0	562,500 60,000
			So the general account is						
500,586	Increasing the wealth of the kingdom	5⅓	2,675,520	68 18	34,488,800	12 18	11 15 4	1 2 8	3,053,700
849,000	Decreasing the wealth of the kingdom	3¼	2,825,000	10 10	9,010,000	3 3	3 7 3	0 4 6	622,500
1,349,586	Neat totals	4 1/13	5,500,520	32 5	43,491,800	7 18	7 9 3	0 8 9	2,401,200

[1] *Political and Commercial Works of Charles Davenant*, collected and revised by Sir C. Whitworth, vol. ii. p. 184 (London, 1761).

TABLE 2.—*Numbers and Occupations of those who were engaged in Agriculture in England and Wales in* 1851, 1861, 1871, *and* 1881.

	1851	1861	1871	1881
Total Population	17,927,609	20,066,224	22,712,266	25,974,439
OCCUPATIONS				
(a) *In Fields and Pastures.*				
Farmers and graziers	249,431	249,735	249,735(a)	223,943(a)
Farmer's, grazier's son, grandson, &c., in the house	111,604	92,321	76,466(b)	75,197(b)
Farm bailiff	10,561	15,698	16,476(c)	19,377(c)
Agricultural labourers, shepherds, and cottagers	965,514	983,824	962,348(d)	870,798(d)
Agricultural students	104	190	760	728
Agricultural implement proprietors or workers	55	1,441	2,160	4,260
Land drainage service	11	1,761	1,255	1,695
Others engaged in agriculture	—	—	1,061	838
(b) *In Woods*				
Woodmen	—	—	7,855	8,151
(c) *In Gardens.*				
Market gardeners	—	—	112,786	65,882(e)
Florists, nurserymen	—	—	7,021	7,755
Domestic gardeners	—	—	(f)	75,188
			119,857	48,825

(a) Shows reduction of 25,964 in number of farmers, or 10 per cent.

(b) Shows a decline in the number of those who, having no other definite occupation, are practically agricultural labourers.

(c) Shows that tenant farmers are giving up holdings and becoming bailiffs.

(d) This decline of 10 per cent. is explained by increase either of agricultural machinery or of pastoral farms.

(e) Owing to difficulty of comparing returns based upon different methods, it is impossible to give the increase of market gardeners, but it seems to be considerable. The increase of florists, &c., is large.

(f) In 1871 a different reckoning was adopted from that of 1881. The sum-totals afford a comparison.

APPENDIX VIII.

TABLE 1.—*Estimated Production of Gold throughout the World from 1852 to 1875.*

(Paper handed in to the Committee on Depression of Silver, by Sir Hector Hay. No. 338 of Session 1876. Appendix, p. 25.)

Years	Average Annual Production in Quinquennial Periods £
1852–56	29,933,000
1857–61	24,633,000
1862–66	22,760,000
1867–71	21,753,000
1872–75 (4 years only)	19,200,000

TABLE 2.—*Estimated Production of Gold and Silver throughout the World in Quinquennial Periods from 1851 to 1880, and in the Years 1881 to 1884. (000's omitted.)*[1]

Years	Gold	Silver
1851–55	27,553	7,975
1856–60	28,745	8,144
1861–65	25,824	9,010
1866–70	26,770	12,051
1871–75	23,809	17,724
1876–80	24,105	22,052
1881	22,027	23,333
1882	20,492	24,921
1883	20,079	26,059
1884	19,530	25,740

[1] See *Report of Commission on Depression of Trade*, 1886 (11), xxiii, Appendix B, Table 5.

TABLE 3.—*Imports and Exports of Gold for the Years 1887-81. (In Thousands of Pounds, 000's omitted.)*

Year	Imports	Exports	Excess of Imports	Excess of Exports
1877	15,452	20,361	—	4,909
1878	20,872	14,969	5,903	—
1879	13,331	17,549	—	4,218
1880	9,459	11,829	—	2,370
1881	9,963	15,499	—	5,536
Total	69,077	80,207	5,903	17,033

TABLE 4.—*The following are the Money Systems adopted in the Principal Nations of the World.*

1. Gold System	2. Gold and Silver System	3. Silver System
England.	France.	Holland.
Australia and New Zealand.	Belgium.	Austria.
Germany.	Italy.	Russia.
Norway.	Switzerland.	Egypt.
Sweden.	Greece.	Japan.
Denmark.	Spain.	China.
Portugal.	Roumania.	India.
Turkey.	United States.	Mexico.
Persia.	Chili.	West Indies.
Brazils.	Venezuela.	
Argentine Republic.	Paraguay.	
Canada.		
S. Africa.		

APPENDIX IX.

Values of Imports of the Undermentioned Articles.

Years	Group 1. Beef, Mutton, Pork, Bacon, Hams, Eggs, Butter, Cheese, &c.	Group 2. Live Cattle, Sheep, and Pigs	Group 3. Fruit (Raw), Nuts (Edible), and Vegetables (Raw)	Group 4. Wheat and Wheat Flour	Group 5. Oats, Indian Corn, Barley, Meal, Hops, Rice, Sugar, &c.	Total of the Groups
	£	£	£	£	£	£
1866–70 (averages)	15,044,181	4,528,203	2,469,991	22,628,516	32,398,540	77,069,431
1871–75 (averages)	23,332,813	5,613,583	4,352,181	30,953,009	44,321,935	108,573,521
1875	28,039,220	7,326,288	4,619,238	32,380,726	47,653,103	120,018,575
1876	31,447,611	7,260,119	5,526,991	27,919,526	48,984,551	121,138,798
1877	31,227,346	6,012,564	6,776,858	40,694,119	55,587,495	140,298,682
1878	33,983,462	7,453,309	6,885,756	31,217,641	50,596,046	133,136,214
1879	33,645,153	7,075,386	7,182,739	39,970,120	49,130,312	137,003,710
1880	39,838,081	10,239,295	8,298,583	39,327,820	52,133,506	149,837,285
1881	39,650,098	8,525,256	5,976,106	40,736,754	49,950,198	144,838,412
1882	35,442,109	9,271,956	6,502,354	44,921,565	50,815,848	146,983,832
1883	40,792,229	11,983,751	6,753,148	43,799,259	54,192,407	157,520,797
1884	39,736,081	10,504,877	6,519,290	30,065,577	43,090,450	129,916,275
1885	38,110,303	8,734,754	6,009,119	33,736,358	42,162,070	128,752,604
1886	36,101,454	7,142,397	6,178,176	26,137,681	37,359,579	112,919,287

APPEN-

TABLE 1.—*Acreage under each Description of Crop, Fallow, and*

Description of Crop and Live Stock	1866	1867	1868	1869
	Acres	Acres	Acres	Acres
Corn crops	9,252,784	9,284,780	9,433,532	9,758,037
Green crops	3,562,434	3,498,163	3,385,866	3,575,067
Other crops—Flax	—	—	17,543	20,923
,, ,, Hops	56,578	64,284	64,488	61,792
Clover and artificial and other grasses in rotation	3,694,224	3,989,974	3,960,008	3,448,726
Permanent pasture not broken up	11,148,814	11,967,288	12,136,036	12,735,897
Bare fallow	964,937	922,558	958,221	738,836
	Number	Number	Number	Number
Live stock—Cattle	4,785,836	4,993,034	5,423,981	5,313,473
,, Sheep	22,048,281	28,910,101	30,711,396	29,538,141
,, Pigs	2,477,619	2,966,979	2,308,539	1,930,452
Horses used for agricultural purposes, unbroken horses and mares, kept solely for breeding	—	—	—	—

Description of Crop and Live Stock	1877	1878	1879	1880
	Acres	Acres	Acres	Acres
Corn crops	9,210,129	9,167,646	8,985,234	8,875,702
Green crops	3,584,846	3,491,010	3,554,318	3,476,653
Other crops—Flax	7,481	7,261	7,055	8,985
,, ,, Hops	71,239	71,789	67,671	66,705
Clover and artificial and other grasses in rotation	4,494,216	4,573,107	4,473,373	4,434,339
Permanent pasture not broken up	13,728,355	13,911,296	14,166,724	14,426,959
Bare fallow	616,147	632,403	721,409	812,566
	Number	Number	Number	Number
Live Stock—Cattle	5,697,933	5,738,128	5,856,356	5,912,046
,, Sheep	28,161,164	28,406,206	28,157,080	26,619,050
,, Pigs	2,498,728	2,483,248	2,091,559	2,000,842
Horses used for agricultural purposes, unbroken horses and mares, kept solely for breeding	1,388,582	1,412,502	1,432,845	1,421,180

APPENDIX X.

Grass, and Number of Horses, Cattle, Sheep, and Pigs, in Great Britain.

	1870	1871	1872	1873	1874	1875	1876
	Acres	Acres	Acres	Acres	Acres	Acres	Acres
	9,548,041	9,675,261	9,573,551	9,458,928	9,431,490	9,451,650	9,184,769
	3,586,730	3,738,180	3,616,383	3,576,486	3,581,270	3,664,107	3,574,249
	23,957	17,306	15,357	14,683	9,394	6,751	7,641
	60,594	60,030	61,927	63,278	65,805	69,171	69,999
	4,504,884	4,369,448	4,515,451	4,366,818	4,340,742	4,354,071	4,540,273
	12,072,856	12,435,442	12,575,606	12,915,929	13,178,012	13,313,621	13,515,994
	601,517	542,840	647,898	706,498	660,206	557,979	651,212
	Number	Number	Number	Number	Number	Number	Number
	5,403,317	5,337,579	5,624,994	5,964,549	6,125,491	6,012,824	5,846,302
	28,397,589	27,119,569	37,921,507	29,427,635	30,313,941	29,167,438	28,172,951
	2,171,138	2,499,602	2,771,749	2,500,259	2,422,832	2,229,918	2,293,620
	1,266,709	1,254,450	1,258,020	1,276,444	1,313,739	1,340,129	1,374,576

	1881	1882	1883	1884	1885	1886	1887
	Acres	Acres	Acres	Acres	Acres	Acres	Acres
	8,847,976	8,833,380	8,618,675	8,484,730	8,392,006	8,200,165	8,145,894
	3,510,568	3,475,660	3,454,579	3,487,703	3,521,612	3,480,480	3,463,706
	6,534	5,220	4,317	2,247	2,490	3,068	3,072
	64,043	65,619	68,016	69,258	71,327	70,127	63,706
	4,342,285	4,327,392	4,395,922	4,381,404	4,654,173	4,689,200	4,781,027
	14,643,397	14,821,675	15,065,373	15,290,820	15,342,478	15,535,279	15,671,395
	795,809	784,425	778,203	749,699	560,322	552,898	485,874
	Number	Number	Number	Number	Number	Number	Number
	5,911,642	5,807,491	5,962,779	6,269,141	6,597,964	6,646,683	6,441,268
	24,581,053	24,319,768	25,068,271	26,068,354	26,534,635	25,520,718	25,958,768
	2,048,090	2,510,402	2,617,757	2,584,391	2,403,380	2,221,475	2,299,323
	1,424,938	1,413,578	1,410,596	1,414,377	1,408,789	1,425,359	1,428,383

STATISTICS OF AGRICULTURE.

TABLE II.—*Acreage under each kind of Crop, Bare Fallow, and Grass, and Horses, Cattle, Sheep, and Pigs, in the Year 1887, in each Division of Great Britain; with the Totals for Great Britain.*

		ENGLAND, 1887	WALES, 1887	SCOTLAND, 1887	GREAT BRITAIN, 1887
		Acres	Acres	Acres	Acres
Total area of land and water		32,597,398	4,721,823	19,466,978	56,786,199
Total acreage under all kinds of crops, bare fallow, and grass [1]		24,922,052	2,831,155	4,862,097	32,615,304
Corn crops	Wheat	2,197,580	69,407	50,337	2,317,324
	Barley or bere	1,759,636	118,920	206,600	2,085,156
	Oats	1,768,123	255,434	1,064,432	3,087,989
	Rye	45,994	1,349	7,817	55,160
	Beans	349,673	2,078	18,963	370,714
	Peas	226,002	2,142	1,407	229,551
	Total	6,347,008	449,330	1,349,556	8,115,894
Green crops	Potatoes	369,243	40,570	149,839	559,652
	Turnips and swedes	1,419,268	70,487	482,532	1,972.287
	Mangold	351,588	7,764	1,338	360,690
	Carrots	14,468	459	1,115	16,042
	Cabbage, k.-rabi, & rape	145,690	1,343	6,640	153,673
	Vetches, &c.[2]	380,286	4,592	16,484	401,362
	Total	2,680,543	125,215	657,948	3,463,706
Clover, sainfoin, & grasses under rotation	For hay	1,708,719	175,119	441,120	2,324,958
	Not for hay	1,116,415	137,255	1,202,399	2,456,069
	Total	2,825,134	312,374	1,643,519	4,781,027
Permanent pasture or grass. Not broken up in rotation [3]	For hay	3,926,513	483,771	152,076	4,562,360
	Not for hay	8,619,990	1,445,375	1,043,670	11,109,035
	Total	12,546,503	1,929,146	1,195,746	15,671,395
Flax		2,746	56	900	3,702
Hops		63,706	..	..	63,706
Bare fallow or uncropped arable land		456,412	15,034	14,428	485,874

[1] Not including nursery-grounds and woods, and that part of the acreage of orchards and market gardens which is not devoted to any of the crops or grass mentioned in the above table.
[2] Except clover and grass, which are separately shown.
[3] Exclusive of heath and mountain land.

Appendix X.—Table II. continued.

		ENGLAND, 1887	WALES, 1887	SCOTLAND, 1887	GREAT BRITAIN, 1887
		Number	Number	Number	Number
Horses[1]	Used solely for agriculture	766,693	72,354	142,083	981,130
	Unbroken horses, and mares kept solely for breeding	330,509	67,774	48,970	447,253
	Total	1,097,202	140,128	191,053	1,428,383
Cattle	Cows and heifers in milk or in calf	1,841,664	282,686	411,930	2,536,280
	Other cattle { 2 years & above	1,160,887	131,934	266,252	1,559,073
	{ Under 2 years	1,021,164	282,617	442,134	2,345,915
	Total	4,023,715	697,237	1,120,316	6,441,268
Sheep	1 year old and above	9,930,719	1,804,465	4,411,065	16,146,249
	Under 1 year old	6,521,789	935,894	2,354.836	9,812,519
	Total	16,452,508	2,740,359	6,765,901	25,958,768
Pigs[2]		1,940,507	223,170	135,646	2,299,323

[1] As returned by *occupiers of land*.—Including ponies.
[2] The number of pigs is exclusive of those kept in towns, and by cottagers with less than a quarter of an acre of land.

APPENDIX XI.

TABLE 1 (a).—*The Land of England and Wales and its Products in* 1688. (*Davenant on Trade*, vol. ii. p. 219.)

	Acres	Value per acre	Rent
		£ s. d.	£
Arable land . . .	9,000,000	0 5 6	2,480,000
Pasture and meadow . .	12,000,000	0 8 8	5,200,000
Woods and coppices . .	3,000,000	0 5 0	750,000
Forests, parks, and commons	3,000,000	0 3 8	570,000
Heaths, moors, mountains, and barren land . .	10,000,000	0 1 0	500,000
Houses and homesteads, gardens and orchards, churches and churchyards	1,000,000	{ The land { The buildings	450,000 2,000,000
Rivers, lakes, meres, and ponds	500,000	0 2 0	50,000
Roads, ways, and waste land	500,000		
In all . .	39,000,000	about 6 2	12,000,000

TABLE 1 (b).—*An Estimate of the Live Stock of England and Wales in* 1688.

	Yearly breed or increase	The whole stock	Value of each besides the skin	Value of the stock
			£ s. d.	£
Beeves, stirks, & calves . .	800,000	4,500,000	2 0 0	9,000,000
Sheep and lambs	3,600,000	12,000,000	0 7 4	4,440,000
Swine and pigs .	1,300,000	2,000,000	0 16 0	1,600,000
Deer and fawns	20,000	100,000	2 0 0	200,000
Goats and kids .	10,000	50,000	0 10 0	25,000
Hares & leverets	12,000	24,000	0 1 6	1,800
Rabbits & conies	2,000,000	1,000,000	0 0 5	20,833
	7,742,000	19,674,000	0 0 0	15,287,633

TABLE 2.—*Arthur Young's Estimate* (1771) *of the* (A) *Area of Cultivation,* (B) *Capital employed by the Farmer,* (C) *Product of the Soil, and* (D) *Live Stock in England and Wales.*

(A) ARABLE STATE OF THE SOIL OF ENGLAND AND WALES.

Acres in all	32,000,000
Arable land	13,518,716
Grass	15,736,185
Wood	2,395,721

(B) CAPITAL EMPLOYED BY THE FARMER.

(i.) Stock in Husbandry.

	Number[1]	Rate	Value
		£ s. d.	£
Draught cattle	684,491	10 0 0	6,844,910
Cows	741,532	7 0 0	5,190,724
Fatting beasts	513,369	12 0 0	6,160,428
Young cattle	912,656	4 0 0	3,650,624
Sheep	22,188,948	0 15 0	16,641,711
Swine	1,711,200	0 12 0	1,026,720
Poultry	—	—	171,120
Total	26,752,196	—	39,686,237
Total of live stock, according to the proportion in stocking farms, 273*l.* to 100*l.* a year	—	—	61,152,000

(ii.) Dead Stock.

	£
Implements at 70*l.* per 100*l.* a year	15,680,000
Furniture ,, ,,	15,680,000
Total	31,360,000

[1] The number of the stock (swine excepted) is the actual number; the value is Young's conjecture.

(B) CAPITAL EMPLOYED BY THE FARMER—*continued*.

(iii.) Sundries.

Including seed, labour, &c. . . £51,520,000

(iv.) Recapitulation.

	£
Live stock	61,152,000
Dead „	31,360,000
Sundries	51,520,000
Total .	144,032,000

(C) PRODUCT OF THE SOIL.

Arable Crops.

Crops	Acres	Product per acre	Total product	Pe· quarter	Value
		Quarters.	Quarters.	s.	£
Wheat .	2,795,008	3 0	8,385,024	40	16,770,048
Barley .	2,623,885	4 0	10,495,540	20	10,495,540
Oats .	1,483,065	4 6	7,044,558	16	5,635,645
Peas .	513,369	2 7	1,475,935	26	1,918,714
Beans .	399,287	4 1	1,647,058	26	2,141,174
		£ s. d.			
Turnips .	1,711,228	2 2 5			3,629,228
Clover .	3,201,425	5 4 0			16,647,410
Total .	12,707,268	—	29,048,115	—	57,237,759

(D) CATTLE.

	Rate per head	Number	Total
	£ s. d.		£
Cows . . .	5 10 0	741,532	4,078,426
Sheep . . .	0 11 8	22,188,948	12,943,551
Fatting beasts . .	5 0 0	513,369	2,566,845
Young cattle . .	1 0 0	912,656	912,656
Swine . . .	0 15 0	1,711,200	1,283,400
Poultry . . .			171,120
Total . .	—	26,067,705	21,955,998

TABLE 3.—*The Proportion of Land cultivated for Different Purposes in England and Wales in 1808.*

(*An Inquiry into the State of National Subsistence.* By W. T. Comber. London, 1808. Appendix XXV.)

Crops.	Acres.
Wheat	3,160,000
Barley and rye	861,000
Oats and beans	2,872,000
Clover, rye, &c.	1,149,000
Roots and cabbages cultivated by the plough	1,150,000
Fallow	2,297,000
Hop-grounds	36,000
Nursery-grounds	9,000
Fruit and kitchen gardens cultivated by the spade	41,000
Pleasure-grounds	16,000
Lands depastured by cattle	17,479,000
Hedgerows, copses, and woods	1,641,000
Ways, water, &c.	1,316,000
Total cultivated area	32,027,000
Commons and waste lands	6,473,000
Total acreage of England and Wales	38,500,000

TABLE 4.—*Mr. W. Couling's General Statement of the Superficial Area of England and Wales in 1827.*

(Select Committee on Emigration, 1827. *Sessional Papers*, 1827, vol. v.)

Territorial divisions	Arable land and gardens	Meadows, pastures, and marshes	Uncultivated improveable wastes	Unimproveable wastes	Total acreage
	Acres	Acres	Acres	Acres	Acres
England	10,252,800	15,379,200	3,454,000	3,256,400	32,342,400
Wales	890,570	2,226,430	530,000	1,105,000	4,752,000
Total	11,143,370	17,605,630	3,984,000	4,361,400	37,094,400

TABLE 5.—*Total Acreage under each kind of Crop, Bare Fallow, and Grass; Total Acreage of Orchards, Market Gardens, Nursery-grounds, and Woods; and Number of each kind of Live stock in Great Britain in each of the Years 1867, 1877, 1887.*

		1867	1877	1887
		Acres	Acres	Acres
Total acreage under all kinds of crops, bare fallow, and grass		29,744,590	31,712,413	32,615,304
Total acreage of permanent pasture		11,967,288	13,728,355	15,671,395
Total acreage of arable land		17,777,302	17,984,058	16,943,909
Corn crops	Wheat	3,367,876	3,168,540	2,317,324
	Barley or bere	2,259,164	2,417,588	2,085,156
	Oats	2,750,487	2,754,179	3,087,989
	Rye	52,865	60,146	55,160
	Beans	536,298	497,879	370,714
	Peas	318,090	311,797	229,551
	Total	9,284,780	9,210,129	8,145,894
Green crops	Potatoes	492,217	512,471	559,652
	Turnips and swedes	2,173,850	2,073,455	1,972,287
	Mangold	258,126	358,055	360,690
	Carrots	15,923	15,953	16,042
	Cabbage, kohl-rabi, & rape	133,692	182,710	153,673
	Vetches & other green crops	424,355	442,202	401,362
	Total	3,498,163	3,584,846	3,463,706
Clover, sainfoin, and grasses under rotation		3,989,974	4,494,216	4,781,027
Flax		17,543	7,481	3,702
Hops		64,284	71,239	63,706
Bare fallow, or uncropped arable land		922,558	616,147	485,874
Orchards, or fruit-trees of any kind		148,221	163,290	202,234
Market gardens		36,204	37,849	62,666
Nursery-grounds		11,779	11,952	12,478
Woods and plantations		2,187,078	2,187,078	2,458,300

Appendix XI.—continued.

		1867	1877	1887
		Number	Number	Number
Horses	Used solely for agriculture	965,515	970,786	981,130
	Unbroken horses & mares kept solely for breeding	301,194	417,796	447,253
	Total	1,266,709	1,388,582	1,428,383
Cattle	Cows and heifers in milk or in calf	2,038,092	2,207,017	2,536,280
	Other cattle: 2 years old and above	1,266,753	1,464,317	1,559,073
	Ditto under 2 years old	1,688,189	2,026,599	2,345,915
	Total	4,993,034	5,697,933	6,441,268
Sheep	1 year old and above	18,449,005	18,145,205	16,146,249
	Under 1 year old	10,470,096	10,015,959	9,812,519
	Total	28,919,101	28,161,164	25,958,768
Pigs		2,966,979	2,498,728	2,299,323

APPENDIX XII.

Return showing Price of Wheat per English Quarter in France, Belgium, and Prussia in the Years 1835, 1845, 1855, and 1885, and the Import Duties on Wheat per English Quarter in the same Countries at the same periods (so far as can be given).

Countries	Price per English Quarter				Import Duty per English Quarter			
	1835	1845	1855	1885	1835	1845	1855	1885
	s. d.	s. d.	s. d.	s. d.	s. d.	s. d.	s. d.	s. d.
France	35 2	45 9	47 2	39 1	sliding scale	do.	do.	1 0½ to 7 May 1885 5 3 after 7 May 1885
Belgium	33 7	46 8	77 1	38 3	8 0	0 4	free	free
Prussia	23 2	35 4	60 0	35 0	no information		2 8	2 2 to 20 Feb. 1885 6 6 after 20 Feb. 1885
England	39 4	50 10	74 8	41 2	sliding scale	do.	free	free

APPENDIX XIII.

TABLE 1.—*Rates in* 1803, 1815, 1827, *and* 1841.

	£
(1) In 1803 the total burden of the rates was	5,848,000
(2) In 1815 ,, ,, ,,	8,164,000
(3) In 1827 ,, ,, ,,	9,489,687
(4) In 1841 ,, ,, ,,	11,187,027

(1) and (2) No figures for the earlier years will supply the items in detail. But for the two latter years the information is more detailed.

(3) 1827—

	£
1. Poor and county rates	7,803,465
2. Highway rates	1,121,834
3. Church rates	564,388
Total	£9,489,687

(4) 1841— (A) DIRECT TAXATION (Rates).

	£
1. Poor rate	5,690,151
2. County and police rate	963,223
3. Highway rate	1,169,891
4. Church rate	506,812
5. Borough rate	246,743
6. Sewer rate (Metropolitan)	75,000
	£8,651,820

(B) INDIRECT TAXATION (Tolls, Fares, and Dues).

Brought forward		£	£8,651,820
1. Borough tolls		172,911	
2. City of London		188,521	
3. Turnpike tolls		1,348,084	
4. Light dues		243,023	
5. Port dues		525,000	
6. Fees in administration of justice		57,668	
			£2,555,207
Total			£11,187,027

TABLE 2.—*Local Taxation in 1873 and 1885 (omitting purely Urban and Metropolitan).*

Urban and Rural	1873	1885
	£	£
Poor Law authorities (extra-Metropolitan)	6,299,124	6,078,942
Burial boards ,,	122,923	168,327
School boards ,,	187,444	1,320,923
Churchwardens (Church rate)	9,246	3,616
County authorities	1,798,487	2,008,048
Commissioners of Sewers	48,724	61,460
Drainage, Embankment, and Conservancy boards	196,962	214,256
Total	8,663,610	9,855,592

Rural		
Highway authorities	1,514,758	1,589,995
Rural Sanitary authorities	174,286	313,724
Inspectors under Lighting and Watching Act (2 & 3 Wm. IV. c. 90)	27,807	22,807
Total	1,716,851	1,926,526
Total Urban and Rural, and Rural	10,380,461	11,782,098

APPENDIX XIV.

ALLOTMENTS IN ENGLAND AND WALES.

THE number of agricultural labourers, farm servants, and cottagers (not including females and shepherds) in England and Wales is 807,608 persons.

The following table shows—(1) How many labourers have (*a*) potato-grounds ; (*b*) cow-runs, whether general or definite (and in the latter case the acreage). (2) The number and size of allotments, whether field gardens or attached to cottages, from under $\frac{1}{8}$ of an acre to 4 acres.

In this table no allotments given by railway companies to their servants are included. Throughout the table the English counties, in which the allotments, &c., are situated, have been classified in four divisions :

I. EASTERN AND NORTH-EASTERN, including Bedford, Cambridge, Essex, Herts, Hunts, Lincoln, Norfolk, Suffolk, East Riding of Yorkshire.

II. SOUTH-EASTERN AND EAST MIDLAND, including Berks, Bucks, Hants, Kent, Leicester, Middlesex, Northants, Notts, Oxford, Rutland, Surrey, Sussex, Warwick.

III. WEST MIDLAND AND SOUTH-WESTERN, including Cornwall, Devon, Dorset, Gloucester, Hereford, Monmouth, Shropshire, Somerset, Wilts, Worcester.

IV. NORTH AND NORTH-WESTERN, including Chester, Cumberland, Derby, Durham, Lancaster, Northumberland, Stafford, Westmoreland, North and West Ridings of Yorkshire.

The first two constitute the corn division ; the last two the grazing division of the country.

APPENDIX XIV.

Appendix XIV.—continued.

Counties	No. of Labourers having Ground for Potatoes	Labourers having Cow-runs — General Run for Cow	Labourers having Cow-runs — Debite Quantity of Land	Total Acreage in latter case	No. of Allotments or Field Gardens not exceeding 4 Acres in extent detached from Cottages in England and Wales — Under ¼ of Acre	Of ¼ and under ½	Of ½ and under 1 Acre	Of 1 to 4 Acres	Average Distance from Cottages — Not exceeding ½ a mile	Average Distance from Cottages — Over ½ but under 1 mile	Average Distance from Cottages — Over 1 mile	No. of Garden Allotments attached to Cottages held by Labourers, &c., of extent ⅛ of an Acre	Average Yearly Rental including Cottage
I. E. & N.-E.	19,144	1,099	510	1,378	20,189	29,861	39,205	8,989				63,590	£ s. d. 4 5 6
II. S.-E. & E.M.	18,569	318	570	891	56,929	44,630	30,088	7,100				55,868	5 6 1
III. W.M.&S.-W.	30,660	519	810	1,383	24,122	30,843	26,033	7,650				71,681	4 7 9
IV. N. & N.-W.	11,672	2,169	1,359	2,016	27,026	11,153	8,493	8,438				39,177	5 9 1
Total in England	80,045	4,135	3,279	5,671	128,566	116,487	103,819	32,177	311,301	56,297	13,451	230,316	Average Rental for England } 4 17 1
Total in Wales	13,263	838	1,214	3,691	3,540	673	736	1,476	7,104	461	453	27,152	Average Rental for Wales } 3 13 11
Total in England & Wales	93,308	4,973	4,193	9,262	132,106	117,160	104,655	33,653	318,405	56,758	13,904	257,468	Average Rental for England and Wales } 4 5 6

APPENDIX XV.

Table of Agricultural Wages in England, 1824, 1836, 1860, 1870, 1881.[1] *It must, however, be noticed that this Table does not include Payments for Piece or Task Work, or Allowances.*

Divisions and Counties	Average Weekly Wages of Men				
	1824	1836	1860	1870	1881
I. *Eastern and North-eastern.*	s. d.	s. d.	s. d.	s. d.	s. d.
Bedford	8 7	9 6	10 3	12 0	13 0
Cambridge . . .	—	9 6	10 0	11 0	—
Essex	9 4	10 4	11 3	11 0	13 6
Hertford	9 0	9 6	10 0	12 0	13 0
Huntingdon . . .	—	9 6	10 9	10 6	—
Lincoln	10 2	12 0	13 0	14 0	13 6
Norfolk	9 1	10 4	10 7	11 6	13 6
Suffolk	8 3	10 4	10 7	11 0	13 6
East Riding . . .	11 8	12 0	13 6	—	17 6
Average . . .	9 5	10 3	11 1	11 7	13 10
II. *South-eastern and East Midland.*					
Berks	—	—	10 0	9 6	12 0
Bucks	—	8 0	—	—	14 0
Hants	8 6	9 6	12 0	10 9	—
Kent	11 9	12 0	12 0	14 0	14 0
Leicester	—	10 0	13 0	13 0	13 0
Middlesex . . .	—	10 6	—	—	—
Northants · . .	8 1	9 0	11 0	11 6	13 0
Notts	10 3	12 0	12 9	13 3	13 6
Oxford	—	9 0	—	—	13 3
Rutland	—	9 0	—	12 6	—
Surrey	10 8	10 6	12 9	13 0	16 0
Sussex	9 7	10 7	11 8	12 0	16 0
Warwick	8 10	10 0	10 9	12 6	16 0
Average . . .	9 8	10 0	11 9	12 2	14 0

[1] The materials from which these Tables of Wages and also that of Prices (Table 3) are principally compiled are Mr. Purdy's paper on

Appendix XV.—continued.

Divisions and Counties	Average Weekly Wages of Men									
	1821		1836		1860		1870		1881	
	s.	d.	s.	d.	s.	d.	s.	d.	s.	d.
III. *West Midland and South-western.*										
Cornwall	—		10	0	11	0	11	0	—	
Devon	7	6	8	0	9	2	10	9	13	6
Dorset	6	11	7	6	9	4	11	0	12	6
Gloucester	9	3	9	0	9	5	10	9	12	6
Hereford	7	1	8	0	9	0	10	3	14	0
Monmouth	10	1	10	6	11	8	13	6	12	0
Shropshire	8	10	9	0	10	0	11	9	14	6
Somerset	8	2	8	8	10	0	10	6	13	0
Wilts	7	7	8	0	9	6	10	9	12	0
Worcester	8	2	9	6	10	0	11	0	—	
Average	8	2	8	10	9	1	11	1	13	0
IV. *North and North-western.*										
Chester	10	8	13	0	11	8	13	6	15	6
Cumberland	12	3	12	0	15	0	15	9	18	0
Derby	10	10	12	0	12	0	14	0	13	6
Durham	11	6	12	0	14	3	16	0	18	0
Lancashire	—		—		—		15	9	17	6
Northumberland	11	5	12	0	14	0	16	0	18	0
Stafford	10	8	12	0	12	6	13	0	—	
Westmoreland	12	0	12	0	14	3	16	4	—	
Yorkshire, North Riding	10	3	12	0	13	6	14	6	17	6
„ West Riding	12	6	12	0	13	6	16	0	17	6
Average	11	3	12	1	13	3	15	2	16	10

Agricultural Wages (Statistical Society, vol. xxiv.); the Evidence before the Agricultural Commissions of 1833, 1836, and 1879-81; the Return of Agricultural Earnings (*Parliamentary Papers*, No. 14, Sess. 1861); the Labour Statistics Return of Wages (*Parliamentary Papers*, 1887, c. 5,172); Mr. Giffen's Presidential Address on the Progress of the Working Classes in the last Half-century (*Statistical Society*, vol. xlvi.); Evidence before the Lords Committee on the Poor, 1830-31; and the Reports of the Poor Law Commissioners, *passim*.

APPENDIX XVI.

Table 1.—*Arthur Young's Calculations of Wages and Prices.*[1]

1. The average wages of agricultural labourers, taking into account extra pay at harvest and haymaking, and commuting food allowances in money, is—in the South and East, 7*s.* 10*d.*; in the North, 7*s.* 1*d.* He adds that in the former case wages had risen by a quarter in the last eighteen years.

2. Prices of provisions, &c. :—

	£	*s.*	*d.*
Bread, per lb.	0	0	1¼
Butter ,,	0	0	6½
Cheese ,,	0	0	3¼
Butcher's meat, per lb.	0	0	3½
House rent, yearly	2	0	0
Firing ,,	1	6	0

Table 2.—*Prices*[2] *of Articles of Food, &c., in* 1815, 1836, 1860, 1887.

Articles		Years							
		1815		1836		1860		1887	
		s.	*d.*	*s.*	*d.*	*s.*	*d.*	*s.*	*d.*
Bread	per 4 lbs.	1	4	0	7½	0	7⅜	0	4½
Butter	per lb.	1	2	1	0	1	0	1	5
Cheese	,,	0	8½	0	7½	0	7¼	0	6
Bacon	,,	0	8½	0	7	0	9¾	0	7
Butcher's meat	,,	—		0	6	0	7¾	0	7
Tea	,,	6	0	5	0	4	0	2	3
Sugar	,,	0	9½	0	7	0	4¾	0	2½
Candles	,,	0	7½	0	6	0	6	0	4
Paraffine	per quart	—		—		—		0	2½

[1] *Eastern Tour* (1770), vol. iv., pp. 311–326; and *Northern Tour* (1771), vol. iv., pp. 293–313.

[2] If these prices appear high, it must be remembered that they are naturally greater when small quantities (as, for instance, ounces of tea) are purchased.

INDEX.

ACREAGE, tables of, since 1866, 264

Agricultural Holdings Acts, 217

Agriculture, Board of, inquiry made in 1816 by, 40, 90; questions appended to their circular letter, 258; their reports and recommendations on enclosures, 69

Agriculture, early systems of, 1; characteristics of, during the Middle Ages, 11; pursuit of, by the monks, 14; first revolution in, from tillage to pasture, 17; early literature of, 29, 248; condition of, in the seventeenth century, 31; general view of, in the eighteenth century, 38–41; obstacles to the advance of, 55; second revolution in, from pasture to tillage, aided by manufacturing development, 64; effects of enclosure legislation on, 74; stimulus imparted to, by improved transport and communication, 78; scientific practice of, in the present century, 86; condition of, during the disastrous period of 1812–45, 87; progress of, from 1845 to 1873, 104; publication of statistics relating to, 113; the present collapse of, its causes, 115, 236; its remedies, 125, 128, 155, 237; effects of monetary disturbances on, 25, 38, 88, 90; French and English, compared, 132; improvements in English, all effected by private enterprise, 148; public teaching of, in France, 149; small number in England of those now occupied in, 158; bearing of the tithe-question on, 166; education in, required for England, 189, 238; need of a State department of, 195; discouraged by present railway rates, 197, 238; and by unfair incidence of local taxation, 201; signs of a third revolution in, to meat and dairy farming, 213; tables of statistics relating to, 264

Allotments, labourers', 231; table of, 277

Althorp (Lord), his devotion to agriculture, 79

American competition, 121

Arable farming, increased attention to, after the Revolution, 41

— land, first separation of, from pasture, 3; crops of, in the Middle Ages, 12

Aristocracy, mediæval, despised farming, 14

Aston Boges, old village customs at, 3; cultivation on the old system at, in the present century, 57

Australia, land registration system of, 184

Austria, agricultural education in, 191

BACON (LORD) on manure, 99

BAK

Bakewell (Robert), 49; his experiments in sheep and cattle breeding, 51
Balks, 5
Belgium, land tenure of, 142
Billyngdon (Thomas) yields his right of common, 27
Blith, advocates drainage, 33 *sqq.*; quoted, 31, 95, 115
Bolingbroke, his interest in agriculture, 78
Bones first used as manure, 80
Borders, 10
Bounty system, 41; table of amounts, &c., paid under the, 254
Bradley's description of Essex drains, 43
Burke, engaged in an agricultural experiment, 79
Butts, 5

CAIRD (SIR JAMES) recommends high farming, 105; obtains agricultural statistics, 113; quoted, 167; his estimate of rentals, 168 *note*
Camden's description of the Gloucestershire sheep-cots, 49
Cassel, farmers' conference at, 130
Castle Combe, Domesday survey of, 15
Cattle, old notions of breeding, 50; Bakewell's attempt to improve, 59; Mr. Coke's improvements in feeding and breeding, 80
Cattle plague in eighteenth century, 39; risk of, 212
Census, agricultural, for last four decades, 260
Chaucer (Geoffrey) quoted, 5 *note*, 9, 14
Chemistry, services of, to agriculture, 99, 109
Cheviot sheep improved on Bakewell's principles, 52
Church rates, 202 *sqq.*; tables of, 275
Civil wars, effect of, on agriculture, 32

COT

Clay lands, drainage of, 95
Climate, deterioration of, after 1764, 40
Clover, first successful cultivation of, in England, 32; field cultivation of, by Townshend, 46; ignorance respecting, 62
Coinage, condition of, in Tudor times, 25
Coke (Judge) prohibits enclosures at Stratford, 28
Coke (Mr., afterwards Earl of Leicester), his agricultural improvements, 79
Colling's (Chas.) Ketton cattle, 53
Common, rights of, their origin, 8; their threefold nature, 18; agreements made to extinguish, 19; example of their commutation by private contract, 27
Common-field system of husbandry, 3; its connection with the disturbances in Skye, 7; extent of its prevalence in 1794, 56; its condemnation and downfall, 65
Commons, enclosures of, commenced, 18; how effected, 26; prohibited by law at Welcombe, 28; Board of Agriculture's recommendations respecting, 70; a national necessity, 74; attended with suffering to the labourers, 74
Compensation for tenants' improvements, 216
Conquest, the, its effect on agriculture, 8
Corn, bounties on exports of, 41, 254; prices of, 12, 25, 26. See also Wheat, &c.
Corn laws, earliest, 21; table of, 252; condition of farming during the period of their greatest stringency, 87; abolition of, its effect on farming, 106; social, of Henry VII., 246
Corn-weeding in the Middle Ages, 11
Cotswolds, the, and sheep-cotting, 49; common fields in, at the end of the last century, 57

COU

County rates, 202 *sqq.*; tables of, 275
Crabbe's description of Suffolk, 43
Crag, a fertiliser used in Suffolk, 43
Crinon (Hector), his description of French peasantry, 136
Crustæ of land, 5
Currency questions, connection of, with agricultural depression, 116; metallic, of principal countries, 262

DAIRY and livestock farming, 221
Dales and dalesmen, 5
Deanston, Smith's thorough drainage experiment at, 97
Demesne land, 9
Denmark, land laws of, 143
Devon cattle, Scott's anachronism about, 53
Devonshire, absence of village communities in, 3
Dishley, stock-breeding at, 51
Distress between 1812 and 1845, 88; agricultural, connection of currency questions with, 116; self-help the best remedy for, 211
Doles, balloting for, 6
Domesday, New, 155
Drage, a kind of barley, 13
Drainage, advocacy of, by Blith, 33; works carried out in the fen district in the seventeenth century, 35; a doggerel poem denouncing, 35; Suffolk and Essex systems of, 43; provided for clay farms, 95
Drills, corn, 101

EDGEWORTH (MISS), popularity of her 'Essay on Irish Bulls,' 79
Education, agricultural, in France, 149, 190, 196; in other countries, 191; need of, for England, 189
Edward III. establishes the woollen manufacture, 22
Elkington (James), drainage system of, 96
Emigration, 234, 241

FEN

Enclosures, beginning of, 18; their effect on the peasantry, 20; high-handed, 26; an instance from Kennet's 'Parochial Antiquities,' 27; extent of, towards the close of the reign of George III., 38; profits derivable from, 68; recommendations of the Board of Agriculture respecting, 70; empowered by Acts of Parliament, 71; not followed by depopulation, 72; hardships caused to the labouring population by, 73; the gain to the nation, 74; increase of, in 1810-14, 89; table of, since 1700, 257
Erskine a student at Holkham, 82
Essex, bad roads of, 60

FAMINE, a frequent result of mediæval agriculture, 11
Farm work in feudal times, 10
Farmers, ignorance of, 59; force of traditional customs among, 61; effects of manufacturing development on their condition, 67; small freeholding or yeomen, suppressed, 83; distress among, after the war, 90; improved class of, 111; popular views of distress among, 115; effect of the depression on, 124, 159; foreign, present condition of, 129; importance of agricultural education to, 194; profession of, 214; their want of security for improvements, 216
Farming, characteristics of, in feudal times, 11; increased interest in, in the sixteenth century, 29; high, a consequence of free trade, 106; future of, 211; livestock and dairy, 213, 220
— common-field system of, 3; extent to which it prevailed towards the end of the eighteenth century, 56; necessity of its abolition, 65
Fens, drainage of the, in the seventeenth century, 34; opposition of the fenmen, 35; shock-

FEU

ing condition of the east and west fens in the succeeding century, 36
Feudalism, agriculture under, 9; emancipation of the land from, 37
Fitzherbert, writings of, 29; quoted, 5, 18, 19, 21, 45, 110
Flat, an ancient division of land, 4
Flemish wool-workers settled in England, 22
Fleta on trinity fields, 3; his estimate of wheat cultivation, 11
Fluke, disease in sheep, Fitzherbert's theory of, 29; extraordinary nostrum for, 59
Foreign competition, 121, 211; felt in other countries than England, 161; extent of, 211
Fortescue's reason for the English victories over the French, 15
Fothers, 5
Fox (C. J.), his interest in agriculture, 79
France, agriculture and peasant proprietorship in, 132; peasant life in, 136; land tenure of, 141; State aid to agriculture in, 149, 190; illustration of its practical working, 196; estimates of land distribution in, 158 *note*; métayage in, 228
Free trade, effect of, on farming, 106
Furlong, an ancient division of land, 4

GAME laws, 215
Gardening, revival of, in the seventeenth century, 31
Garstons, 3
Geology, services of, to agriculture, 100, 109
George III., farming tastes of, 79
Germany, depression of farming in, 130; agrarian legislation of, 142; agricultural education in, 191
Gilbert (Dr.), 109, 114
Gold, supply of, its relation to agricultural depression, 119; tables showing production of, 261

HUN

Gores, 5
Goschen (Rt. Hon. G. J.) quoted, 160, 205
Grain crops in the Middle Ages, 13
Grasses, artificial, culture of, 108
Gresley (Sir T.), cattle-breeding by, 52
Grey (John, of Dilston) establishes farming in Northumberland, 102
Guano, British, 99

HALSBURY (LORD), Land Bill of, 182, 184, 187
Hams, 6
Harrison quoted, 13 *note*, 26; his theory of sheep rot, 29
Hartlib, his remedy for fluke, 59; his enumeration of manures, 99 *note*; his notices of agriculture in the seventeenth century, 31 *sqq.*
Harvesting in the Middle Ages, 12
Harvests, bad, as a cause of the present depression, 121
Hawsted Manor in the fourteenth century, 11; lease covenant respecting manure at, 44
Hedges, prevalence of, in Devonshire, 3; construction of, in the eighteenth century, 7; Henry VII., laws of, against pasture farms, 246
Henslow (Professor) shows the use of coprolites for manure, 100
Heraldry, illustration of contempt for farming from, 14
Herefordshire, roads of, 60
Highway rates, 202 *sqq.*; tables of, 275
Holkham, Mr. Coke's enterprise at, 79; the sheep-shearings at, 82
Hooker (Richard) tending sheep in a common field, 5
Hops, introduction of, into England, 31
Horses, Suffolk, 42; State encouragement to breeding of, 195
Houghton recommends turnip cultivation, 33
Hundred Years' War, its effect on agriculture, 19

IMPORTS, agricultural, since 1866, table of, 263
Improvements, compensation for, 216
Ings divided into doles, 6
Ireland, ignorant agricultural practices in, 62

JOHNSTONE (JOHN), his work on drainage, 96

KENNET'S instance of a cession of common rights, 27
King (Gregory), his classification of the population in 1688, 158

LABOURERS, agricultural, wages of, in the seventeenth century, 32; in the reign of Henry VI., 25; table of weekly wages of, 279; early attracted to manufacture, 66; decline in number of, 111; effect of the depression on, 124, 159; past and present condition of, 224; how to secure small holdings for, 227; lodgings of, 230; allotments for, 231, 277; emigration for, 234
Lammas Day, land customs of, 5
Land, property in, *see* Property; agitation, the, 126; nationalisation of, 141; distribution of, in England and Wales, 155; decreased letting value of, 159; transfer of, by registration, 184; tables of crops and livestock on, since 1866, 264-7
— laws, reform of the, 181
— tax, 202
Landlords, effect of the agricultural depression on, 123, 159; a natural growth, 141; number of, in England and Wales, 146, 155; the real gainers by their losses, 160; need of agricultural education for, 193
Landowners, small number of, in England, 158
Landshires, 5

Lavergne (M. de), his estimate of land division in France, 158 *note*
Lawes (Sir John) obtains an artificial manure from bonedust, 100; his services to agriculture, 114
Leases, farmers', 58; Mr. Coke's, at Holkham, 82; want of security for improvements under, 216; under Lord Tollemache, 219
Leicester (Earl of). *See* Coke
Leicester sheep, 51
Liebig, agricultural chemistry of, 99
Lincoln Heath, value of enclosures shown on, 70
Lincolnshire, waste condition of, in former times, 44; change effected by the adoption of Townshend's system in, 45; value of improved farming shown in, 103
Local Government, abuses of, 208
Local taxation, 201 *sqq.*; tables of, 275
Lynches on the Wiltshire and Sussex downs, 2

MACHINES, agricultural, 109
Manors, lords of, origin of their rights, 8; division of the land of, after the Conquest, 9; as illustrated by the Domesday Book, 15; first enclosures by, 18; results of their withdrawal from the agrarian partnership, 20
Manure, bones first used for, 80; neglect of, in early agriculture, 98; researches of modern chemists on, 99
Markham (Gervase) quoted, 29, 25; his 'Farewell to Husbandry' quoted, 99
Marling revived by Lord Townshend, 45
Marshall, his theory of lynches, 1; discovers evidences of the wild-field-grass system, 2; his description of the Warwickshire ram, 50; quoted, 55, 60, 96
Mascall's theory of sheep rot, 29

MAS

Maslin, bread so called, 13
Meat, prices of, in 1843-6, and 1870-3, 108 *note*
Merton, statute of, authorises enclosures, 19; re-enacted, 22
Métayage, 228
Molesworth (Lord) wishes to make Tusser's poem a class-book, 30
'Monday men' tenants, 16
Money systems of the principal countries, 262
Monks, practice of agriculture by, 14; drainage of fen district by, 34
Moreton's leam, 35
Moryson, his 'Itinerary' quoted, 13

NANCY, decision of the Agricultural Congress at, 129
Naseby, late survival of the common-field system at, 57
New Zealand as an agricultural labourers' settlement, 234
Norfolk, Lord Townshend's agricultural improvements in, 44; roads of, 60; agricultural improvement of, effected by Mr. Coke, 80
Northumberland, farming in, 102

ODAMS, manure of, 100
Oxen, employment of, in farm work, 13
Oxgangs, 5

PARKES (JOSIAH), 98
Pasture, first separation of, from arable land, 3; tillage forsaken for, 22; return to, 64; legislation against farming, 246
Peasant proprietors, condition of, in France, 132
— proprietorship means extinction of Free Trade, 161; the agitation for, 128; not capable of flourishing universally in Britain, 131; socially advantageous, 138; not to be established by legislation, 139; incompatible with

PUN

the modern social system, 140; co-exists with landlordism on the Continent, 141; need of State aid to, as shown in France, 148
Peasantry, condition and obligations of, in feudal times, 9; improved condition of, after 1350, 14; disastrous consequences of sheep-farming to, 23
Pickering, Vale of, late continuance of the common-field system at, 57
Pightels, 5
Plat (Sir Hugh) on the origin of 'setting corn,' 100
Plot, his 'Nat. Hist. of Oxfordshire' quoted, 10, 33, 45
Ploughing in mediæval times, 10; in Suffolk, 43; examples of waste of power in, 61; by the tail, 62
Pole, local variations in length of the, 4
Poor law of 1733, 39; evils of the, during the war period, 75, 224
— rates, 202 *sqq.*; tables of, 275
Population, table of, in 1688, 259
Prices, fall of, in 1819-22, 93
Primogeniture, law of, 181
Property in land, 125; duty of the State to uphold, 147; how to cheapen and facilitate the transfer of, 182
Protection, historical associations of, 87, 163; encouraged gambling, 105; wretched system of farming under, 112; the creed of a peasant proprietary, 161; working of, abroad, 163; impossibility of reviving, in England, 166; local taxation of, persisting with Free Trade prices, 203; no remedy for the present depression, 211
Provisions, prices of, 281
Prussia, agrarian legislation of, 142; land registration system of, 186; agricultural education in, 191
Punches, Suffolk horses so called, 42

Pusey (Mr.), his Committee on Agricultural Customs, 103, 107; recognises need for tenant right, 112
Pykes, 5

QUARTLEY (Mr.), Devon cattle-breeder, 53

RAFFEISEN'S land-bank system, 227
Railway rates, revision of, in the interests of farmers, 197
Rainfall, increased, in the latter half of the eighteenth century, 40
Raps, 5
Rates, 201 *sqq.*; tables of, 275
Reed's drainage pipes, 98
Rigs, 5
Roads, bad, an obstacle to agricultural progress, 60
Rogers (Prof. Thorold), his 'Hist. of Agriculture and Prices' quoted, 11
Roots, culture of, 108
Roses, wars of the, their effect on agriculture, 21
Rothwell, common-field cultivation at, in 1797, 57
Rous (John) denounces sheep-farming, 24
Rupee, Indian, reduced value of, 120
Russia, agricultural education in, 192 *note*
Rye, cultivation of, in former times, 13
Ryeland sheep, 48

SALISBURY Plain, traces of extinct villages in, 1
Scott (Sir W.), his anachronism about Devon cattle, 53; 'Waverley' quoted, 51
Scragg's machine for making drainage pipes, 98
Seebohm, his theory of lynches, 2; his inquiries into manorial rights, 8

Serfs, 10
Shakespeare resists an invasion of his rights of common, 28
Sheep, diseases of, early theories as to, 29; rot in 1735, 39; cotting of, 48; diseases in, extraordinary nostrum for, 59
Sheep-farming for wool, *see* Wool; for meat, Bakewell's experiments in, 49
Shot, an ancient division of land, 4
Silver, depreciation of, 120; tables showing production of, 261
Skye, crofters of, in 1750, 7
Smith of Deanston, his system of thorough drainage, 97
Smithfield, sizes of cattle and sheep sold at, in 1710 and 1795, 53
Sologne district, reclamation of, 153
Southdown sheep improved on Bakewell's principles, 52
Sprengel, agricultural chemistry of, 99
Stewkley, common-field cultivation at, in the end of the last century, 57
Stillingfleet, his knowledge of grasses, 81
Stogoursey, late survival of the dual system of common-field husbandry at, 4, 7
Stratford-on-Avon, an enclosure prohibited at, 28
Suffolk, farming in, prior to Lord Townshend's agricultural reform, 42

TAXATION, local, 201; tables of, 275
Taylor (Samuel), on the use of corn drills, 101
Tenant-right, connection of, with improved farming, 112
Tenants' improvements question, 216
Tillage, reaction from pasture to, 64; abandoned for sheep-farming, 22
Tithe question, the, 166; to be solved by redemption, 173

TOL

Tollemache leases, 219
Tomkins's improvement of Hereford cattle, 53
Torrens Act, 184
Townshend (Lord), his system of husbandry, 42; receives the nickname of Turnip Townshend, 47; profitable results of his system, 47
Township described, 3
Tull (Jethro) on the field cultivation of turnips and clover, 46; quoted, 62
Tùn, the Anglo-Saxon, 3
Turnips, first successful cultivation of, in England, 32; field cultivation of, by Townshend, 46; ignorance and prejudice respecting, 62
Turnpike roads, 60
Tusser, his agricultural knowledge, 30; quoted, 6, 10, 31, 55, 65

UNITED STATES, agricultural competition of, with England, 121; Central Department of Agriculture in, 196 *note*

VETERINARY science in France, 152
Village communities, sites of the oldest, 1; farming system of, 3; imposition of feudal manors on, 8
Villein, status and duties of the, 9
Villeins' land, 9
Vines, ancient culture of, 13

WAGES, rates of, 12, 25, 32, 40, 279
Walpole (Sir R.), his interest in agriculture, 78
Webb (Jonas), his Babraham flock of South-Downs, 52
Webster of Canley, cattle breeding by, 52

YOU

Welcombe, failure of an attempted enclosure at, 28
Westminster, statute of, authorises enclosures, 19
Weston (Sir Richard) succeeds in cultivating turnips and clover, 32
Wheat, unsteady prices of, in the Middle Ages, 12; prices of, in the seventeenth century, 32; between 1713 and 1764, 39; foreign duties laid on, 41; cultivation of, established by Mr. Coke in Norfolk, 80; high prices of, in the early years of the present century, 88; importation of, from America, 121; not grown profitably under Protection, 163; minimum Protection for, 165; tables of prices of, in England, 243; in France, Belgium, and Prussia, 274
Wight, Isle of, pasture-farming forbidden in, 246
Wild-field-grass system of husbandry, 2
Wool, culture of, 21; its disastrous effects on the lower peasantry, 23; exportation of, forbidden, 41; value of English, 48
Worlidge recommends turnip cultivation, 33
Württemberg, agricultural education in, 192

YARDLANDS explained, 57
Young (Arthur), outline of his career, 62; denounces the open-field system, 65; his argument against small farmers, 74; his agricultural estimates for 1771, 269; his calculations of wages and prices for 1771, 281; quoted, 32, 55, 58, 59, 60, 70, 72, 73, 79, 95, 114, 139, 169, 215, 228, 232

THE BADMINTON LIBRARY.
EDITED BY
THE DUKE OF BEAUFORT, K.G. AND A. E. T. WATSON.

HUNTING. By the DUKE OF BEAUFORT, K.G. and MOWBRAY
MORRIS. With Contributions by the EARL OF SUFFOLK and BERK-
SHIRE, Rev. E. W. L. DAVIES, DIGBY COLLINS, and ALFRED E. T.
WATSON. With Coloured Frontispiece and 53 Illustrations on Wood
by J. STURGESS, J. CHARLTON, and AGNES M. BIDDULPH. Fourth
Edition. Crown 8vo. 10s. 6d.

FISHING. By H. CHOLMONDELEY-PENNELL. With Contri-
butions by the MARQUIS of EXETER, HENRY R. FRANCIS, M.A. Major
JOHN P. TRAHERNE, G. CHRISTOPHER DAVIES, R. B. MARSTON, &c.
Vol. I. Salmon, Trout, and Grayling. With Frontispiece, and 150 Illustrations of
Tackle, &c. Third Edition. Crown 8vo. 10s. 6d.
Vol. II. Pike and other Coarse Fish. With Frontispiece and 58 Illustrations of
Tackle, &c. Third Edition. Crown 8vo. 10s. 6d.

RACING AND STEEPLE-CHASING. RACING: By the
EARL OF SUFFOLK AND BERKSHIRE and W. G. CRAVEN. With a
Contribution by the Hon. F. LAWLEY. STEEPLE-CHASING: By
ARTHUR COVENTRY and ALFRED E. T. WATSON. With Coloured
Frontispiece and 56 Illustrations by J. STURGESS. Second Edition.
Crown 8vo. 10s. 6d.

SHOOTING. By LORD WALSINGHAM and Sir RALPH PAYNE-
GALLWEY, Bart. With Contributions by Lord LOVAT, Lord CHARLES
LENNOX KERR, the Hon. G. LASCELLES, and A. J. STUART-WORTLEY.
With 21 Full-page Illustrations and 149 Woodcuts in the Text by
A. J. STUART-WORTLEY, HARPER PENNINGTON, C. WHYMPER, J. G.
MILLAIS, G. E. LODGE, and J. H. OSWALD BROWN.
Vol. I. Field and Covert. Second Edition. Crown 8vo. 10s. 6d.
Vol. II. Moor and Marsh. Second Edition. Crown 8vo. 10s. 6d.

CYCLING. By VISCOUNT BURY, K.C.M.G. and G. LACY
HILLIER. With 19 Plates and 61 Woodcuts in the Text by VISCOUNT
BURY and JOSEPH PENNELL. Crown 8vo. 10s. 6d.

ATHLETICS AND FOOTBALL. By MONTAGUE SHEARMAN.
With an Introduction by Sir RICHARD WEBSTER, Q.C. M.P. and
a Contribution on Paper Chasing by WALTER RYE. With 6 Full-
page Illustrations and 45 Woodcuts in the Text from Drawings by
STANLEY BERKELEY, and from Instantaneous Photographs by
G. MITCHELL. Crown 8vo. 10s. 6d.

IN PREPARATION.

RIDING.	CRICKET.
DRIVING.	TENNIS, &c.
FENCING.	GOLF, &c.
BOATING.	YACHTING.

London: LONGMANS, GREEN, & CO.

BOOKS FOR THE COUNTRY.

A BOOK on ANGLING; or, Treatise on the Art of Fishing in every branch, including full Illustrated Lists of Salmon Flies By FRANCIS FRANCIS. Post 8vo. Portraits and Plates 15s.

The FLY-FISHER'S ETYMOLOGY. By ALFRED RONALDS. With 20 Coloured Plates. 8vo. 14s.

The SEA-FISHERMAN; comprising the Chief Methods of Hook and Line Fishing in the British and other Seas, and Remarks on Nets, Boats, and Boating. By J. C. WILCOCKS. Profusely Illustrated with Woodcuts of Leads, Baited Hooks, &c. New and Cheaper Edition (the Fourth). Crown 8vo. 6s.

The SCIENCE of AGRICULTURE. By FREDERICK JAMES LLOYD, Lecturer on Agriculture, King's College, London. 8vo. 12s.

ARTIFICIAL MANURES; their Chemical Selection and Scientific Application to Agriculture. By GEORGES VILLE. Translated and edited by W. CROOKES, F.R.S. With 31 Plates. 8vo. 21s.

HOW to MAKE the LAND PAY; or, Profitable Industries connected with the Land. By H. P. DUNSTER, M.A. Crown 8vo. 5s.

A TREATISE on the DISEASES of the OX; being a Manual of Bovine Pathology specially adapted for the use of Veterinary Practitioners and Students. By J. H. STEEL M.R.C.V.S With 2 Plates and 117 Woodcuts. 8vo. 15s.

A TREATISE on the DISEASES of the DOG; being a Manual of Canine Pathology. Especially adapted for the Use of Veterinary Practitioners and Students. By JOHN HENRY STEEL, M.R.C.V.S. With 88 Illustrations. 8vo. 10s. 6d.

HORSES and STABLES. By Major-General Sir F. FITZWYGRAM, Bart. With 19 pages of Illustrations. 8vo. 5s.

The HORSE. By WILLIAM YOUATT. Revised and Enlarged by W. WATSON, M.R.C.V.S. 8vo. Woodcuts. 7s. 6d.

The DOG. By WILLIAM YOUATT. Revised and Enlarged. 8vo. Woodcuts. 6s.

The DOG in HEALTH and DISEASE. By 'STONEHENGE.' With 84 Wood Engravings. 8vo. 7s. 6d.

The GREYHOUND. By 'STONEHENGE.' With 25 Portraits of Greyhounds, &c. Square crown 8vo. 15s.

London: LONGMANS, GREEN, & CO.

JUNE 1883.

GENERAL LISTS OF WORKS
PUBLISHED BY
Messrs. LONGMANS, GREEN, & CO.
LONDON AND NEW YORK.

HISTORY, POLITICS, HISTORICAL MEMOIRS, &c.

Abbey's The English Church and its Bishops, 1700–1800. 2 vols. 8vo. 24s.
Abbey and Overton's English Church in the Eighteenth Century. Cr. 8vo. 7s. 6d.
Arnold's Lectures on Modern History. 8vo. 7s. 6d.
Bagwell's Ireland under the Tudors. Vols. 1 and 2. 2 vols. 8vo. 32s.
Ball's The Reformed Church of Ireland, 1537-1886. 8vo. 7s. 6d.
Boultbee's History of the Church of England, Pre-Reformation Period. 8vo. 15s.
Buckle's History of Civilisation. 3 vols. crown 8vo. 24s.
Canning (George) Some Official Correspondence of. 2 vols. 8vo. 28s.
Cox's (Sir G. W.) General History of Greece. Crown 8vo. Maps, 7s. 6d.
Creighton's Papacy during the Reformation. 8vo. Vols. 1 & 2, 32s. Vols. 3 & 4, 24s.
De Tocqueville's Democracy in America. 2 vols. crown 8vo, 16s.
Doyle's English in America: Virginia, Maryland, and the Carolinas, 8vo. 18s.
— — — The Puritan Colonies, 2 vols. 8vo. 36s.
Epochs of Ancient History. Edited by the Rev. Sir G. W. Cox, Bart. and C. Sankey, M.A. With Maps. Fcp. 8vo. price 2s. 6d. each.

Beesly's Gracchi, Marius, and Sulla.
Capes's Age of the Antonines.
— Early Roman Empire.
Cox's Athenian Empire.
— Greeks and Persians.
Curteis's Rise of the Macedonian Empire.

Ihne's Rome to its Capture by the Gauls.
Merivale's Roman Triumvirates.
Sankey's Spartan and Theban Supremacies.
Smith's Rome and Carthage, the Punic Wars.

Epochs of Modern History. Edited by C. Colbeck, M.A. With Maps. Fcp. 8vo. 2s. 6d. each.

Church's Beginning of the Middle Ages.
Cox's Crusades.
Creighton's Age of Elizabeth.
Gairdner's Houses of Lancaster and York.
Gardiner's Puritan Revolution.
— Thirty Years' War.
— (Mrs.) French Revolution, 1789-1795.
Hale's Fall of the Stuarts.
Johnson's Normans in Europe.

Longman's Frederick the Great and the Seven Years' War.
Ludlow's War of American Independence.
M'Carthy's Epoch of Reform, 1830–1850.
Moberly's The Early Tudors.
Morris's Age of Queen Anne.
— The Early Hanoverians.
Seebohm's Protestant Revolution.
Stubbs's The Early Plantagenets.
Warburton's Edward III.

Epochs of Church History. Edited by the Rev. Mandell Creighton, M.A. Fcp. 8vo. price 2s. 6d. each.

Brodrick's A History of the University of Oxford.
Carr's The Church and the Roman Empire.
Hunt's England and the Papacy.
Mullinger's The University of Cambridge.
Overton's The Evangelical Revival in the Eighteenth Century.
Perry's The Reformation in England.

Plummer's The Church of the Early Fathers.
Stephens' Hildebrand and his Times.
Tozer's The Church and the Eastern Empire.
Tucker's The English Church in other Lands.
Wakeman's The Church and the Puritans.

⁎ *Other Volumes in preparation.*

LONGMANS, GREEN, & CO., London and New York.

Freeman's Historical Geography of Europe. 2 vols. 8vo. 31*s*. 6*d*.
Froude's English in Ireland in the 18th Century. 3 vols. crown 8vo. 18*s*.
— History of England. Popular Edition. 12 vols. crown 8vo. 3*s*. 6*d*. each.
Gardiner's History of England from the Accession of James I. to the Outbreak of the Civil War. 10 vols. crown 8vo. 60*s*.
— History of the Great Civil War, 1642-1649 (3 vols.) Vol. 1, 1642-1644, 8vo. 21*s*.
Greville's Journal of the Reigns of King George IV., King William IV., and Queen Victoria. Cabinet Edition. 8 vols. crown 8vo. 6*s*. each.
Historic Towns. Edited by E. A. Freeman, D.C.L. and the Rev. William Hunt, M.A. With Maps and Plans. Crown 8vo. 3*s*. 6*d*. each.

London. By W. E. Loftie.	Bristol. By the Rev. W. Hunt.
Exeter. By E. A. Freeman.	Oxford. By the Rev. C. W. Boase.
Cinque Ports. By Montagu Burrows.	Colchester. By the Rev. E. O. Cutts.

Lecky's History of England in the Eighteenth Century. Vols. 1 & 2, 1700-1760, 8vo. 36*s*. Vols. 3 & 4, 1760-1784, 8vo. 36*s*. Vols. 5 & 6, 1784-1793, 36*s*.
— History of European Morals. 2 vols. crown 8vo. 16*s*.
— — Rationalism in Europe. 2 vols. crown 8vo. 16*s*.
Longman's Life and Times of Edward III. 2 vols. 8vo. 28*s*.
Macaulay's Complete Works. Library Edition. 8 vols. 8vo. £5. 5*s*.
— — — Cabinet Edition. 16 vols. crown 8vo. £4. 16*s*.
— History of England :—
Student's Edition. 2 vols. cr. 8vo. 12*s*. | Cabinet Edition. 8 vols. post 8vo. 48*s*.
People's Edition. 4 vols. cr. 8vo. 16*s*. | Library Edition. 5 vols. 8vo. £4.
Macaulay's Critical and Historical Essays, with Lays of Ancient Rome In One Volume :—
Authorised Edition. Cr. 8vo. 2*s*. 6*d*. | Popular Edition. Cr. 8vo. 2*s*. 6*d*.
or 3*s*. 6*d*. gilt edges. |
Macaulay's Critical and Historical Essays :—
Student's Edition. 1 vol. cr. 8vo. 6*s*. | Cabinet Edition. 4 vols. post 8vo. 24*s*.
People's Edition. 2 vols. cr. 8vo. 8*s*. | Library Edition. 3 vols. 8vo. 36*s*.
Macaulay's Speeches corrected by Himself. Crown 8vo. 3*s*. 6*d*.
Malmesbury's (Earl of) Memoirs of an Ex-Minister. Crown 8vo. 7*s*. 6*d*.
May's Constitutional History of England, 1760-1870. 3 vols. crown 8vo. 18*s*.
— Democracy in Europe. 2 vols. 8vo. 32*s*.
Merivale's Fall of the Roman Republic. 12mo. 7*s*. 6*d*.
— General History of Rome, B.C. 753-A.D. 476. Crown 8vo. 7*s*. 6*d*.
— History of the Romans under the Empire. 8 vols. post 8vo. 48*s*.
Nelson's (Lord) Letters and Despatches. Edited by J. K. Laughton. 8vo. 16*s*.
Pears' The Fall of Constantinople. 8vo. 16*s*.
Richey's Short History of the Irish People. 8vo. 14*s*.
Saintsbury's Manchester : a Short History. Crown 8vo. 3*s*. 6*d*.
Seebohm's Oxford Reformers—Colet, Erasmus, & More. 8vo. 14*s*.
Short's History of the Church of England. Crown 8vo. 7*s*. 6*d*.
Smith's Carthage and the Carthaginians. Crown 8vo. 10*s*. 6*d*.
Taylor's Manual of the History of India. Crown 8vo. 7*s*. 6*d*.
Todd's Parliamentary Government in England (2 vols.) Vol. 1, 8vo. 21*s*.
Tuttle's History of Prussia under Frederick the Great, 1740-1756. 2 vols. crown 8vo. 18*s*.

LONGMANS, GREEN, & CO., London and New York.

Vitzthum's St. Petersburg and London, 1852-1864. 2 vols. 8vo. 30s.
Walpole's History of England, from 1815. 5 vols. 8vo. Vols. 1 & 2, 1815-1832, 36s.
 Vol. 3, 1832-1841, 18s. Vols. 4 & 5, 1841-1858, 36s.
Wylie's History of England under Henry IV. Vol. 1, crown 8vo. 10s. 6d.

BIOGRAPHICAL WORKS

Armstrong's (E. J.) Life and Letters. Edited by G. F. Armstrong. Fcp. 8vo. 7s. 6d.
Bacon's Life and Letters, by Spedding. 7 vols. 8vo. £4. 4s.
Bagehot's Biographical Studies. 1 vol. 8vo. 12s.
Carlyle's Life, by J. A. Froude. Vols. 1 & 2, 1795-1835, 8vo. 32s. Vols. 3 & 4, 1834-1881, 8vo. 32s.
— (Mrs.) Letters and Memorials. 3 vols. 8vo. 36s.
Doyle (Sir F. H.) Reminiscences and Opinions. 8vo. 16s.
English Worthies. Edited by Andrew Lang. Crown 8vo. each 1s. sewed; 1s. 6d. cloth.

    Charles Darwin. By Grant Allen.
    Shaftesbury (The First Earl). By H. D. Traill.
    Admiral Blake. By David Hannay.
    Marlborough. By Geo. Saintsbury.
    Steele. By Austin Dobson.
    Ben Jonson. By J. A. Symonds.
    George Canning. By Frank H. Hill.
    Claverhouse. By Mowbray Morris.

Fox (Charles James) The Early History of. By Sir G. O. Trevelyan, Bart. Crown 8vo. 6s.
Froude's Cæsar; a Sketch. Crown 8vo. 6s.
Hamilton's (Sir W. R.) Life, by Graves. Vols. 1 and 2, 8vo. 15s. each.
Havelock's Life, by Marshman. Crown 8vo. 3s. 6d.
Jenkin's (Fleeming) Papers, Literary, Scientific, &c. With Memoir by R. L. Stevenson. 2 vols. 8vo. 32s.
Laughton's Studies in Naval History. 8vo. 10s. 6d.
Macaulay's (Lord) Life and Letters. By his Nephew, Sir G. O. Trevelyan, Bart. Popular Edition, 1 vol. crown 8vo. 6s. Cabinet Edition, 2 vols. post 8vo. 12s. Library Edition, 2 vols. 8vo. 36s.
Mendelssohn's Letters. Translated by Lady Wallace. 2 vols. cr. 8vo. 5s. each.
Müller's (Max) Biographical Essays. Crown 8vo. 7s. 6d.
Newman's Apologia pro Vitâ Suâ. Crown 8vo. 6s.
Pasteur (Louis) His Life and Labours. Crown 8vo. 7s. 6d.
Shakespeare's Life (Outlines of), by Halliwell-Phillipps. 2 vols. royal 8vo. 10s. 6d.
Southey's Correspondence with Caroline Bowles. 8vo. 14s.
Stephen's Essays in Ecclesiastical Biography. Crown 8vo. 7s. 6d.
Taylor's (Sir Henry) Correspondence. 8vo. 16s.
Wellington's Life, by Gleig. Crown 8vo. 6s.

MENTAL AND POLITICAL PHILOSOPHY, FINANCE, &c.

Adam's Public Debts; an Essay on the Science of Finance. 8vo. 12s. 6d.
Amos's View of the Science of Jurisprudence. 8vo. 18s.
— Primer of the English Constitution. Crown 8vo. 6s.
Bacon's Essays, with Annotations by Whately. 8vo. 10s. 6d.
— Works, edited by Spedding. 7 vols. 8vo. 73s. 6d.
Bagehot's Economic Studies, edited by Hutton. 8vo. 10s. 6d.
— The Postulates of English Political Economy. Crown 8vo. 2s. 6d.

LONGMANS, GREEN, & CO., London and New York.

General Lists of Works.

Bain's Logic, Deductive and Inductive. Crown 8vo. 10s. 6d.
 Part I. Deduction, 4s. | ' Part II. Induction, 6s. 6d.
— Mental and Moral Science. Crown 8vo. 10s. 6d.
— The Senses and the Intellect. 8vo. 15s.
— The Emotions and the Will. 8vo. 15s.
Crozier's Civilisation and Progress. 8vo. 5s.
Crump's Short Enquiry into the Formation of English Political Opinion. 8vo. 7s. 6d.
Dowell's A History of Taxation and Taxes in England. 8vo. Vols. 1 & 2, 21s. Vols. 3 & 4, 21s.
Green's (Thomas Hill) Works. (3 vols.) Vols. 1 & 2, Philosophical Works. 8vo. 16s. each.
Hume's Essays, edited by Green & Grose. 2 vols. 8vo. 28s.
— Treatise of Human Nature, edited by Green & Grose. 2 vols. 8vo. 28s.
Kirkup's An Enquiry into Socialism. Crown 8vo. 5s.
Ladd's Elements of Physiological Psychology. 8vo. 21s.
Lang's Custom and Myth : Studies of Early Usage and Belief. Crown 8vo. 7s. 6d.
— Myth, Ritual, and Religion. 2 vols. crown 8vo. 21s.
Leslie's Essays in Political and Moral Philosophy. 8vo. 10s. 6d.
Lewes's History of Philosophy. 2 vols. 8vo. 32s.
Lubbock's Origin of Civilisation. 8vo. 18s.
Macleod's The Elements of Economics. (2 vols.) Vol. 1, cr. 8vo. 7s. 6d. Vol. 2, Part I. cr. 8vo. 7s. 6d.
— The Elements of Banking. Crown 8vo. 5s.
— The Theory and Practice of Banking. Vol. 1, 8vo. 12s. Vol. 2, 14s.
Max Müller's The Science of Thought. 8vo. 21s.
Mill's (James) Analysis of the Phenomena of the Human Mind. 2 vols. 8vo. 28s.
Mill (John Stuart) on Representative Government. Crown 8vo. 2s.
—   — on Liberty. Crown 8vo. 1s. 4d.
—   — Examination of Hamilton's Philosophy. 8vo. 16s.
—   — Logic. Crown 8vo. 5s.
—   — Principles of Political Economy. 2 vols. 8vo. 30s. People's Edition, 1 vol. crown 8vo. 5s.
—   — Utilitarianism. 8vo. 5s.
—   — Three Essays on Religion, &c. 8vo. 5s.
Mulhall's History of Prices since 1850. Crown 8vo. 6s.
Sandars's Institutes of Justinian, with English Notes. 8vo. 18s.
Seebohm's English Village Community. 8vo. 16s.
Sully's Outlines of Psychology. 8vo. 12s. 6d.
— Teacher's Handbook of Psychology. Crown 8vo. 6s. 6d.
Swinburne's Picture Logic. Post 8vo. 5s.
Thompson's A System of Psychology. 2 vols. 8vo. 36s.
— The Problem of Evil. 8vo. 10s. 6d.
— The Religious Sentiments of the Human Mind. 8vo. 7s. 6d.
Thomson's Outline of Necessary Laws of Thought. Crown 8vo. 6s.
Twiss's Law of Nations in Time of War. 8vo. 21s.
—   — in Time of Peace. 8vo. 15s.
Webb's The Veil of Isis. 8vo. 10s. 6d.
Whately's Elements of Logic. Crown 8vo. 4s. 6d.
—   — Rhetoric. Crown 8vo. 4s. 6d.
Wylie's Labour, Leisure, and Luxury. Crown 8vo. 6s.
Zeller's History of Eclecticism in Greek Philosophy. Crown 8vo. 10s. 6d.
— Plato and the Older Academy. Crown 8vo. 18s.

LONGMANS, GREEN, & CO., London and New York.

Zeller's Pre-Socratic Schools. 2 vols. crown 8vo. 30s.
— Socrates and the Socratic Schools. Crown 8vo. 10s. 6d.
— Stoics, Epicureans, and Sceptics. Crown 8vo. 15s.
— Outlines of the History of Greek Philosophy. Crown 8vo. 10s. 6d.

MISCELLANEOUS WORKS.

A. K. H. B., The Essays and Contributions of. Crown 8vo.
    Autumn Holidays of a Country Parson. 3s. 6d.
    Changed Aspects of Unchanged Truths. 3s. 6d.
    Common-Place Philosopher in Town and Country. 3s. 6d.
    Critical Essays of a Country Parson. 3s. 6d.
    Counsel and Comfort spoken from a City Pulpit. 3s. 6d.
    Graver Thoughts of a Country Parson. Three Series. 3s. 6d. each.
    Landscapes, Churches, and Moralities. 3s. 6d.
    Leisure Hours in Town. 3s. 6d. Lessons of Middle Age. 3s. 6d.
    Our Homely Comedy ; and Tragedy. 3s. 6d.
    Our Little Life. Essays Consolatory and Domestic. Two Series. 3s. 6d.
    Present-day Thoughts. 3s. 6d. [each.
    Recreations of a Country Parson. Three Series. 3s. 6d. each.
    Seaside Musings on Sundays and Week-Days. 3s. 6d.
    Sunday Afternoons in the Parish Church of a University City. 3s. 6d.
Armstrong's (Ed. J.) Essays and Sketches. Fcp. 8vo. 5s.
Arnold's (Dr. Thomas) Miscellaneous Works. 8vo. 7s. 6d.
Bagehot's Literary Studies, edited by Hutton. 2 vols. 8vo. 28s.
Beaconsfield (Lord), The Wit and Wisdom of. Crown 8vo. 1s. boards; 1s. 6d. cl.
Farrar's Language and Languages. Crown 8vo. 6s.
Froude's Short Studies on Great Subjects. 4 vols. crown 8vo. 24s.
Huth's The Marriage of Near Kin. Royal 8vo. 21s.
Lang's Letters to Dead Authors. Fcp. 8vo. 6s. 6d.
— Books and Bookmen. Crown 8vo. 6s. 6d.
Macaulay's Miscellaneous Writings. 2 vols. 8vo. 21s. 1 vol. crown 8vo. 4s. 6d.
— Miscellaneous Writings and Speeches. Crown 8vo. 6s.
— Miscellaneous Writings, Speeches, Lays of Ancient Rome, &c. Cabinet Edition. 4 vols. crown 8vo. 24s.
— Writings, Selections from. Crown 8vo. 6s.
Max Müller's Lectures on the Science of Language. 2 vols. crown 8vo. 16s.
— — Lectures on India. 8vo. 12s. 6d.
— — Biographies of Words and the Home of the Aryas. Crown 8vo. 7s. 6d.
Oliver's Astronomy for Amateurs. Crown 8vo. 7s. 6d.
Proctor's Chance and Luck. Crown 8vo. 5s.
Smith (Sydney) The Wit and Wisdom of. Crown 8vo. 1s. boards; 1s. 6d. cloth.

ASTRONOMY.

Herschel's Outlines of Astronomy. Square crown 8vo. 12s.
Proctor's Larger Star Atlas. Folio, 15s. or Maps only, 12s. 6d.
— New Star Atlas. Crown 8vo. 5s.
— Light Science for Leisure Hours. 3 Series. Crown 8vo. 5s. each.
— The Moon. Crown 8vo. 6s.
— Other Worlds than Ours. Crown 8vo. 5s.
— Studies of Venus-Transits. 8vo. 5s.
— Orbs Around Us. Crown 8vo. 5s.
— Universe of Stars. 8vo. 10s. 6d.
— Old and New Astronomy. 12 Parts. 2s. 6d. each. (In course of publication.)
Webb's Celestial Objects for Common Telescopes. Crown 8vo. 9s.

LONGMANS, GREEN, & CO., London and New York.

General Lists of Works.

THE 'KNOWLEDGE' LIBRARY.
Edited by RICHARD A. PROCTOR.

How to Play Whist. Crown 8vo. 5s.
Home Whist. 16mo. 1s.
The Poetry of Astronomy. Cr. 8vo. 6s.
Nature Studies. Crown 8vo. 6s.
Leisure Readings. Crown 8vo. 6s.
The Stars in their Seasons. Imp. 8vo. 5s.
Myths and Marvels of Astronomy. Crown 8vo. 6s.

Pleasant Ways in Science. Cr. 8vo. 6s.
Star Primer. Crown 4to. 2s. 6d.
The Seasons Pictured. Demy 4to. 5s.
Strength and Happiness. Cr. 8vo. 5s.
Rough Ways made Smooth. Cr. 8vo. 5s.
The Expanse of Heaven. Cr. 8vo. 5s.
Our Place among Infinities. Cr. 8vo. 5s.
The Great Pyramid. Cr. 8vo. 6s.

CLASSICAL LANGUAGES AND LITERATURE.

Æschylus, The Eumenides of. Text, with Metrical English Translation, by J. F. Davies. 8vo. 7s.
Aristophanes' The Acharnians, translated by R. Y. Tyrrell. Crown 8vo. 2s. 6d.
Aristotle's The Ethics, Text and Notes, by Sir Alex. Grant, Bart. 2 vols. 8vo. 32s.
— The Nicomachean Ethics, translated by Williams, crown 8vo. 7s. 6d.
— The Politics, Books I. III. IV. (VII.) with Translation, &c. by Bolland and Lang. Crown 8vo. 7s. 6d.
Becker's *Charicles* and *Gallus*, by Metcalfe. Post 8vo. 7s. 6d. each.
Cicero's Correspondence, Text and Notes, by R. Y. Tyrrell. Vols. 1 & 2, 8vo. 12s. each.
Mahaffy's Classical Greek Literature. Crown 8vo. Vol. 1, The Poets, 7s. 6d. Vol. 2, The Prose Writers, 7s. 6d.
Plato's Parmenides, with Notes, &c. by J. Maguire. 8vo. 7s. 6d.
Virgil's Works, Latin Text, with Commentary, by Kennedy. Crown 8vo. 10s. 6d.
— Æneid, translated into English Verse, by Conington. Crown 8vo. 9s.
— — — — — — by W. J. Thornhill. Cr. 8vo. 7s. 6d.
— Poems, — — Prose, by Conington. Crown 8vo. 9s.
Witt's Myths of Hellas, translated by F. M. Younghusband. Crown 8vo. 3s. 6d.
— The Trojan War, — — Fcp. 8vo. 2s.
— The Wanderings of Ulysses, — Crown 8vo. 3s. 6d.

NATURAL HISTORY, BOTANY, & GARDENING.

Dixon's Rural Bird Life. Crown 8vo. Illustrations, 5s.
Hartwig's Aerial World, 8vo. 10s. 6d.
— Polar World, 8vo. 10s. 6d.
— Sea and its Living Wonders. 8vo. 10s. 6d.
— Subterranean World, 8vo. 10s. 6d.
— Tropical World, 8vo. 10s. 6d.
Lindley's Treasury of Botany. 2 vols. fcp. 8vo. 12s.
Loudon's Encyclopædia of Gardening. 8vo. 21s.
— — Plants. 8vo. 42s.
Rivers's Orchard House. Crown 8vo. 5s.
— Miniature Fruit Garden. Fcp. 8vo. 4s.
Stanley's Familiar History of British Birds. Crown 8vo. 6s.
Wood's Bible Animals. With 112 Vignettes. 8vo. 10s. 6d.
— Homes Without Hands, 8vo. 10s. 6d.
— Insects Abroad, 8vo. 10s. 6d.
— Horse and Man. 8vo. 14s.
— Insects at Home. With 700 Illustrations. 8vo. 10s. 6d.

LONGMANS, GREEN, & CO., London and New York.

General Lists of Works.

Wood's Out of Doors. Crown 8vo. 5s.
— Petland Revisited. Crown 8vo. 7s. 6d.
— Strange Dwellings. Crown 8vo. 5s. Popular Edition, 4to. 6d.

CHEMISTRY ENGINEERING, & GENERAL SCIENCE.

Arnott's Elements of Physics or Natural Philosophy. Crown 8vo. 12s. 6d.
Barrett's English Glees and Part-Songs: their Historical Development. Crown 8vo. 7s. 6d.
Bourne's Catechism of the Steam Engine. Crown 8vo. 7s. 6d.
— Handbook of the Steam Engine. Fcp. 8vo. 9s.
— Recent Improvements in the Steam Engine. Fcp. 8vo. 6s.
Buckton's Our Dwellings, Healthy and Unhealthy. Crown 8vo. 3s. 6d.
Clerk's The Gas Engine. With Illustrations. Crown 8vo. 7s. 6d.
Clodd's The Story of Creation. Illustrated. Crown 8vo. 6s.
Crookes's Select Methods in Chemical Analysis. 8vo. 24s.
Culley's Handbook of Practical Telegraphy. 8vo. 16s.
Fairbairn's Useful Information for Engineers. 3 vols. crown 8vo. 31s. 6d.
— Mills and Millwork. 1 vol. 8vo. 25s.
Forbes' Lectures on Electricity. Crown 8vo. 5s.
Galloway's Principles of Chemistry Practically Taught. Crown 8vo. 6s. 6d.
Ganot's Elementary Treatise on Physics, by Atkinson. Large crown 8vo. 15s.
— Natural Philosophy, by Atkinson. Crown 8vo. 7s. 6d.
Grove's Correlation of Physical Forces. 8vo. 15s.
Haughton's Six Lectures on Physical Geography. 8vo. 15s.
Helmholtz on the Sensations of Tone. Royal 8vo. 28s.
Helmholtz's Lectures on Scientific Subjects. 2 vols. crown 8vo. 7s. 6d. each.
Hudson and Gosse's The Rotifera or 'Wheel Animalcules.' With 30 Coloured Plates. 6 parts. 4to. 10s. 6d. each. Complete, 2 vols. 4to. £3. 10s.
Hullah's Lectures on the History of Modern Music. 8vo. 8s. 6d.
— Transition Period of Musical History. 8vo. 10s. 6d.
Jackson's Aid to Engineering Solution. Royal 8vo. 21s.
Jago's Inorganic Chemistry, Theoretical and Practical. Fcp. 8vo. 2s. 6d.
Kolbe's Short Text-Book of Inorganic Chemistry. Crown 8vo. 7s. 6d.
Lloyd's Treatise on Magnetism. 8vo. 10s. 6d.
Macalister's Zoology and Morphology of Vertebrate Animals. 8vo. 10s. 6d.
Macfarren's Lectures on Harmony. 8vo. 12s.
— Addresses and Lectures. Crown 8vo. 6s. 6d.
Martin's Navigation and Nautical Astronomy. Royal 8vo. 18s.
Meyer's Modern Theories of Chemistry. 8vo. 18s.
Miller's Elements of Chemistry, Theoretical and Practical. 3 vols. 8vo. Part I. Chemical Physics, 16s. Part II. Inorganic Chemistry, 24s. Part III. Organic Chemistry, price 31s. 6d.
Mitchell's Manual of Practical Assaying. 8vo. 31s. 6d.
— Dissolution and Evolution and the Science of Medicine. 8vo. 16s.
Noble's Hours with a Three-inch Telescope. Crown 8vo. 4s. 6d.
Northcott's Lathes and Turning. 8vo. 18s.
Owen's Comparative Anatomy and Physiology of the Vertebrate Animals. 3 vols. 8vo. 73s. 6d.
Piesse's Art of Perfumery. Square crown 8vo. 21s.

LONGMANS, GREEN, & CO., London and New York.

8 General Lists of Works.

Richardson's The Health of Nations; Works and Life of Edwin Chadwick, C.B. 2 vols. 8vo. 28s.
— The Commonhealth; a Series of Essays. Crown 8vo. 6s.
Schellen's Spectrum Analysis. 8vo. 31s. 6d.
Scott's Weather Charts and Storm Warnings. Crown 8vo. 6s.
Sennett's Treatise on the Marine Steam Engine. 8vo. 21s.
Smith's Air and Rain. 8vo. 24s.
Stoney's The Theory of the Stresses on Girders, &c. Royal 8vo. 36s.
Tilden's Practical Chemistry. Fcp. 8vo. 1s. 6d.
Tyndall's Faraday as a Discoverer. Crown 8vo. 3s. 6d.
— Floating Matter of the Air. Crown 8vo. 7s. 6d.
— Fragments of Science. 2 vols. post 8vo. 16s.
— Heat a Mode of Motion. Crown 8vo. 12s.
— Lectures on Light delivered in America. Crown 8vo. 5s.
— Lessons on Electricity. Crown 8vo. 2s. 6d.
— Notes on Electrical Phenomena. Crown 8vo. 1s. sewed, 1s. 6d. cloth.
— Notes of Lectures on Light. Crown 8vo. 1s. sewed, 1s. 6d. cloth.
— Researches on Diamagnetism and Magne-Crystallic Action. Cr. 8vo. 12s.
— Sound, with Frontispiece and 203 Woodcuts. Crown 8vo. 10s. 6d.
Unwin's The Testing of Materials of Construction. Illustrated. 8vo. 21s.
Watts' Dictionary of Chemistry. New Edition (4 vols.). Vol. 1, 8vo. 42s.
Wilson's Manual of Health-Science. Crown 8vo. 2s. 6d.

THEOLOGICAL AND RELIGIOUS WORKS.

Arnold's (Rev. Dr. Thomas) Sermons. 6 vols. crown 8vo. 5s. each.
Boultbee's Commentary on the 39 Articles. Crown 8vo. 6s.
Browne's (Bishop) Exposition of the 39 Articles. 8vo. 16s.
Bullinger's Critical Lexicon and Concordance to the English and Greek New Testament. Royal 8vo. 15s.
Colenso on the Pentateuch and Book of Joshua. Crown 8vo. 6s.
Conder's Handbook of the Bible. Post 8vo. 7s. 6d.
Conybeare & Howson's Life and Letters of St. Paul :—
    Library Edition, with Maps, Plates, and Woodcuts. 2 vols. square crown 8vo. 21s.
    Student's Edition, revised and condensed, with 46 Illustrations and Maps. 1 vol. crown 8vo. 6s.
Cox's (Homersham) The First Century of Christianity. 8vo. 12s.
Davidson's Introduction to the Study of the New Testament. 2 vols. 8vo. 30s.
Edersheim's Life and Times of Jesus the Messiah. 2 vols. 8vo. 24s.
— Prophecy and History in relation to the Messiah. 8vo. 12s.
Ellicott's (Bishop) Commentary on St. Paul's Epistles. 8vo. Corinthians I. 16s. Galatians, 8s. 6d. Ephesians, 8s. 6d. Pastoral Epistles, 10s. 6d. Philippians, Colossians and Philemon, 10s. 6d. Thessalonians, 7s. 6d.
— Lectures on the Life of our Lord. 8vo. 12s.
Ewald's Antiquities of Israel, translated by Solly. 8vo. 12s. 6d.
— History of Israel, translated by Carpenter & Smith. 8 vols. 8vo. Vols. 1 & 2, 24s. Vols. 3 & 4, 21s. Vol. 5, 18s. Vol. 6, 16s. Vol. 7, 21s. Vol. 8, 18s.
Hobart's Medical Language of St. Luke. 8vo. 16s.
Hopkins's Christ the Consoler. Fcp. 8vo. 2s. 6d.

LONGMANS, GREEN, & CO., London and New York.

General Lists of Works.

Jameson's Sacred and Legendary Art. 6 vols. square 8vo.
    Legends of the Madonna. 1 vol. 21*s*.
    — — — Monastic Orders 1 vol. 21*s*.
    — — — Saints and Martyrs. 2 vols. 31*s*. 6*d*.
    — — — Saviour. Completed by Lady Eastlake. 2 vols. 42*s*.
Jukes's New Man and the Eternal Life. Crown 8vo. 6*s*.
  — Second Death and the Restitution of all Things. Crown 8vo. 3*s*. 6*d*.
  — Types of Genesis. Crown 8vo. 7*s*. 6*d*.
  — The Mystery of the Kingdom. Crown 8vo. 3*s*. 6*d*.
  — The Names of God in Holy Scripture. Crown 8vo. 4*s*. 6*d*.
Lenormant's New Translation of the Book of Genesis. Translated into English. 8vo. 10*s*. 6*d*.
Lyra Germanica : Hymns translated by Miss Winkworth. Fcp. 8vo. 5*s*.
Macdonald's (G.) Unspoken Sermons. Two Series, Crown 8vo. 3*s*. 6*d*. each.
  — The Miracles of our Lord. Crown 8vo. 3*s*. 6*d*.
Manning's Temporal Mission of the Holy Ghost. Crown 8vo. 8*s*. 6*d*.
Martineau's Endeavours after the Christian Life. Crown 8vo. 7*s*. 6*d*.
  — Hymns of Praise and Prayer. Crown 8vo. 4*s*. 6*d*. 32mo. 1*s*. 6*d*.
  — Sermons, Hours of Thought on Sacred Things. 2 vols. 7*s*. 6*d*. each.
Max Müller's Origin and Growth of Religion. Crown 8vo. 7*s*. 6*d*.
  — Science of Religion. Crown 8vo. 7*s*. 6*d*.
Monsell's Spiritual Songs for Sundays and Holidays. Fcp. 8vo. 5*s*. 18mo. 2*s*.
Newman's Apologia pro Vitâ Suâ. Crown 8vo. 6*s*.
  — The Arians of the Fourth Century. Crown 8vo. 6*s*.
  — The Idea of a University Defined and Illustrated. Crown 8vo. 7*s*.
  — Historical Sketches. 3 vols. crown 8vo. 6*s*. each.
  — Discussions and Arguments on Various Subjects. Crown 8vo. 6*s*.
  — An Essay on the Development of Christian Doctrine. Crown 8vo. 6*s*.
  — Certain Difficulties Felt by Anglicans in Catholic Teaching Considered. Vol. 1, crown 8vo. 7*s*. 6*d*. Vol. 2, crown 8vo. 5*s*. 6*d*.
  — The Via Media of the Anglican Church, Illustrated in Lectures, &c. 2 vols. crown 8vo. 6*s*. each.
  — Essays, Critical and Historical. 2 vols. crown 8vo. 12*s*.
  — Essays on Biblical and on Ecclesiastical Miracles. Crown 8vo. 6*s*.
  — An Essay in Aid of a Grammar of Assent. 7*s*. 6*d*.
  — Select Treatises of St. Athanasius in Controversy with the Arians. Translated. 2 vols. crown 8vo. 15*s*.
Overton's Life in the English Church (1660–1714). 8vo. 14*s*.
Roberts' Greek the Language of Christ and His Apostles. 8vo. 18*s*.
Supernatural Religion. Complete Edition. 3 vols. 8vo. 36*s*.
Younghusband's The Story of Our Lord told in Simple Language for Children. Illustrated. Crown 8vo. 2*s*. 6*d*. cloth plain ; 3*s*. 6*d*. cloth extra, gilt edges.

TRAVELS, ADVENTURES, &c.

Baker's Eight Years in Ceylon. Crown 8vo. 5*s*.
  — Rifle and Hound in Ceylon. Crown 8vo. 5*s*.
Brassey's Sunshine and Storm in the East. Library Edition, 8vo. 21*s*. Cabinet Edition, crown 8vo. 7*s*. 6*d*. Popular Edition, 4to. 6*d*.

LONGMANS, GREEN, & CO., London and New York.

Brassey's Voyage in the 'Sunbeam.' Library Edition, 8vo. 21s. Cabinet Edition, crown 8vo. 7s. 6d. School Edition, fcp. 8vo. 2s. Popular Edition, 4to. 6d.
— In the Trades, the Tropics, and the 'Roaring Forties.' Cabinet Edition, crown 8vo. 17s. 6d. Popular Edition, 4to. 6d.
Crawford's Reminiscences of Foreign Travel. Crown 8vo. 5s.
Froude's Oceana; or, England and her Colonies. Cr. 8vo. 2s. boards; 2s. 6d. cloth.
— The English in the West Indies. 8vo. 18s.
Howitt's Visits to Remarkable Places. Crown 8vo. 5s.
James's The Long White Mountain; or, a Journey in Manchuria. 8vo. 24s.
Lindt's Picturesque New Guinea. 4to. 42s.
Pennell's Our Sentimental Journey through France and Italy. Illustrated. Crown 8vo. 6s.
Riley's Athos; or, The Mountain of the Monks. 8vo. 21s.
Three in Norway. By Two of Them. Illustrated. Crown 8vo. 2s. boards; 2s. 6d. cloth.

WORKS OF FICTION.

Anstey's The Black Poodle, &c. Crown 8vo. 2s. boards; 2s. 6d. cloth.
Beaconsfield's (The Earl of) Novels and Tales. Hughenden Edition, with 2 Portraits on Steel and 11 Vignettes on Wood. 11 vols. crown 8vo. £2. 2s.
Cheap Edition, 11 vols. crown 8vo. 1s. each, boards; 1s. 6d. each, cloth.

Lothair.	Contarini Fleming.
Sybil.	Alroy, Ixion, &c.
Coningsby.	The Young Duke, &c.
Tancred.	Vivian Grey.
Venetia.	Endymion.
Henrietta Temple.	

Gilkes' Boys and Masters. Crown 8vo. 3s. 6d.
Haggard's (H. Rider) She: a History of Adventure. Crown 8vo. 6s.
— — Allan Quatermain. Illustrated. Crown 8vo. 6s.
Harte (Bret) On the Frontier. Three Stories. 16mo. 1s.
— — By Shore and Sedge. Three Stories. 16mo. 1s.
— — In the Carquinez Woods. Crown 8vo. 1s. boards; 1s. 6d. cloth.
Lyall's (Edna) The Autobiography of a Slander. Fcp. 1s. sewed.
Melville's (Whyte) Novels. 8 vols. fcp. 8vo. 1s. each, boards; 1s. 6d. each, cloth.

Digby Grand.	Good for Nothing.
General Bounce.	Holmby House.
Kate Coventry.	The Interpreter.
The Gladiators.	The Queen's Maries.

Molesworth's (Mrs.) Marrying and Giving in Marriage. Crown 8vo. 2s. 6d.
Novels by the Author of 'The Atelier du Lys':
The Atelier du Lys; or, An Art Student in the Reign of Terror. Crown 8vo. 2s. 6d.
Mademoiselle Mori: a Tale of Modern Rome. Crown 8vo. 2s. 6d.
In the Olden Time: a Tale of the Peasant War in Germany. Crown 8vo. 2s. 6d.
Hester's Venture. Crown 8vo. 2s. 6d.
Oliphant's (Mrs.) Madam. Crown 8vo. 1s. boards; 1s. 6d. cloth.
— — In Trust: the Story of a Lady and her Lover. Crown 8vo. 1s. boards; 1s. 6d. cloth.
Payn's (James) The Luck of the Darrells. Crown 8vo. 1s. boards; 1s. 6d. cloth.
— — Thicker than Water. Crown 8vo. 1s. boards; 1s. 6d. cloth.
Reader's Fairy Prince Follow-my-Lead. Crown 8vo. 2s. 6d.
— The Ghost of Brankinshaw; and other Tales. Fcp. 8vo. 2s. 6d.

LONGMANS, GREEN, & CO., London and New York.

Sewell's (Miss) Stories and Tales. Crown 8vo. 1s. each, boards ; 1s. 6d. cloth ; 2s. 6d. cloth extra, gilt edges.

Amy Herbert. Cleve Hall.
The Earl's Daughter.
Experience of Life.
Gertrude. Ivors.

A Glimpse of the World.
Katharine Ashton.
Laneton Parsonage.
Margaret Percival. Ursula.

Stevenson's (R. L.) The Dynamiter. Fcp. 8vo. 1s. sewed ; 1s. 6d. cloth.
— — Strange Case of Dr. Jekyll and Mr. Hyde. Fcp. 8vo. 1s. sewed ; 1s. 6d. cloth.
Trollope's (Anthony) Novels. Fcp. 8vo. 1s. each, boards ; 1s. 6d. cloth.
The Warden | Barchester Towers.

POETRY AND THE DRAMA.

Armstrong's (Ed. J.) Poetical Works. Fcp. 8vo. 5s.
— (G. F.) Poetical Works :—

Poems, Lyrical and Dramatic. Fcp. 8vo. 6s.
Ugone : a Tragedy. Fcp. 8vo. 6s.
A Garland from Greece. Fcp. 8vo. 9s.
King Saul. Fcp. 8vo. 5s.
King David. Fcp. 8vo. 6s.
King Solomon. Fcp. 8vo. 6s.

Stories of Wicklow. Fcp. 8vo. 9s.
Mephistopheles in Broadcloth : a Satire. Fcp. 8vo. 4s.
Victoria Regina et Imperatrix : a Jubilee Song from Ireland, 1887. 4to. 2s. 6d.

Ballads of Berks. Edited by Andrew Lang. Fcp. 8vo. 6s.
Bowen's Harrow Songs and other Verses. Fcp. 8vo. 2s. 6d. ; or printed on hand-made paper, 5s.
Bowdler's Family Shakespeare. Medium 8vo. 14s. 6 vols. fcp. 8vo. 21s.
Dante's Divine Comedy, translated by James Innes Minchin. Crown 8vo. 15s.
Goethe's Faust, translated by Birds. Large crown 8vo. 12s. 6d.
— — translated by Webb. 8vo. 12s. 6d.
— — edited by Selss. Crown 8vo. 5s.
Ingelow's Poems. 2 Vols. fcp. 8vo. 12s. ; Vol. 3, fcp. 8vo. 5s.
— Lyrical and other Poems. Fcp. 8vo. 2s. 6d. cloth, plain ; 3s. cloth, gilt edges.
Kendall's (Mrs.) Dreams to Sell. Fcp. 8vo. 6s.
Macaulay's Lays of Ancient Rome. Illustrated by Scharf. 4to. 10s. 6d. Popular Edition, fcp. 4to. 6d. swd., 1s. cloth.
— Lays of Ancient Rome, with Ivry and the Armada. Illustrated by Weguelin. Crown 8vo. 3s. 6d. gilt edges.
Nesbit's Lays and Legends. Crown 8vo. 5s.
Newman's The Dream of Gerontius. 16mo. 6d. sewed ; 1s. cloth.
— Verses on Various Occasions. Fcp. 8vo. 6s.
Reader's Voices from Flowerland, a Birthday Book, 2s. 6d. cloth, 3s. 6d. roan.
Southey's Poetical Works. Medium 8vo. 14s.
Stevenson's A Child's Garden of Verses. Fcp. 8vo. 5s.
Virgil's Æneid, translated by Conington. Crown 8vo. 9s.
— Poems, translated into English Prose. Crown 8vo. 9s.

AGRICULTURE, HORSES, DOGS, AND CATTLE.

Fitzwygram's Horses and Stables. 8vo. 5s.
Lloyd's The Science of Agriculture. 8vo. 12s.
Loudon's Encyclopædia of Agriculture. 21s.
Prothero's Pioneers and Progress of English Farming. Crown 8vo. 5s.
Steel's Diseases of the Ox, a Manual of Bovine Pathology. 8vo. 15s.
— — — Dog. 8vo. 10s. 6d.

LONGMANS, GREEN, & CO., London and New York.

Stonehenge's Dog in Health and Disease. Square crown 8vo. 7s. 6d.
— Greyhound. Square crown 8vo. 15s.
Taylor's Agricultural Note Book. Fcp. 8vo. 2s. 6d.
Ville on Artificial Manures, by Crookes. 8vo. 21s.
Youatt's Work on the Dog. 8vo. 6s.
— — — — Horse. 8vo. 7s. 6d.

SPORTS AND PASTIMES.

The Badminton Library of Sports and Pastimes. Edited by the Duke of Beaufort and A. E. T. Watson. With numerous Illustrations. Cr. 8vo. 10s. 6d. each.
  Hunting, by the Duke of Beaufort, &c.
  Fishing, by H. Cholmondeley-Pennell, &c. 2 vols.
  Racing, by the Earl of Suffolk, &c.
  Shooting, by Lord Walsingham, &c. 2 vols.
  Cycling. By Viscount Bury.
  Athletics and Football. By Montague Shearman, &c.
  Boating. By W. B. Woodgate, &c.
  Cricket. By A. G. Steel, &c.
  Driving. By the Duke of Beaufort, &c.
  ₊ *Other Volumes in preparation.*
Campbell-Walker's Correct Card, or How to Play at Whist. Fcp. 8vo. 2s. 6d.
Ford's Theory and Practice of Archery, revised by W. Butt. 8vo. 14s.
Francis's Treatise on Fishing in all its Branches. Post 8vo. 15s.
Longman's Chess Openings. Fcp. 8vo. 2s. 6d.
Pease's The Cleveland Hounds as a Trencher-Fed Pack. Royal 8vo. 18s.
Pole's Theory of the Modern Scientific Game of Whist. Fcp. 8vo. 2s. 6d.
Proctor's How to Play Whist. Crown 8vo. 5s.
Ronalds's Fly-Fisher's Entomology. 8vo. 14s.
Wilcocks's Sea-Fisherman. Post 8vo. 6s.

ENCYCLOPÆDIAS, DICTIONARIES, AND BOOKS OF REFERENCE.

Acton's Modern Cookery for Private Families. Fcp 8vo. 4s. 6d.
Ayre's Treasury of Bible Knowledge. Fcp. 8vo. 6s.
Cabinet Lawyer (The), a Popular Digest of the Laws of England. Fcp. 8vo. 9s.
Cates's Dictionary of General Biography. Medium 8vo. 28s.
Gwilt's Encyclopædia of Architecture. 8vo. 52s. 6d.
Keith Johnston's Dictionary of Geography, or General Gazetteer. 8vo. 42s.
M'Culloch's Dictionary of Commerce and Commercial Navigation. 8vo. 63s.
Maunder's Biographical Treasury. Fcp. 8vo. 6s.
  — Historical Treasury. Fcp. 8vo. 6s.
  — Scientific and Literary Treasury. Fcp. 8vo. 6s.
  — Treasury of Bible Knowledge, edited by Ayre. Fcp. 8vo. 6s.
  — Treasury of Botany, edited by Lindley & Moore. Two Parts, 12s.
  — Treasury of Geography. Fcp. 8vo. 6s.
  — Treasury of Knowledge and Library of Reference. Fcp. 8vo. 6s.
  — Treasury of Natural History. Fcp. 8vo. 6s.
Quain's Dictionary of Medicine. Medium 8vo. 31s. 6d., or in 2 vols. 34s.
Reeve's Cookery and Housekeeping. Crown 8vo. 5s.
Rich's Dictionary of Roman and Greek Antiquities. Crown 8vo. 7s. 6d.
Roget's Thesaurus of English Words and Phrases. Crown 8vo. 10s. 6d.
Willich's Popular Tables, by Marriott. Crown 8vo. 10s. 6d.

WORKS BY MRS. DE SALIS.

Savouries à la Mode. Fcp. 8vo. 1s.
Entrées à la Mode. Fcp. 8vo. 1s. 6d.
Soups and Dressed Fish à la Mode. Fcp. 8vo. 1s. 6d.

Sweets and Supper Dishes, à la Mode. Fcp. 8vo. 1s. 6d.
Oysters à la Mode. Fcp. 8vo. 1s. 6d.
Vegetables à la Mode. Fcp. 8vo. 1s. 6d.

LONGMANS, GREEN, & CO., London and New York.

A SELECTION OF EDUCATIONAL WORKS.

TEXT-BOOKS OF SCIENCE.
FULLY ILLUSTRATED.

Abney's Treatise on Photography. Fcp. 8vo. 3s. 6d.
Anderson's Strength of Materials. 3s. 6d.
Armstrong's Organic Chemistry. 3s. 6d.
Ball's Elements of Astronomy. 6s.
Barry's Railway Appliances. 3s. 6d.
Bauerman's Systematic Mineralogy. 6s.
— Descriptive Mineralogy. 6s.
Bloxam and Huntington's Metals. 5s.
Glazebrook's Physical Optics. 6s.
Glazebrook and Shaw's Practical Physics. 6s.
Gore's Art of Electro-Metallurgy. 6s.
Griffin's Algebra and Trigonometry. 3s. 6d. Notes and Solutions, 3s. 6d.
Holmes's The Steam Engine. 6s.
Jenkin's Electricity and Magnetism. 3s. 6d.
Maxwell's Theory of Heat. 3s. 6d.
Merrifield's Technical Arithmetic and Mensuration. 3s. 6d. Key, 3s. 6d.
Miller's Inorganic Chemistry. 3s. 6d.
Preece and Sivewright's Telegraphy. 5s.
Rutley's Study of Rocks, a Text-Book of Petrology. 4s. 6d.
Shelley's Workshop Appliances. 4s. 6d.
Thomé's Structural and Physiological Botany. 6s.
Thorpe's Quantitative Chemical Analysis. 4s. 6d.
Thorpe and Muir's Qualitative Analysis. 3s. 6d.
Tilden's Chemical Philosophy. 3s. 6d. With Answers to Problems. 4s. 6d.
Unwin's Elements of Machine Design. 6s.
Watson's Plane and Solid Geometry. 3s. 6d.

THE GREEK LANGUAGE.

Bloomfield's College and School Greek Testament. Fcp. 8vo. 5s.
Bolland & Lang's Politics of Aristotle. Post 8vo. 7s. 6d.
Collis's Chief Tenses of the Greek Irregular Verbs. 8vo. 1s.
— Pontes Graeci, Stepping-Stone to Greek Grammar. 12mo. 3s. 6d.
— Praxis Graeca, Etymology. 12mo. 2s. 6d.
— Greek Verse-Book, Praxis Iambica. 12mo. 4s. 6d.
Farrar's Brief Greek Syntax and Accidence. 12mo. 4s. 6d.
— Greek Grammar Rules for Harrow School. 12mo. 1s. 6d.
Geare's Notes on Thucydides. Book I. Fcp. 8vo. 2s. 6d.

LONGMANS, GREEN, & CO., London and New York.

14   A Selection of Educational Works.

Hewitt's Greek Examination-Papers. 12mo. 1s. 6d.
Isbister's Xenophon's Anabasis, Books I. to III. with Notes. 12mo. 3s. 6d.
Kennedy's Greek Grammar. 12mo. 4s. 6d.
Liddell & Scott's English-Greek Lexicon. 4to. 36s.; Square 12mo. 7s. 6d.
Mahaffy's Classical Greek Literature. Crown 8vo. Poets, 7s. 6d. Prose Writers, 7s. 6d.
Morris's Greek Lessons. Square 18mo. Part I. 2s. 6d.; Part II. 1s.
Parry's Elementary Greek Grammar. 12mo. 3s. 6d.
Plato's Republic, Book I. Greek Text, English Notes by Hardy. Crown 8vo. 3s.
Sheppard and Evans's Notes on Thucydides. Crown 8vo. 7s. 6d.
Thucydides, Book IV. with Notes by Barton and Chavasse. Crown 8vo. 5s.
Valpy's Greek Delectus, improved by White. 12mo. 2s. 6d. Key, 2s. 6d.
White's Xenophon's Expedition of Cyrus, with English Notes. 12mo. 7s. 6d.
Wilkins's Manual of Greek Prose Composition. Crown 8vo. 5s. Key, 5s.
— Exercises in Greek Prose Composition. Crown 8vo. 4s. 6d. Key, 2s. 6d.
— New Greek Delectus. Crown 8vo. 3s. 6d. Key, 2s. 6d.
— Progressive Greek Delectus. 12mo. 4s. Key, 2s. 6d.
— Progressive Greek Anthology. 12mo. 5s.
— Scriptores Attici, Excerpts with English Notes. Crown 8vo. 7s. 6d.
— Speeches from Thucydides translated. Post 8vo. 6s.
Yonge's English-Greek Lexicon. 4to. 21s.; Square 12mo. 8s. 6d.

THE LATIN LANGUAGE.

Bradley's Latin Prose Exercises. 12mo. 3s. 6d. Key, 5s.
— Continuous Lessons in Latin Prose. 12mo. 5s. Key, 5s. 6d.
— Cornelius Nepos, improved by White. 12mo. 3s. 6d.
— Eutropius, improved by White. 12mo. 2s. 6d.
— Ovid's Metamorphoses, improved by White. 12mo. 4s. 6d.
— Select Fables of Phædrus, improved by White. 12mo. 2s. 6d.
Collis's Chief Tenses of Latin Irregular Verbs. 8vo. 1s.
— Pontes Latini, Stepping-Stone to Latin Grammar. 12mo. 3s. 6d.
Hewitt's Latin Examination-Papers. 12mo. 1s. 6d.
Isbister's Cæsar, Books I.-VII. 12mo. 4s.; or with Reading Lessons, 4s. 6d.
— Cæsar's Commentaries, Books I.-V. 12mo. 3s. 6d.
— First Book of Cæsar's Gallic War. 12mo. 1s. 6d.
Jerram's Latiné Reddenda. Crown 8vo. 1s. 6d.
Kennedy's Child's Latin Primer, or First Latin Lessons. 12mo. 2s.
— Child's Latin Accidence. 12mo. 1s.
— Elementary Latin Grammar. 12mo. 3s. 6d.
— Elementary Latin Reading Book, or Tirocinium Latinum. 12mo. 2s.
— Latin Prose, Palæstra Stili Latini. 12mo. 6s.
— Latin Vocabulary. 12mo. 2s. 6d.
— Subsidia Primaria, Exercise Books to the Public School Latin Primer. I. Accidence and Simple Construction, 2s. 6d. II. Syntax, 3s. 6d.
— Key to the Exercises in Subsidia Primaria, Parts I. and II. price 5s.
— Subsidia Primaria, III. the Latin Compound Sentence. 12mo. 1s.

LONGMANS, GREEN, & CO., London and New York.

A Selection of Educational Works. 15

Kennedy's Curriculum Stili Latini. 12mo. 4s. 6d. Key, 7s. 6d.
— Palæstra Latina, or Second Latin Reading Book. 12mo. 5s.
Moody's Eton Latin Grammar. 12mo. 2s. 6d. The Accidence separately, 1s.
Morris's Elementa Latina. Fcp. 8vo. 1s. 6d. Key, 2s. 6d.
Parry's Origines Romanæ, from Livy, with English Notes. Crown 8vo. 4s.
The Public School Latin Primer. 12mo. 2s. 6d.
— — — Grammar, by Rev. Dr. Kennedy. Post 8vo. 7s. 6d.
Prendergast's Mastery Series, Manual of Latin. 12mo. 2s. 6d.
Rapier's Introduction to Composition of Latin Verse. 12mo. 3s. 6d. Key, 2s. 6d.
Sheppard and Turner's Aids to Classical Study. 12mo. 5s. Key, 6s.
Valpy's Latin Delectus, improved by White. 12mo. 2s. 6d. Key, 3s. 6d.
Virgil's Æneid, translated into English Verse by Conington. Crown 8vo. 9s.
— Works, edited by Kennedy. Crown 8vo. 10s. 6d.
— — translated into English Prose by Conington. Crown 8vo. 9s.
Walford's Progressive Exercises in Latin Elegiac Verse. 12mo. 2s. 6d. Key, 5s.
White and Riddle's Large Latin-English Dictionary. 1 vol. 4to. 21s.
White's Concise Latin-Eng. Dictionary for University Students. Royal 8vo. 12s.
— Junior Students' Eng.-Lat. & Lat.-Eng. Dictionary. Square 12mo. 5s.
Separately { The Latin-English Dictionary, price 3s.
{ The English-Latin Dictionary, price 3s.
Yonge's Latin Gradus. Post 8vo. 9s.; or with Appendix, 12s.

WHITE'S GRAMMAR-SCHOOL GREEK TEXTS.

Æsop (Fables) & Palæphatus (Myths). 32mo. 1s.
Euripides, Hecuba. 2s.
Homer, Iliad, Book I. 1s.
— Odyssey, Book I. 1s.
Lucian, Select Dialogues. 1s.
Xenophon, Anabasis, Books I. III. IV. V. & VI. 1s. 6d. each ; Book II. 1s. ; Book VII. 2s.

Xenophon, Book I. without Vocabulary. 3d.
St. Matthew's and St. Luke's Gospels. 2s. 6d. each.
St. Mark's and St. John's Gospels. 1s. 6d. each.
The Acts of the Apostles. 2s. 6d.
St. Paul's Epistle to the Romans. 1s. 6d.

The Four Gospels in Greek, with Greek-English Lexicon. Edited by John T. White, D.D. Oxon. Square 32mo. price 5s.

WHITE'S GRAMMAR-SCHOOL LATIN TEXTS.

Cæsar, Gallic War, Books I. & II. V. & VI. 1s. each. Book I. without Vocabulary, 3d.
Cæsar, Gallic War, Books III. & IV. 9d. each.
Cæsar, Gallic War, Book VII. 1s. 6d.
Cicero, Cato Major (Old Age). 1s. 6d.
Cicero, Lælius (Friendship). 1s. 6d.
Eutropius, Roman History, Books I. & II. 1s. Books III. & IV. 1s.
Horace, Odes, Books I. II. & IV. 1s. each.
Horace, Odes, Book III. 1s. 6d.
Horace, Epodes and Carmen Seculare. 1s.

Nepos, Miltiades, Simon, Pausanias, Aristides. 9d.
Ovid, Selections from Epistles and Fasti. 1s.
Ovid, Select Myths from Metamorphoses. 9d.
Phædrus, Select Easy Fables.
Phædrus, Fables, Books I. & II. 1s.
Sallust, Bellum Catilinarium. 1s. 6d.
Virgil, Georgics, Book IV. 1s.
Virgil, Æneid, Books I. to VI. 1s. each. Book I. without Vocabulary, 3d.
Virgil, Æneid, Books VII. to XII. 1s. 6d. each.

LONGMANS, GREEN, & CO., London and New York.

THE FRENCH LANGUAGE.

Albitès's How to Speak French. Fcp. 8vo. 5s. 6d.
— Instantaneous French Exercises. Fcp. 2s. Key, 2s.
Cassal's French Genders. Crown 8vo. 3s. 6d.
Cassal & Karcher's Graduated French Translation Book. Part I. 3s. 6d.
Part II. 5s. Key to Part I. by Professor Cassal, price 5s.
Contanseau's Practical French and English Dictionary. Post 8vo. 3s. 6d.
— Pocket French and English Dictionary. Square 18mo. 1s. 6d.
— Premières Lectures. 12mo. 2s. 6d.
— First Step in French. 12mo. 2s. 6d. Key, 3s.
— French Accidence. 12mo. 2s. 6d.
— — Grammar. 12mo. 4s. Key, 3s.
Contanseau's Middle-Class French Course. Fcp. 8vo. :—

Accidence, 8d.	French Translation-Book, 8d.
Syntax, 8d.	Easy French Delectus, 8d.
French Conversation-Book, 8d.	First French Reader, 8d.
First French Exercise-Book, 8d.	Second French Reader, 8d.
Second French Exercise-Book, 8d.	French and English Dialogues, 8d.

Contanseau's Guide to French Translation. 12mo. 3s. 6d. Key 3s. 6d.
— Prosateurs et Poètes Français. 12mo. 5s.
— Précis de la Littérature Française. 12mo. 3s. 6d.
— Abrégé de l'Histoire de France. 12mo. 2s. 6d.
Féval's Chouans et Bleus, with Notes by C. Sankey, M.A. Fcp. 8vo. 2s. 6d.
Jerram's Sentences for Translation into French. Cr. 8vo. 1s. Key, 2s. 6d.
Prendergast's Mastery Series, French. 12mo. 2s. 6d.
Souvestre's Philosophe sous les Toits, by Stièvenard. Square 18mo. 1s. 6d.
Stepping-Stone to French Pronunciation. 18mo. 1s.
Stièvenard's Lectures Françaises from Modern Authors. 12mo. 4s. 6d.
— Rules and Exercises on the French Language. 12mo. 3s. 6d.
Tarver's Eton French Grammar. 12mo. 6s. 6d.

THE GERMAN LANGUAGE.

Blackley's Practical German and English Dictionary. Post 8vo. 3s. 6d.
Buchheim's German Poetry, for Repetition. 18mo. 1s. 6d.
Collis's Card of German Irregular Verbs. 8vo. 2s.
Fischer-Fischart's Elementary German Grammar. Fcp. 8vo. 2s. 6d.
Just's German Grammar. 12mo. 1s. 6d.
— German Reading Book. 12mo. 3s. 6d.
Longman's Pocket German and English Dictionary. Square 18mo. 2s. 6d.
Naftel's Elementary German Course for Public Schools. Fcp. 8vo.

German Accidence. 9d.	German Prose Composition Book. 9d.
German Syntax. 9d.	First German Reader. 9d.
First German Exercise-Book. 9d.	Second German Reader. 9d.
Second German Exercise-Book. 9d.	

Prendergast's Mastery Series, German. 12mo. 2s. 6d.
Quick's Essentials of German. Crown 8vo. 3s. 6d.
Selss's School Edition of Goethe's Faust. Crown 8vo. 5s.
— Outline of German Literature. Crown 8vo. 4s. 6d.
Wirth's German Chit-Chat. Crown 8vo. 2s. 6d.

LONGMANS, GREEN, & CO., London and New York.

www.ingramcontent.com/pod-product-compliance
Lightning Source LLC
Chambersburg PA
CBHW030756230426
43667CB00007B/989